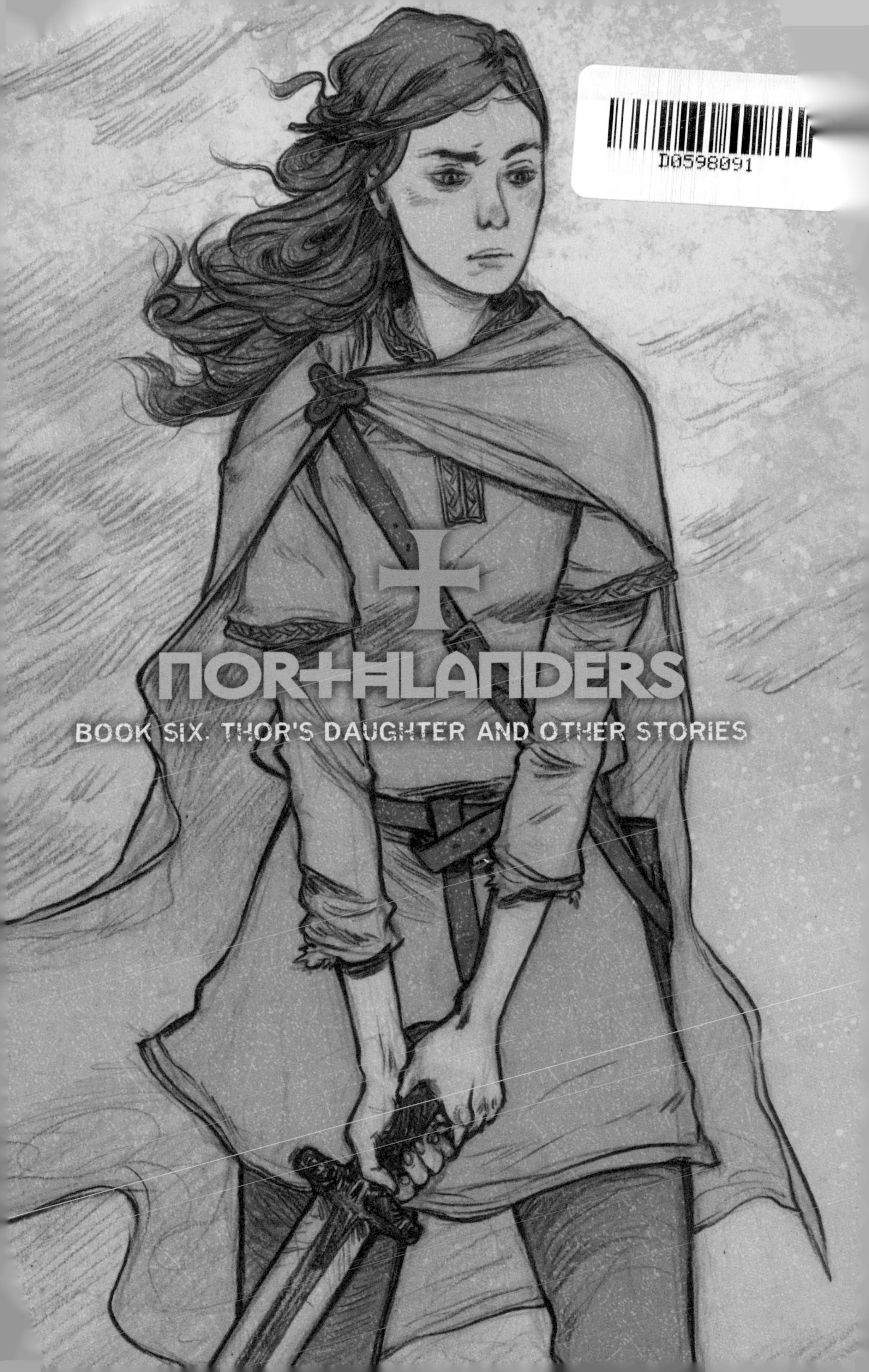

NORTHLANDERS
BOOK SIX: THOR'S DAUGHTER AND OTHER STORIES

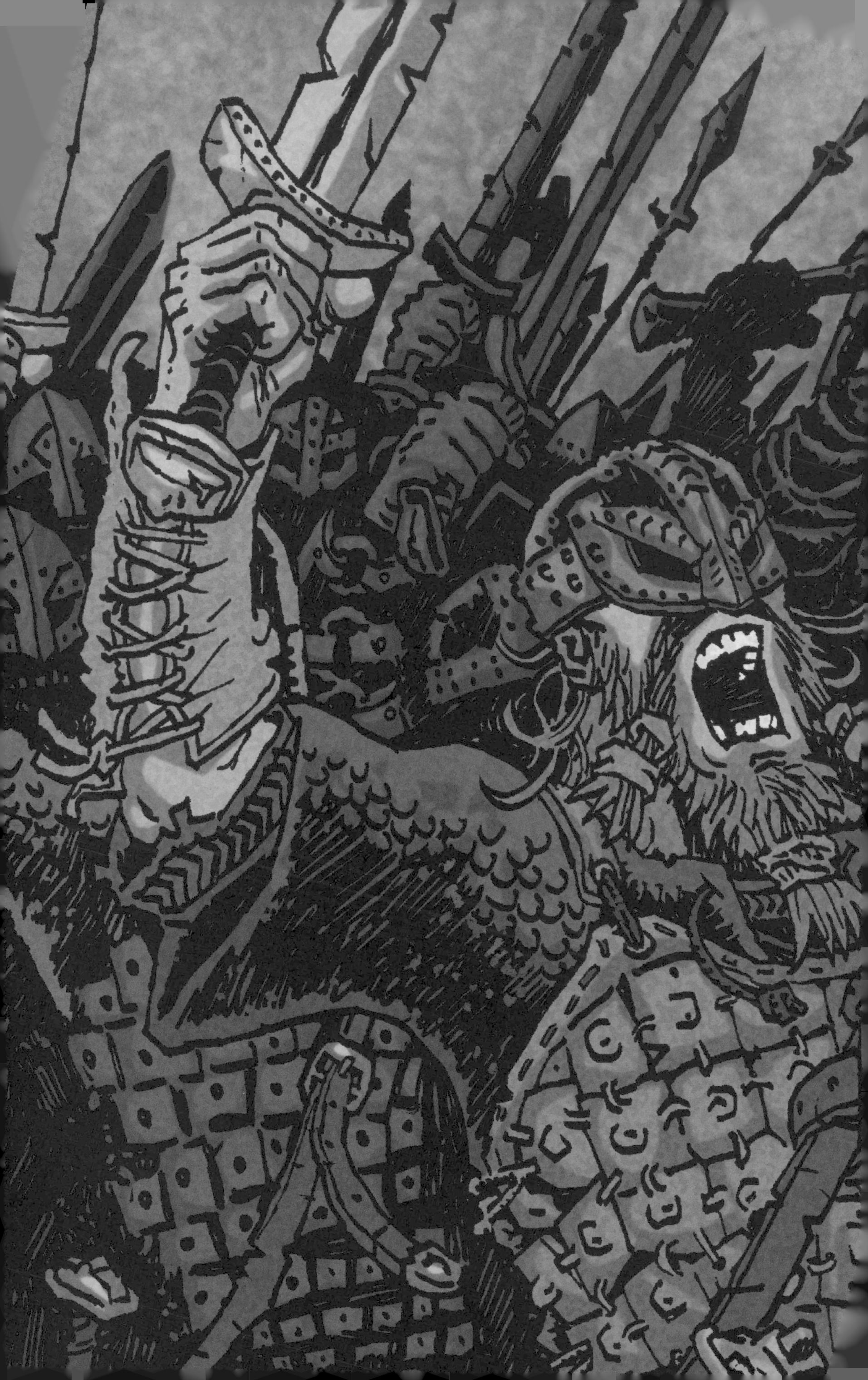

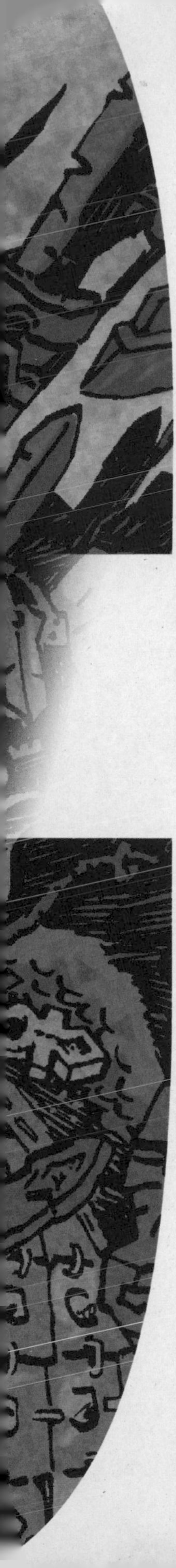

NORTHLANDERS

BOOK SIX: THOR'S DAUGHTER AND OTHER STORIES

Brian Wood Writer

Simon Gane
Artist - "THE SIEGE OF PARIS"

Matthew Woodson
Artist - "THE HUNT"

Marian Churchland
Artist - "THOR'S DAUGHTER"

Dave McCaig Colorist

Travis Lanham Letterer

Cover art and
original series covers by
Massimo Carnevale

Cover design by **Brian Wood**

Northlanders created by
Brian Wood

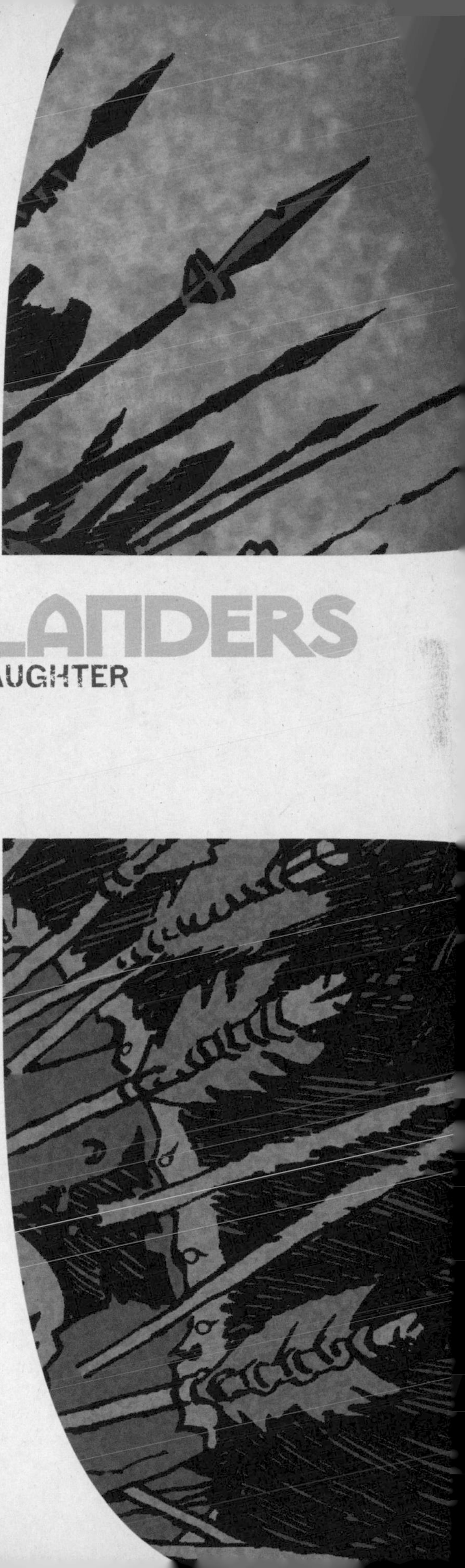

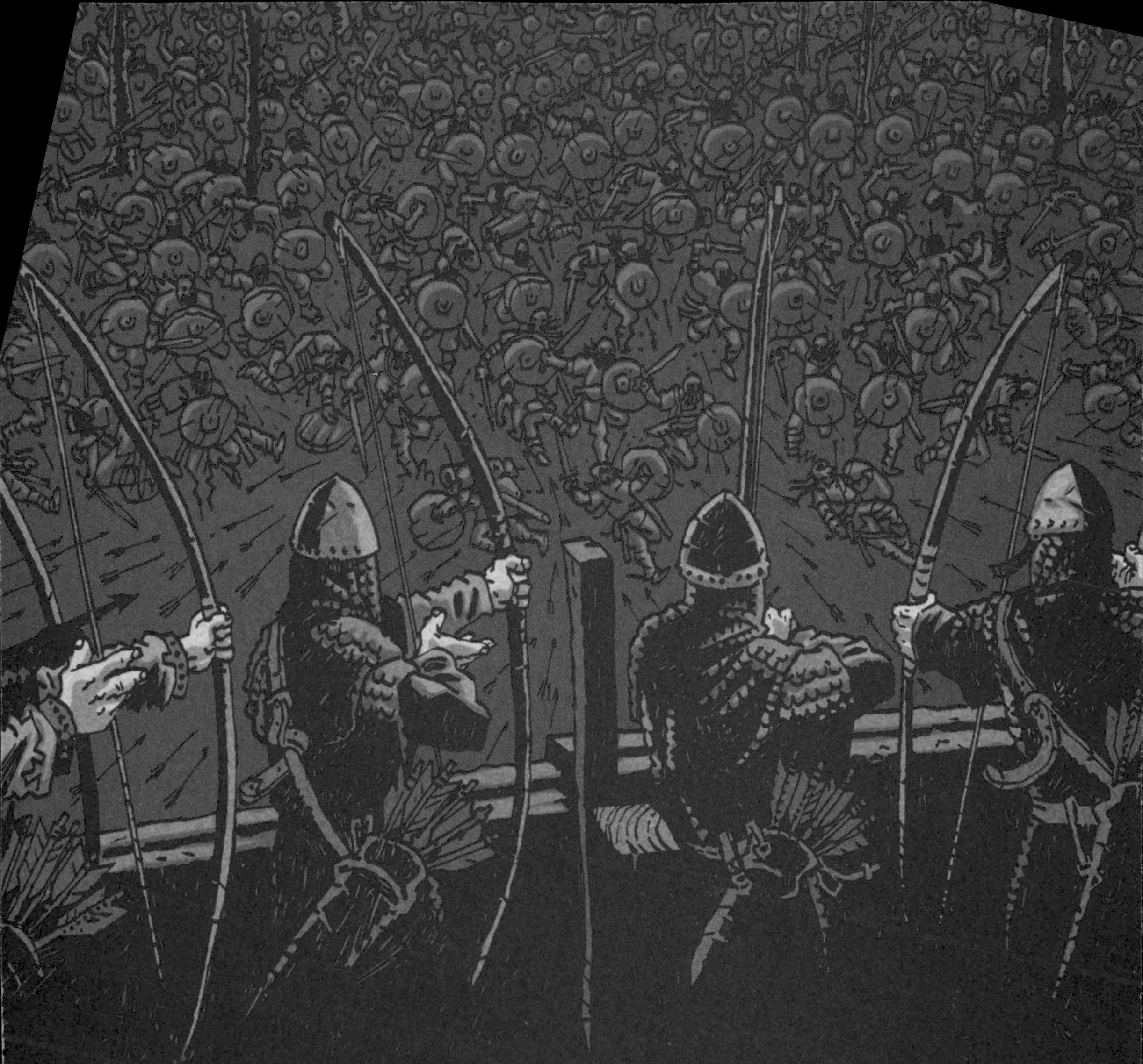

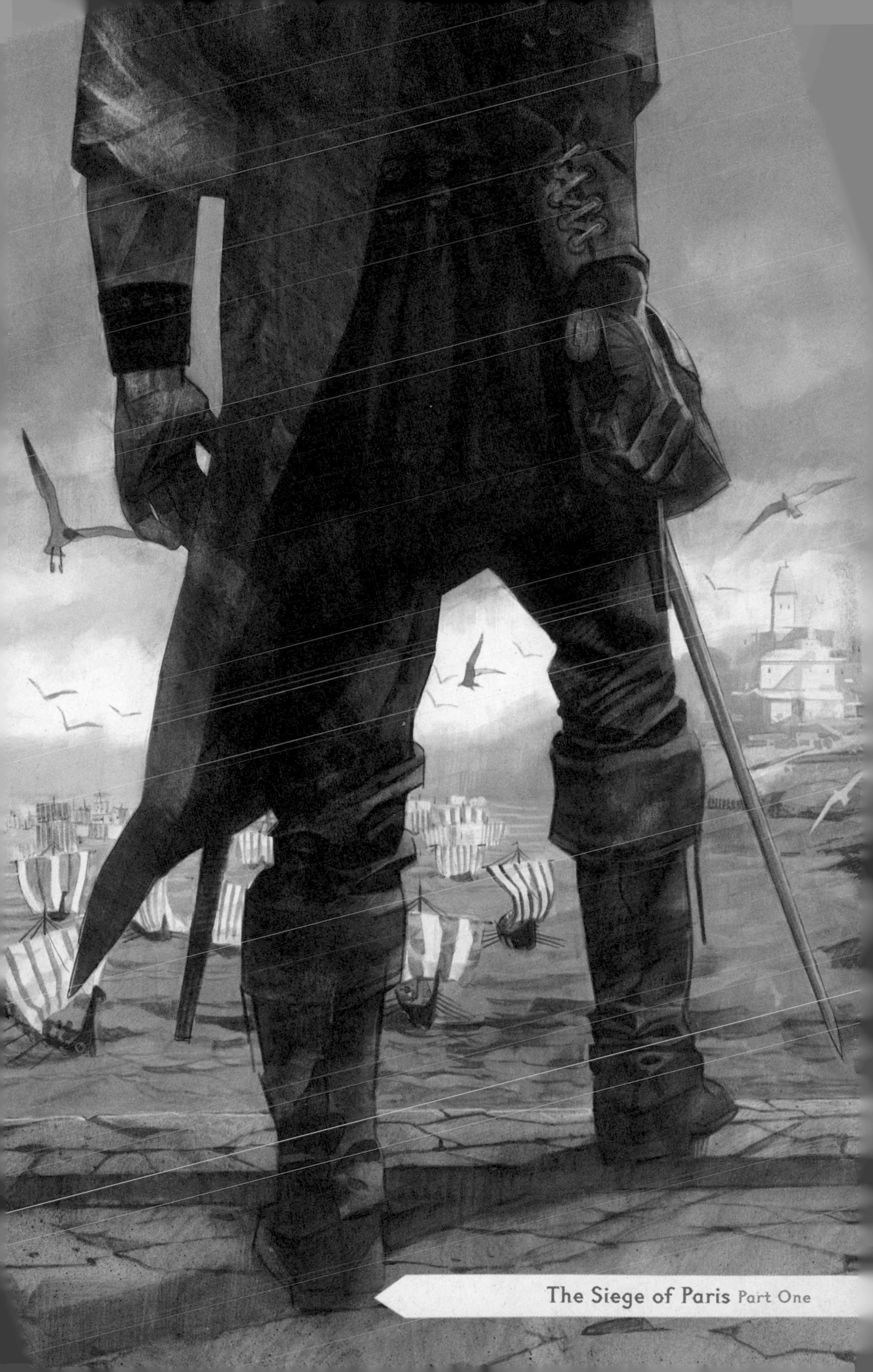
The Siege of Paris Part One

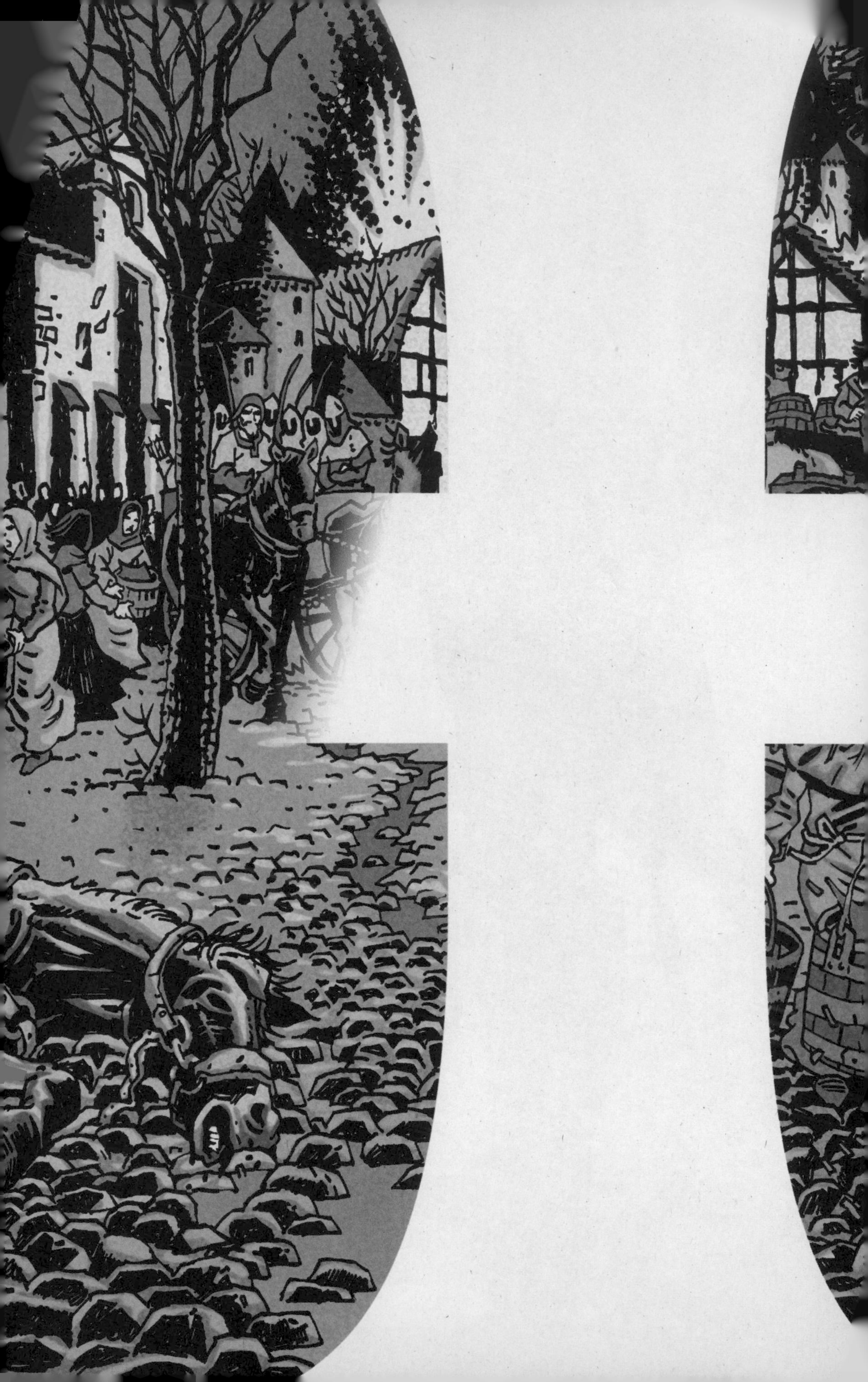

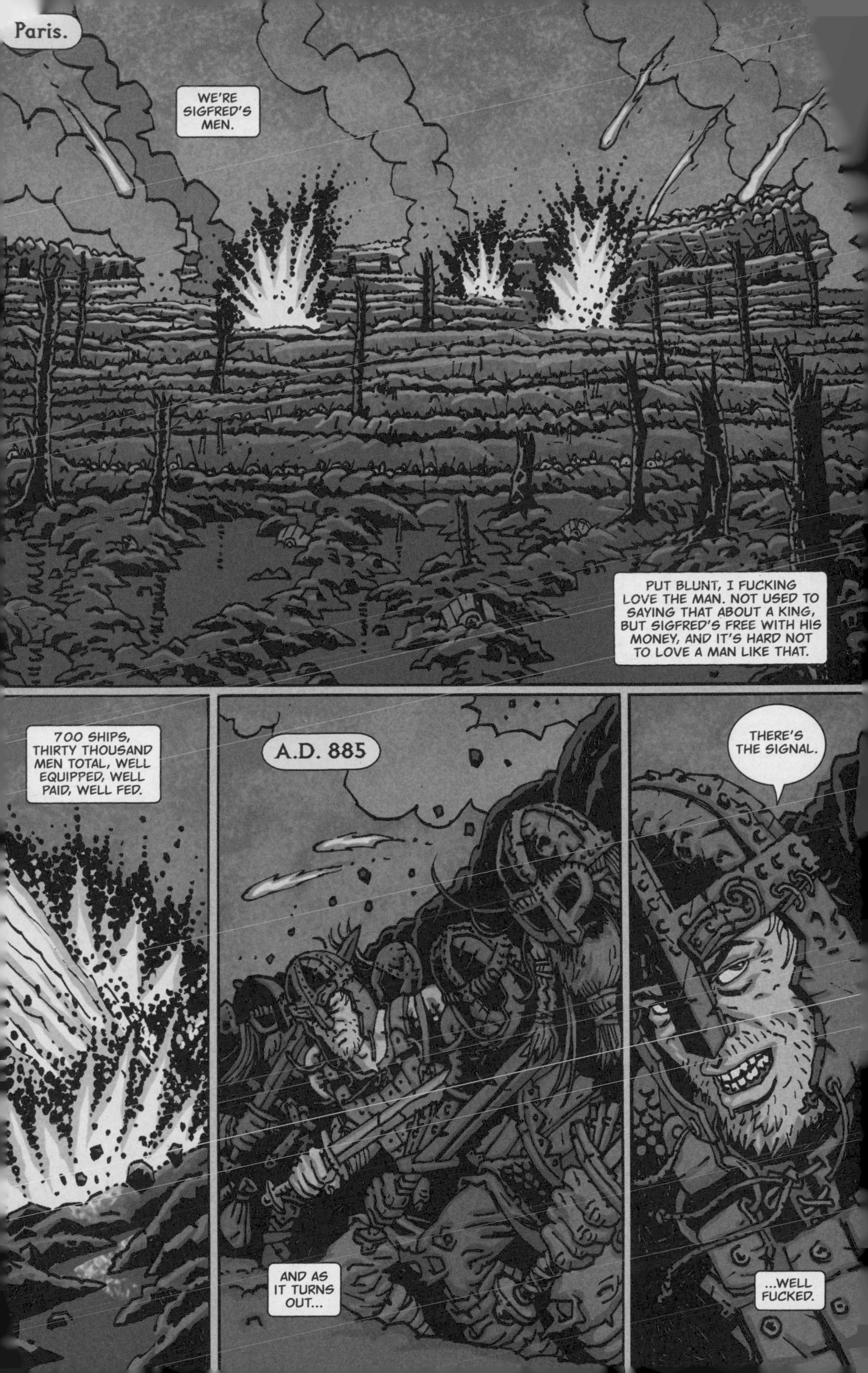
Paris.
WE'RE SIGFRED'S MEN.
PUT BLUNT, I FUCKING LOVE THE MAN. NOT USED TO SAYING THAT ABOUT A KING, BUT SIGFRED'S FREE WITH HIS MONEY, AND IT'S HARD NOT TO LOVE A MAN LIKE THAT.
700 SHIPS, THIRTY THOUSAND MEN TOTAL, WELL EQUIPPED, WELL PAID, WELL FED.
A.D. 885
AND AS IT TURNS OUT...
THERE'S THE SIGNAL.
...WELL FUCKED.

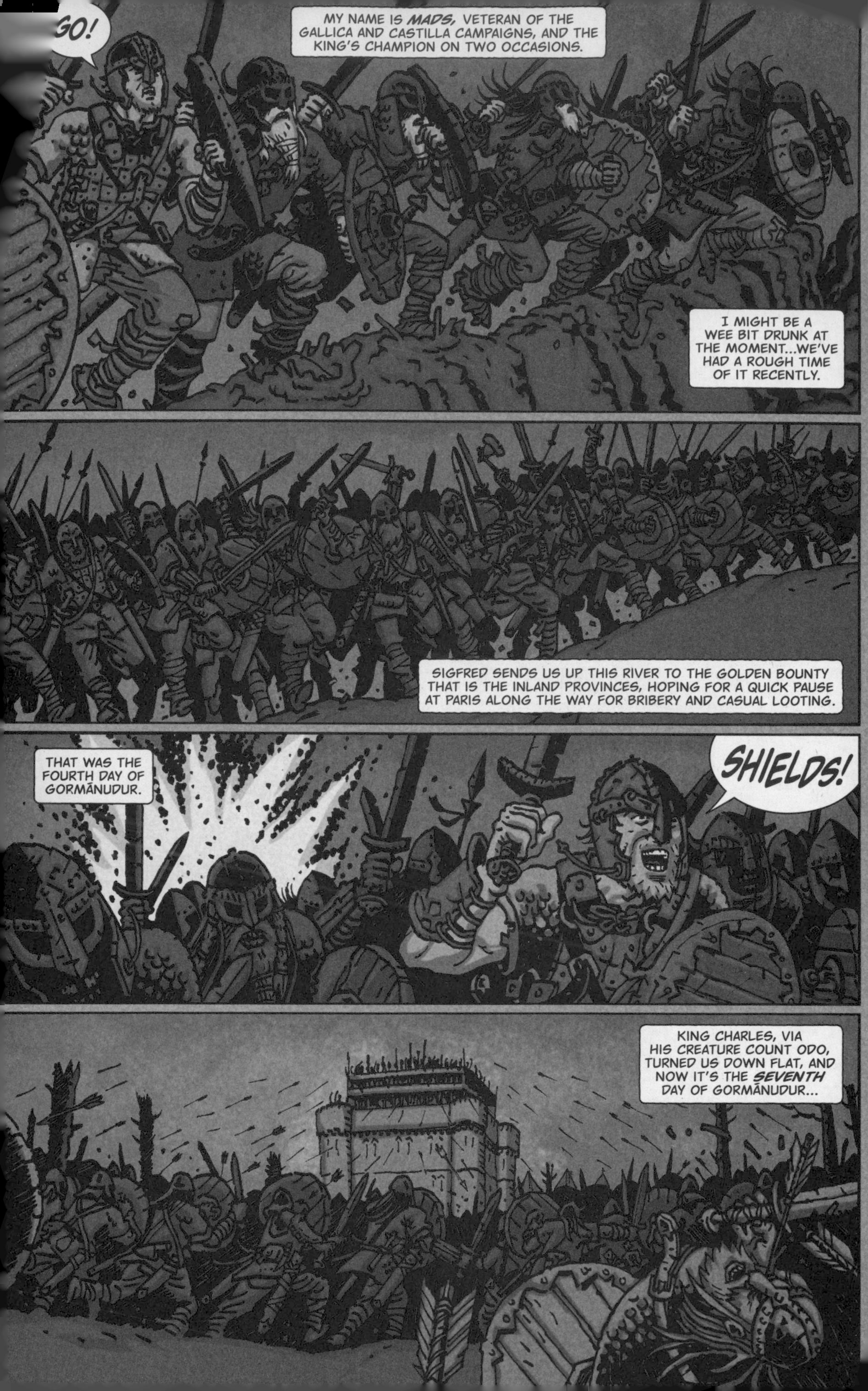
GO!
MY NAME IS MADS, VETERAN OF THE GALLICA AND CASTILLA CAMPAIGNS, AND THE KING'S CHAMPION ON TWO OCCASIONS.
I MIGHT BE A WEE BIT DRUNK AT THE MOMENT...WE'VE HAD A ROUGH TIME OF IT RECENTLY.
SIGFRED SENDS US UP THIS RIVER TO THE GOLDEN BOUNTY THAT IS THE INLAND PROVINCES, HOPING FOR A QUICK PAUSE AT PARIS ALONG THE WAY FOR BRIBERY AND CASUAL LOOTING.
THAT WAS THE FOURTH DAY OF GORMĀNUDUR.
SHIELDS!
KING CHARLES, VIA HIS CREATURE COUNT ODO, TURNED US DOWN FLAT, AND NOW IT'S THE SEVENTH DAY OF GORMĀNUDUR...

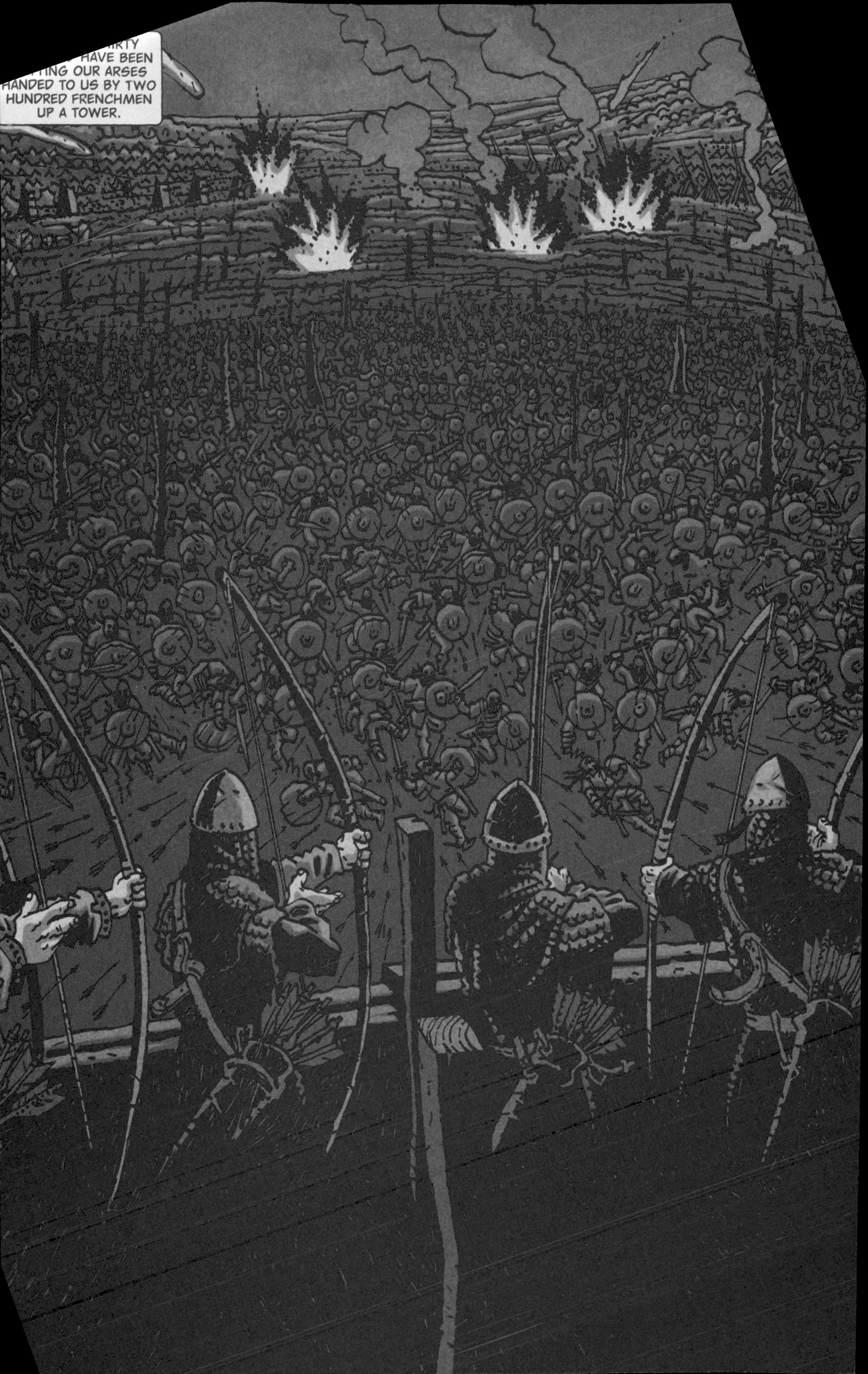
...HAVE BEEN
...ING OUR ARSES
HANDED TO US BY TWO
HUNDRED FRENCHMEN
UP A TOWER.

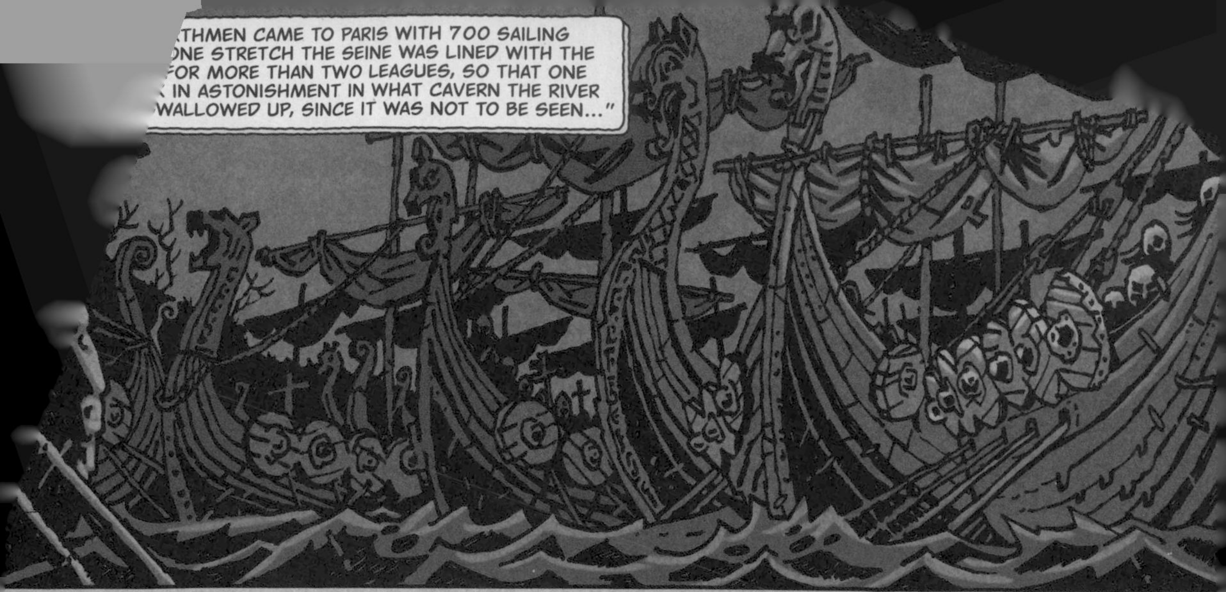
THMEN CAME TO PARIS WITH 700 SAILING
ONE STRETCH THE SEINE WAS LINED WITH THE
FOR MORE THAN TWO LEAGUES, SO THAT ONE
IN ASTONISHMENT IN WHAT CAVERN THE RIVER
WALLOWED UP, SINCE IT WAS NOT TO BE SEEN..."

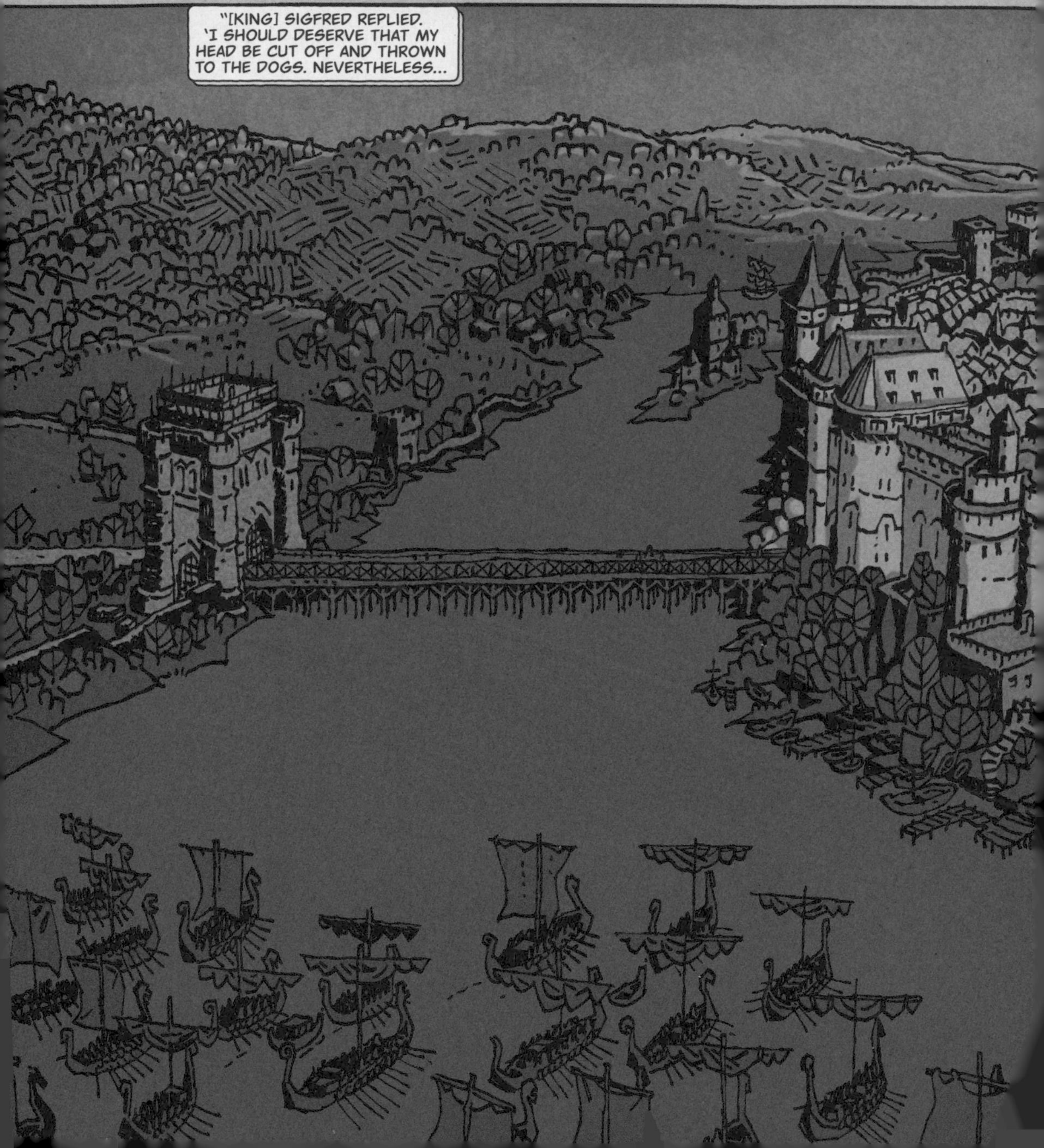
"[KING] SIGFRED REPLIED. 'I SHOULD DESERVE THAT MY HEAD BE CUT OFF AND THROWN TO THE DOGS. NEVERTHELESS...

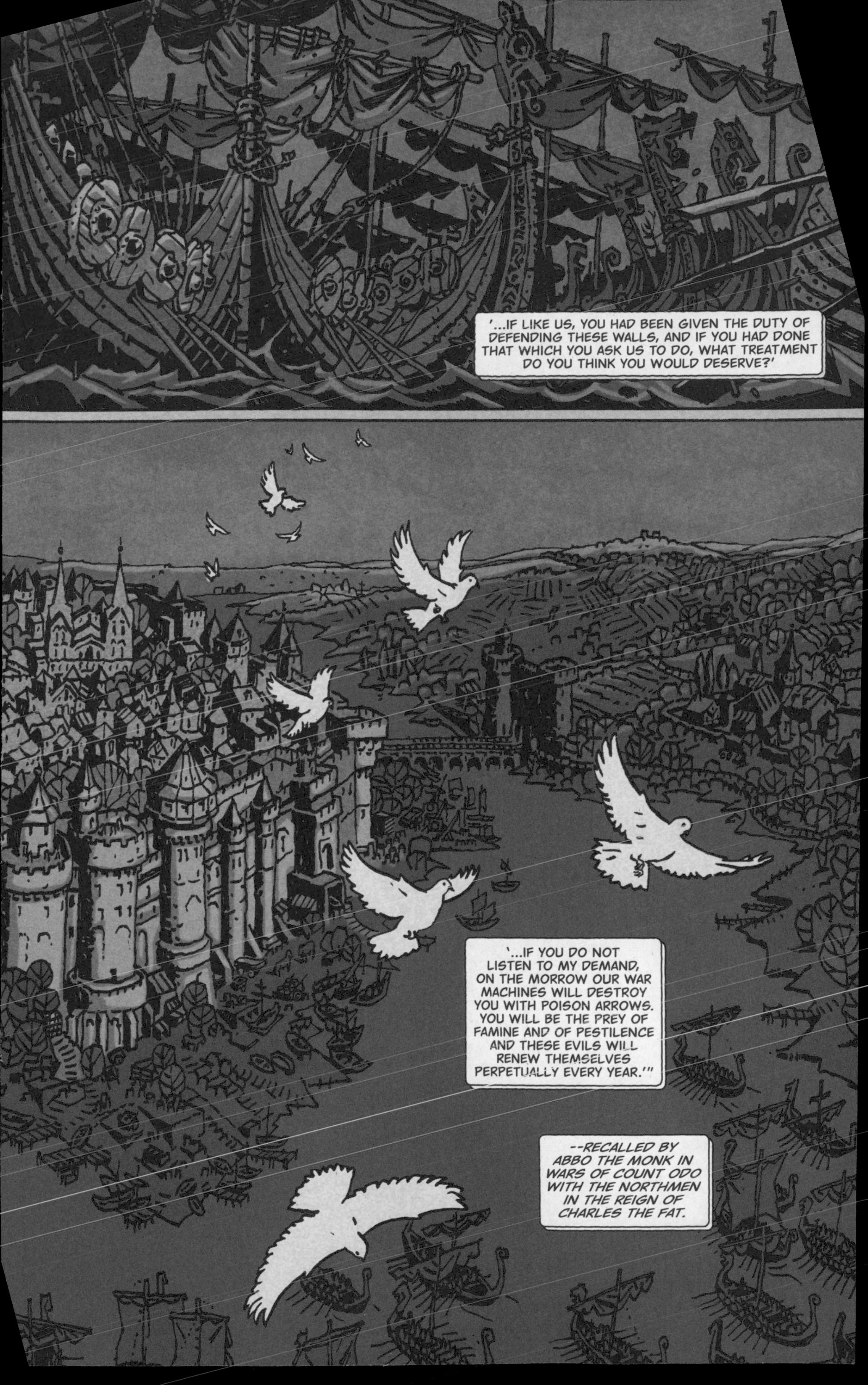
'...IF LIKE US, YOU HAD BEEN GIVEN THE DUTY OF DEFENDING THESE WALLS, AND IF YOU HAD DONE THAT WHICH YOU ASK US TO DO, WHAT TREATMENT DO YOU THINK YOU WOULD DESERVE?'
'...IF YOU DO NOT LISTEN TO MY DEMAND, ON THE MORROW OUR WAR MACHINES WILL DESTROY YOU WITH POISON ARROWS. YOU WILL BE THE PREY OF FAMINE AND OF PESTILENCE AND THESE EVILS WILL RENEW THEMSELVES PERPETUALLY EVERY YEAR.'"
--RECALLED BY ABBO THE MONK IN WARS OF COUNT ODO WITH THE NORTHMEN IN THE REIGN OF CHARLES THE FAT.

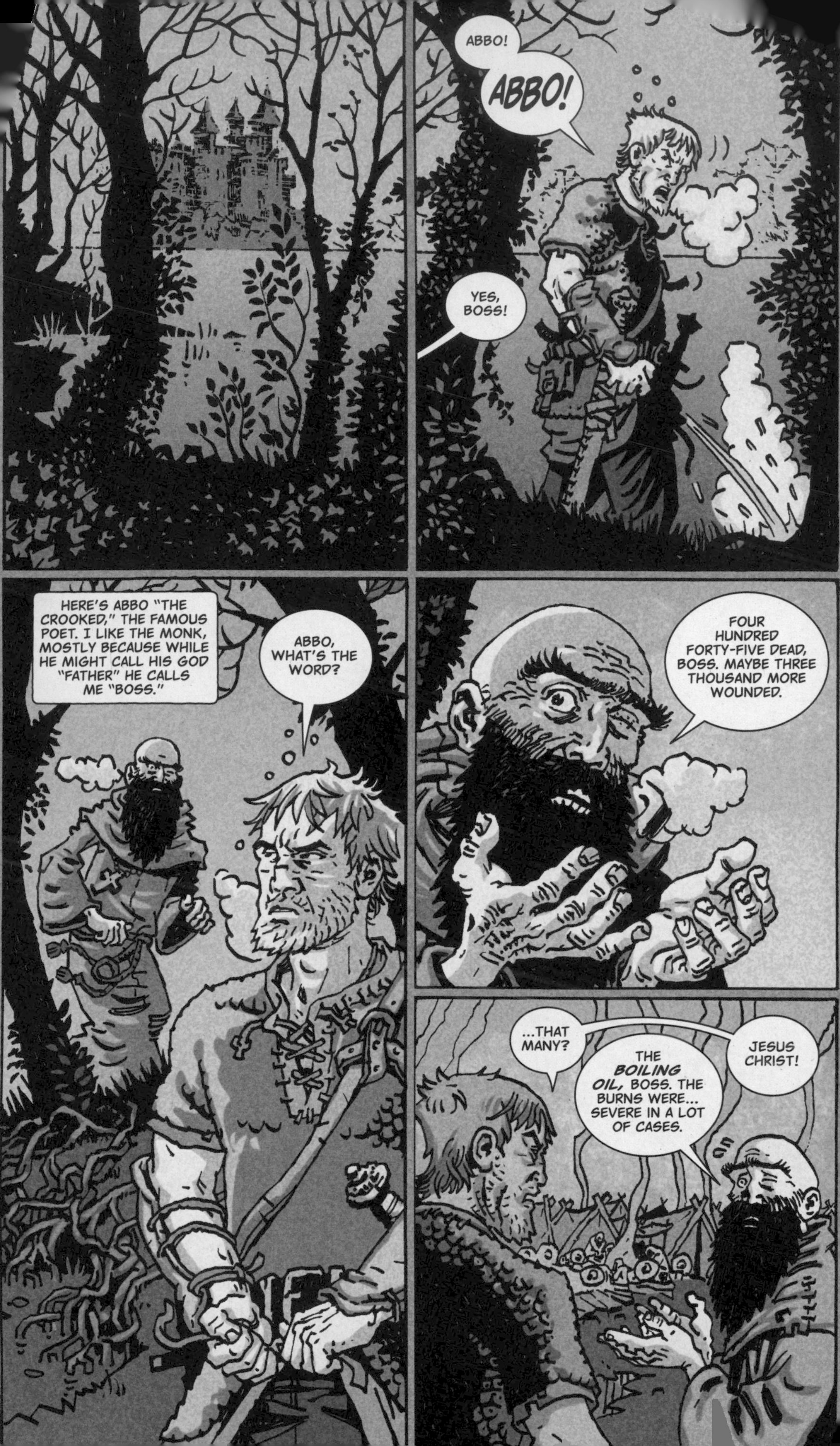
ABBO!
ABBO!
YES, BOSS!
HERE'S ABBO "THE CROOKED," THE FAMOUS POET. I LIKE THE MONK, MOSTLY BECAUSE WHILE HE MIGHT CALL HIS GOD "FATHER" HE CALLS ME "BOSS."
ABBO, WHAT'S THE WORD?
FOUR HUNDRED FORTY-FIVE DEAD, BOSS. MAYBE THREE THOUSAND MORE WOUNDED.
...THAT MANY?
THE BOILING OIL, BOSS. THE BURNS WERE... SEVERE IN A LOT OF CASES.
JESUS CHRIST!

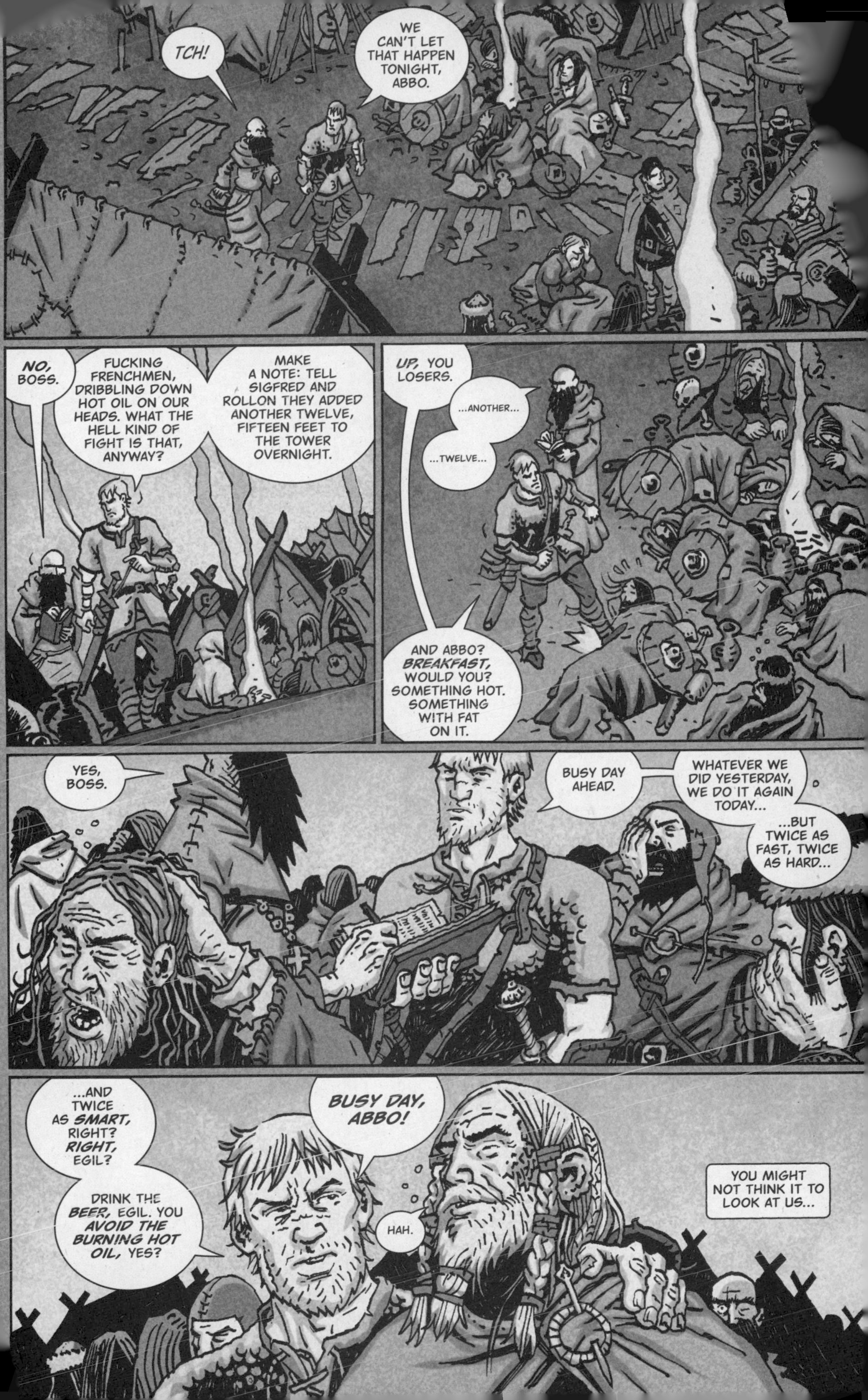
TCH!
WE CAN'T LET THAT HAPPEN TONIGHT, ABBO.
NO, BOSS.
FUCKING FRENCHMEN, DRIBBLING DOWN HOT OIL ON OUR HEADS. WHAT THE HELL KIND OF FIGHT IS THAT, ANYWAY?
MAKE A NOTE: TELL SIGFRED AND ROLLON THEY ADDED ANOTHER TWELVE, FIFTEEN FEET TO THE TOWER OVERNIGHT.
UP, YOU LOSERS.
...ANOTHER...
...TWELVE...
AND ABBO? BREAKFAST, WOULD YOU? SOMETHING HOT. SOMETHING WITH FAT ON IT.
YES, BOSS.
BUSY DAY AHEAD.
WHATEVER WE DID YESTERDAY, WE DO IT AGAIN TODAY...
...BUT TWICE AS FAST, TWICE AS HARD...
...AND TWICE AS SMART, RIGHT? RIGHT, EGIL?
BUSY DAY, ABBO!
DRINK THE BEER, EGIL. YOU AVOID THE BURNING HOT OIL, YES?
HAH.
YOU MIGHT NOT THINK IT TO LOOK AT US...

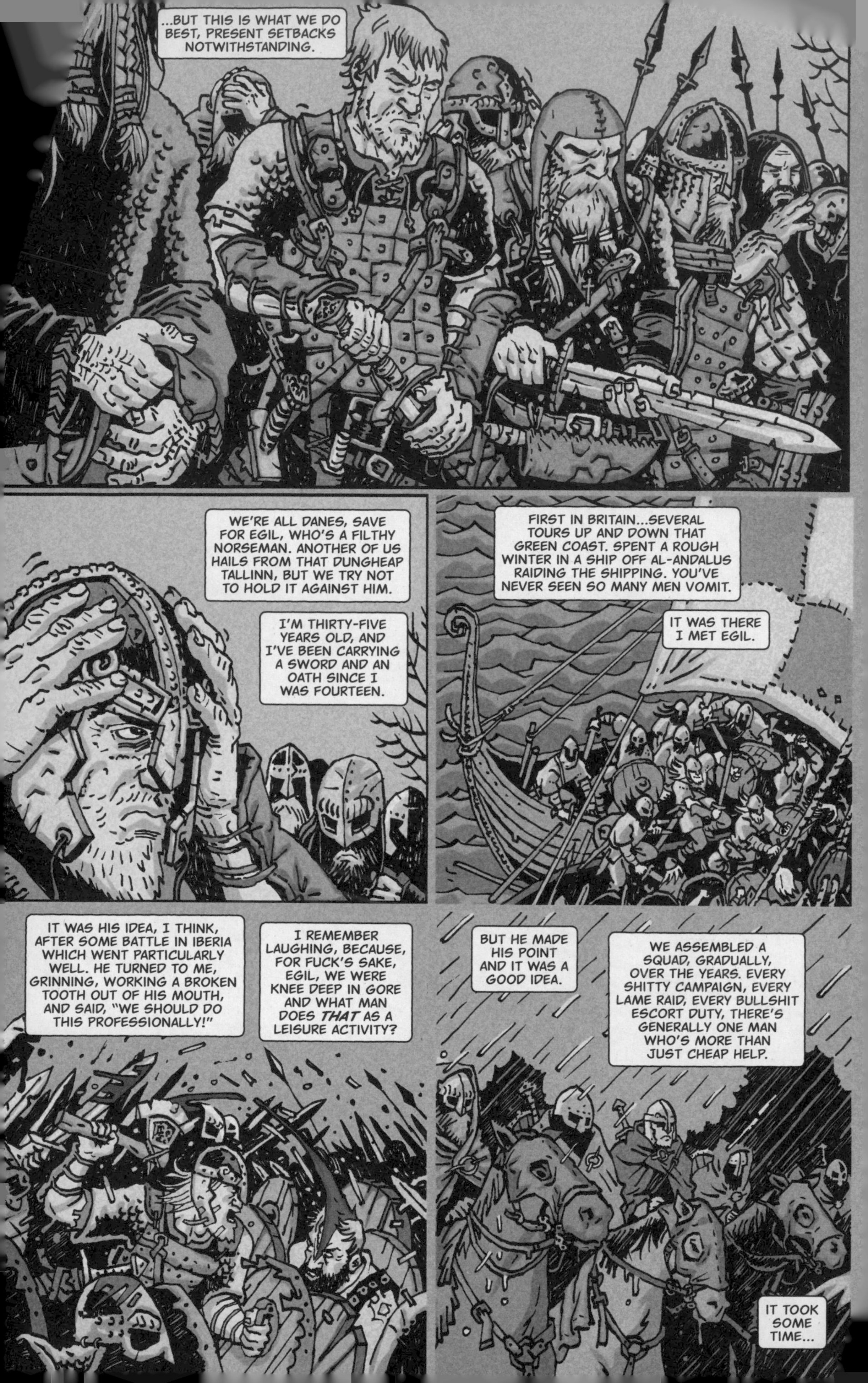
...BUT THIS IS WHAT WE DO BEST, PRESENT SETBACKS NOTWITHSTANDING.
WE'RE ALL DANES, SAVE FOR EGIL, WHO'S A FILTHY NORSEMAN. ANOTHER OF US HAILS FROM THAT DUNGHEAP TALLINN, BUT WE TRY NOT TO HOLD IT AGAINST HIM.
I'M THIRTY-FIVE YEARS OLD, AND I'VE BEEN CARRYING A SWORD AND AN OATH SINCE I WAS FOURTEEN.
FIRST IN BRITAIN...SEVERAL TOURS UP AND DOWN THAT GREEN COAST. SPENT A ROUGH WINTER IN A SHIP OFF AL-ANDALUS RAIDING THE SHIPPING. YOU'VE NEVER SEEN SO MANY MEN VOMIT.
IT WAS THERE I MET EGIL.
IT WAS HIS IDEA, I THINK, AFTER SOME BATTLE IN IBERIA WHICH WENT PARTICULARLY WELL. HE TURNED TO ME, GRINNING, WORKING A BROKEN TOOTH OUT OF HIS MOUTH, AND SAID, "WE SHOULD DO THIS PROFESSIONALLY!"
I REMEMBER LAUGHING, BECAUSE, FOR FUCK'S SAKE, EGIL, WE WERE KNEE DEEP IN GORE AND WHAT MAN DOES *THAT* AS A LEISURE ACTIVITY?
BUT HE MADE HIS POINT AND IT WAS A GOOD IDEA.
WE ASSEMBLED A SQUAD, GRADUALLY, OVER THE YEARS. EVERY SHITTY CAMPAIGN, EVERY LAME RAID, EVERY BULLSHIT ESCORT DUTY, THERE'S GENERALLY ONE MAN WHO'S MORE THAN JUST CHEAP HELP.
IT TOOK SOME TIME...

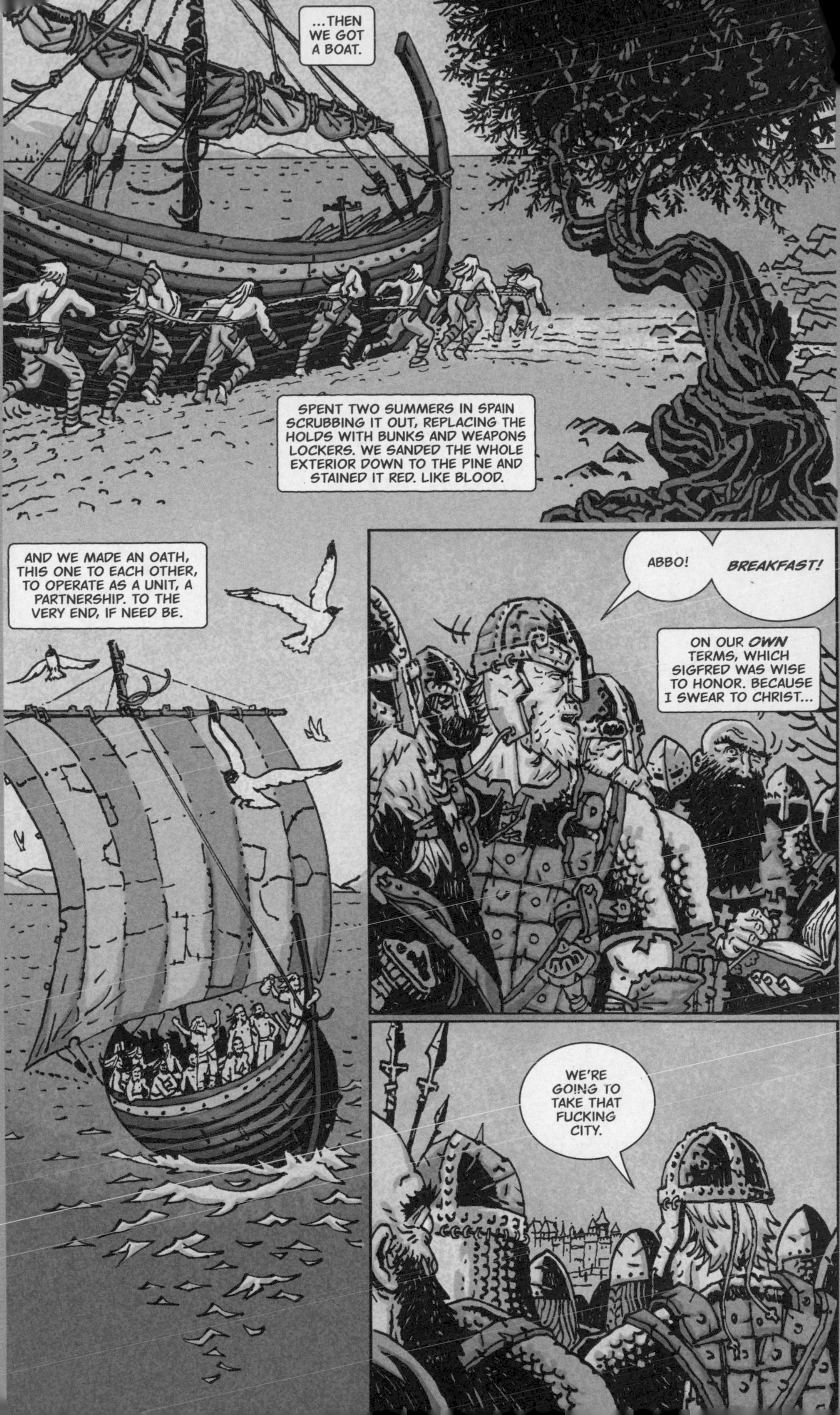
...THEN WE GOT A BOAT.
SPENT TWO SUMMERS IN SPAIN SCRUBBING IT OUT, REPLACING THE HOLDS WITH BUNKS AND WEAPONS LOCKERS. WE SANDED THE WHOLE EXTERIOR DOWN TO THE PINE AND STAINED IT RED. LIKE BLOOD.
AND WE MADE AN OATH, THIS ONE TO EACH OTHER, TO OPERATE AS A UNIT, A PARTNERSHIP. TO THE VERY END, IF NEED BE.
ABBO!
BREAKFAST!
ON OUR *OWN* TERMS, WHICH SIGFRED WAS WISE TO HONOR. BECAUSE I SWEAR TO CHRIST...
WE'RE GOING TO TAKE THAT FUCKING CITY.

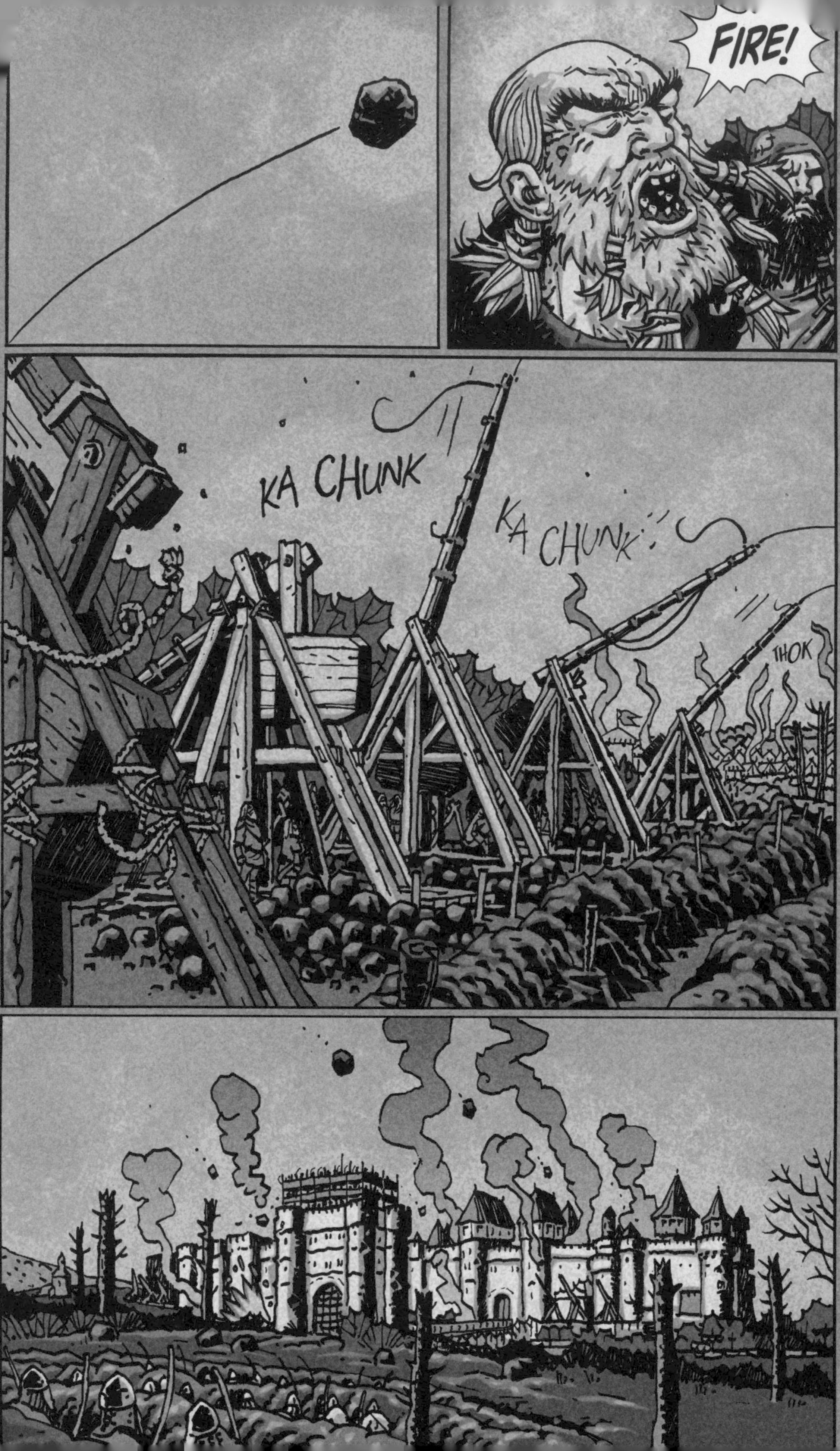
FIRE!
KA CHUNK
KA CHUNK
THOK

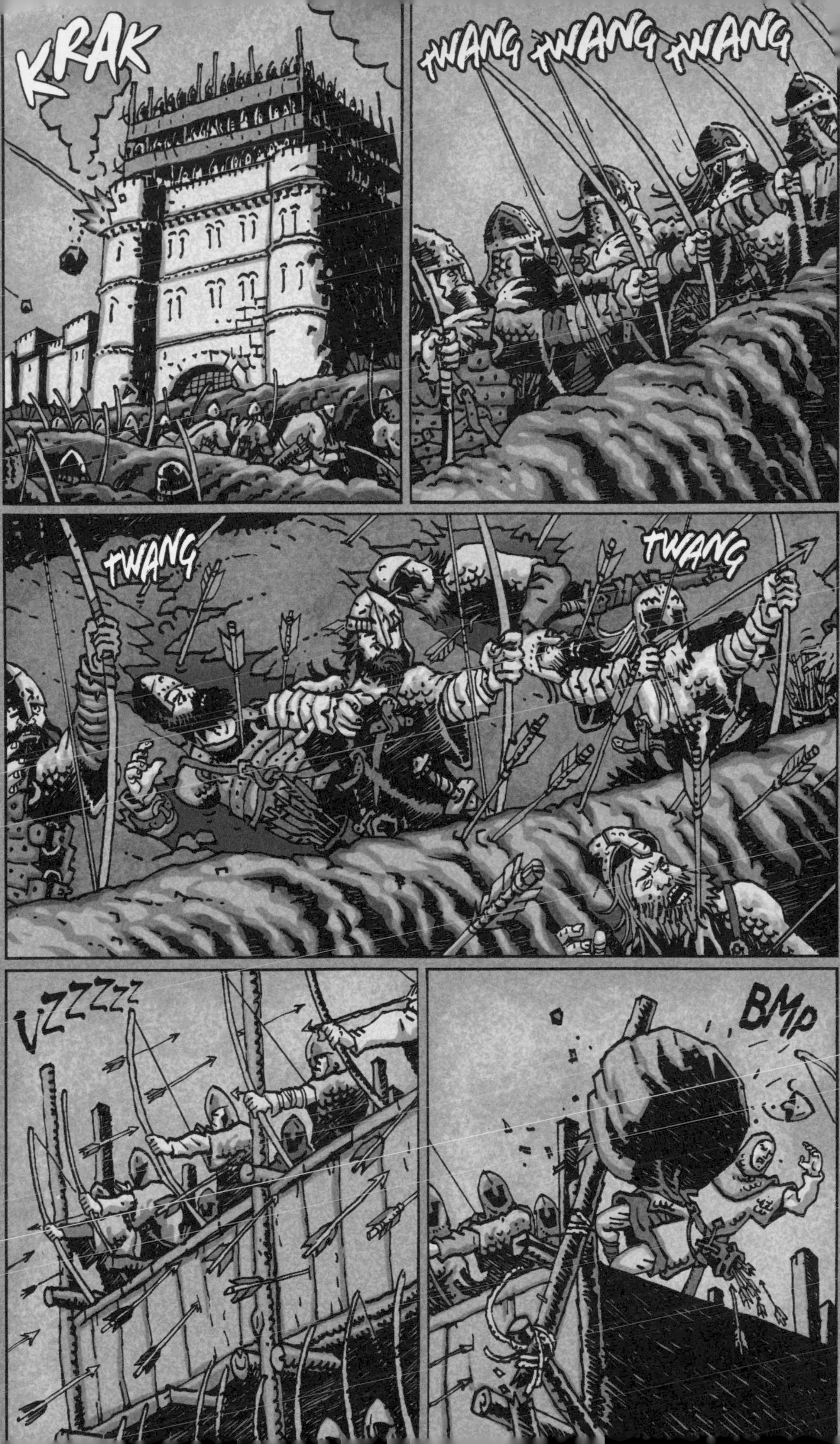
KRAK
TWANG TWANG TWANG
TWANG
TWANG
VZZZZZ
BMP

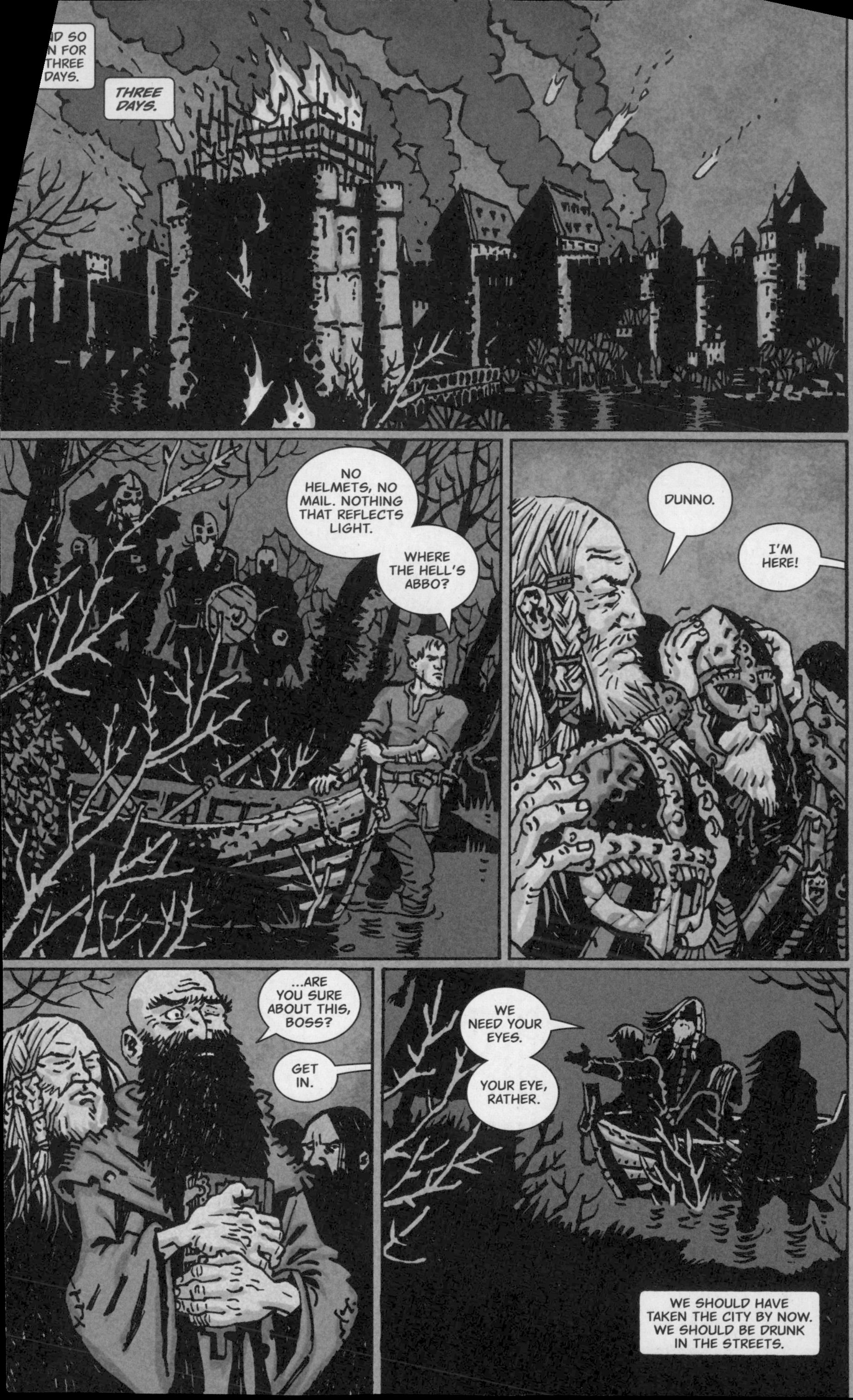

ND SO N FOR THREE DAYS.
THREE DAYS.
NO HELMETS, NO MAIL. NOTHING THAT REFLECTS LIGHT.
WHERE THE HELL'S ABBO?
DUNNO.
I'M HERE!
...ARE YOU SURE ABOUT THIS, BOSS?
GET IN.
WE NEED YOUR EYES.
YOUR EYE, RATHER.
WE SHOULD HAVE TAKEN THE CITY BY NOW. WE SHOULD BE DRUNK IN THE STREETS.

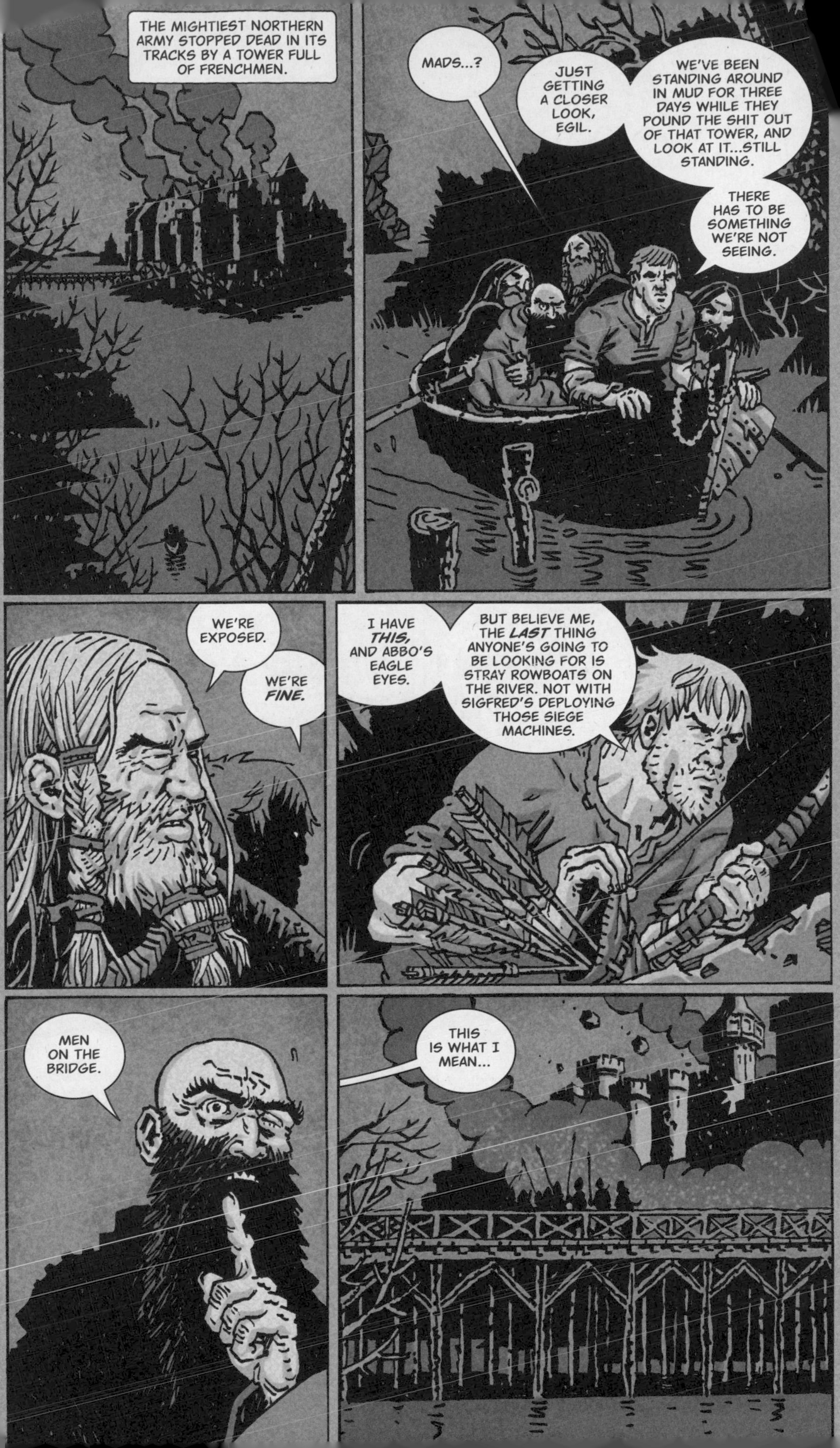
THE MIGHTIEST NORTHERN ARMY STOPPED DEAD IN ITS TRACKS BY A TOWER FULL OF FRENCHMEN.
MADS...?
JUST GETTING A CLOSER LOOK, EGIL.
WE'VE BEEN STANDING AROUND IN MUD FOR THREE DAYS WHILE THEY POUND THE SHIT OUT OF THAT TOWER, AND LOOK AT IT...STILL STANDING.
THERE HAS TO BE SOMETHING WE'RE NOT SEEING.
WE'RE EXPOSED.
WE'RE FINE.
I HAVE THIS, AND ABBO'S EAGLE EYES.
BUT BELIEVE ME, THE LAST THING ANYONE'S GOING TO BE LOOKING FOR IS STRAY ROWBOATS ON THE RIVER. NOT WITH SIGFRED'S DEPLOYING THOSE SIEGE MACHINES.
MEN ON THE BRIDGE.
THIS IS WHAT I MEAN...

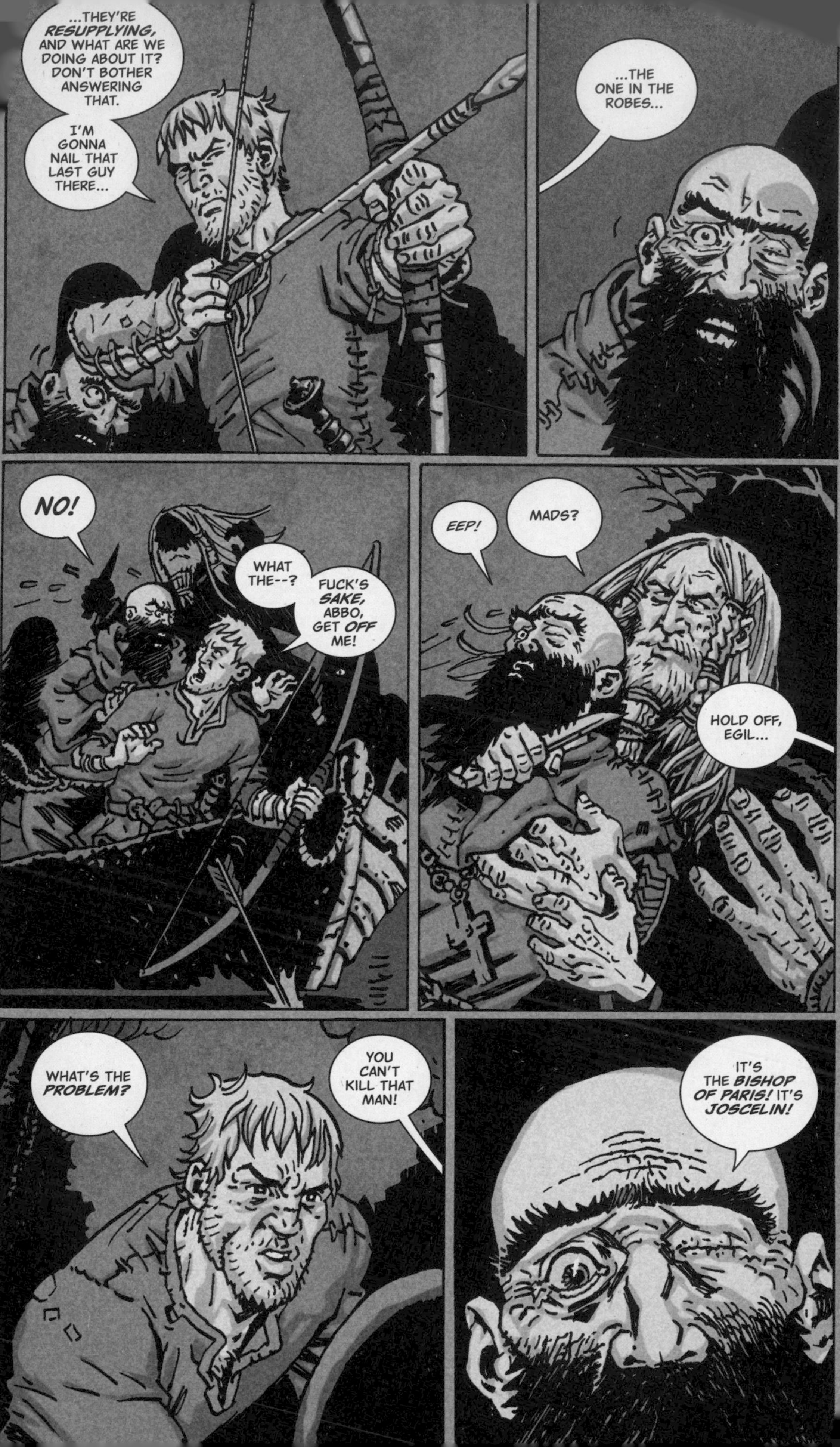
...THEY'RE RESUPPLYING, AND WHAT ARE WE DOING ABOUT IT? DON'T BOTHER ANSWERING THAT.
I'M GONNA NAIL THAT LAST GUY THERE...
...THE ONE IN THE ROBES...
NO!
WHAT THE--?
FUCK'S SAKE, ABBO, GET OFF ME!
EEP!
MADS?
HOLD OFF, EGIL...
WHAT'S THE PROBLEM?
YOU CAN'T KILL THAT MAN!
IT'S THE BISHOP OF PARIS! IT'S JOSCELIN!

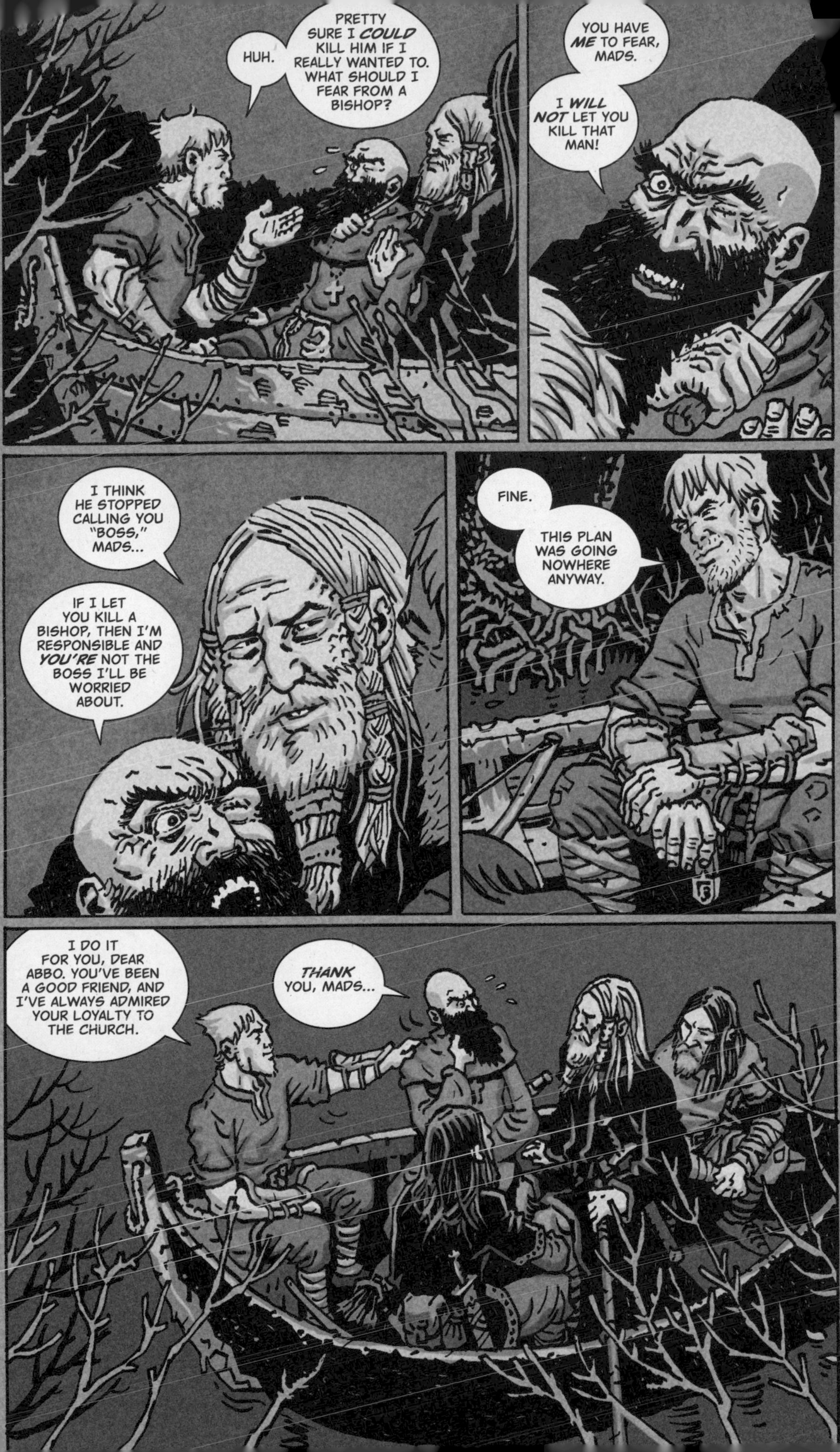
HUH.
PRETTY SURE I COULD KILL HIM IF I REALLY WANTED TO. WHAT SHOULD I FEAR FROM A BISHOP?
YOU HAVE ME TO FEAR, MADS.
I WILL NOT LET YOU KILL THAT MAN!
I THINK HE STOPPED CALLING YOU "BOSS," MADS...
IF I LET YOU KILL A BISHOP, THEN I'M RESPONSIBLE AND YOU'RE NOT THE BOSS I'LL BE WORRIED ABOUT.
FINE.
THIS PLAN WAS GOING NOWHERE ANYWAY.
I DO IT FOR YOU, DEAR ABBO. YOU'VE BEEN A GOOD FRIEND, AND I'VE ALWAYS ADMIRED YOUR LOYALTY TO THE CHURCH.
THANK YOU, MADS...

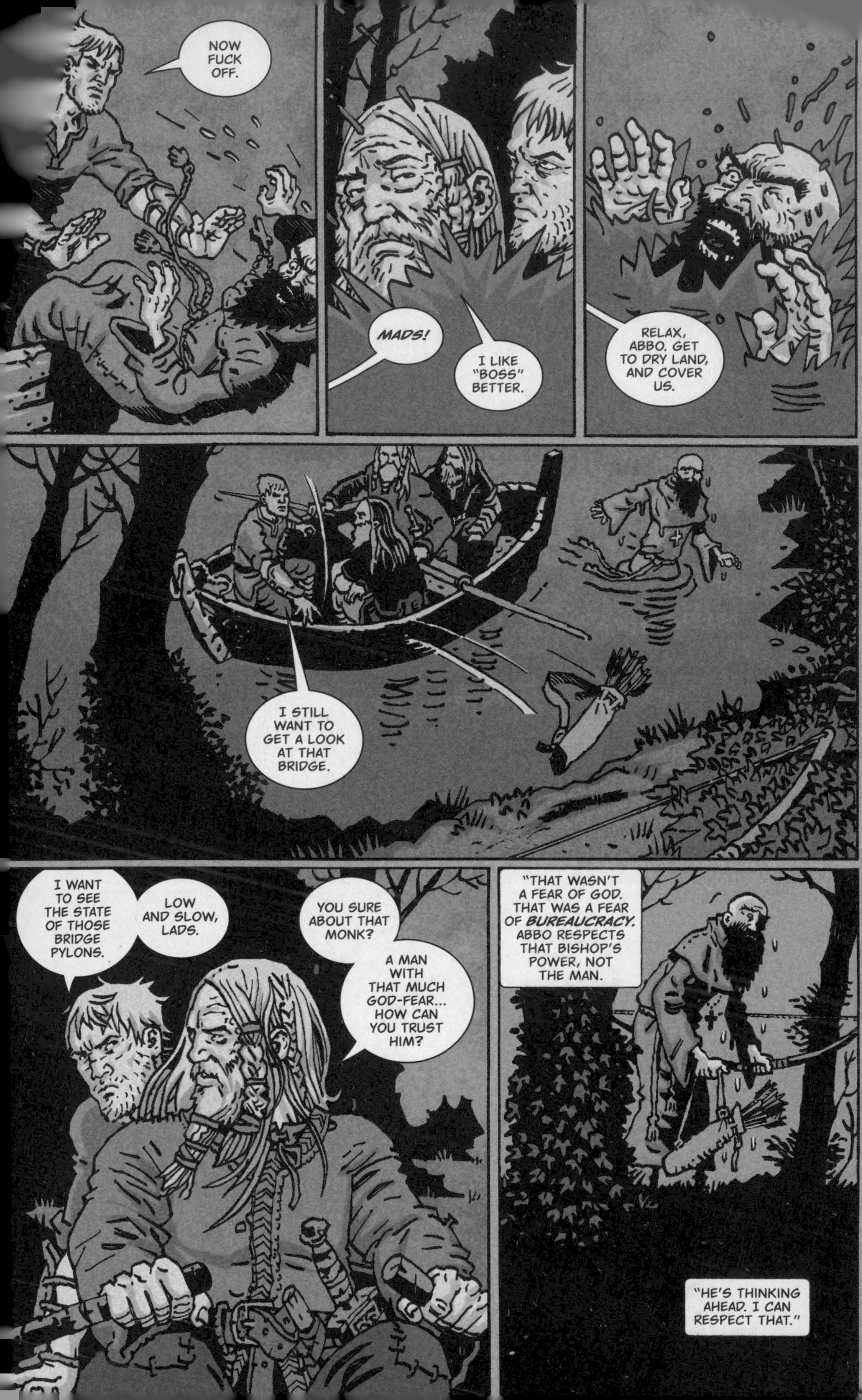
NOW FUCK OFF.
MADS!
I LIKE "BOSS" BETTER.
RELAX, ABBO. GET TO DRY LAND, AND COVER US.
I STILL WANT TO GET A LOOK AT THAT BRIDGE.
I WANT TO SEE THE STATE OF THOSE BRIDGE PYLONS.
LOW AND SLOW, LADS.
YOU SURE ABOUT THAT MONK?
A MAN WITH THAT MUCH GOD-FEAR... HOW CAN YOU TRUST HIM?
"THAT WASN'T A FEAR OF GOD. THAT WAS A FEAR OF BUREAUCRACY. ABBO RESPECTS THAT BISHOP'S POWER, NOT THE MAN.
"HE'S THINKING AHEAD. I CAN RESPECT THAT."

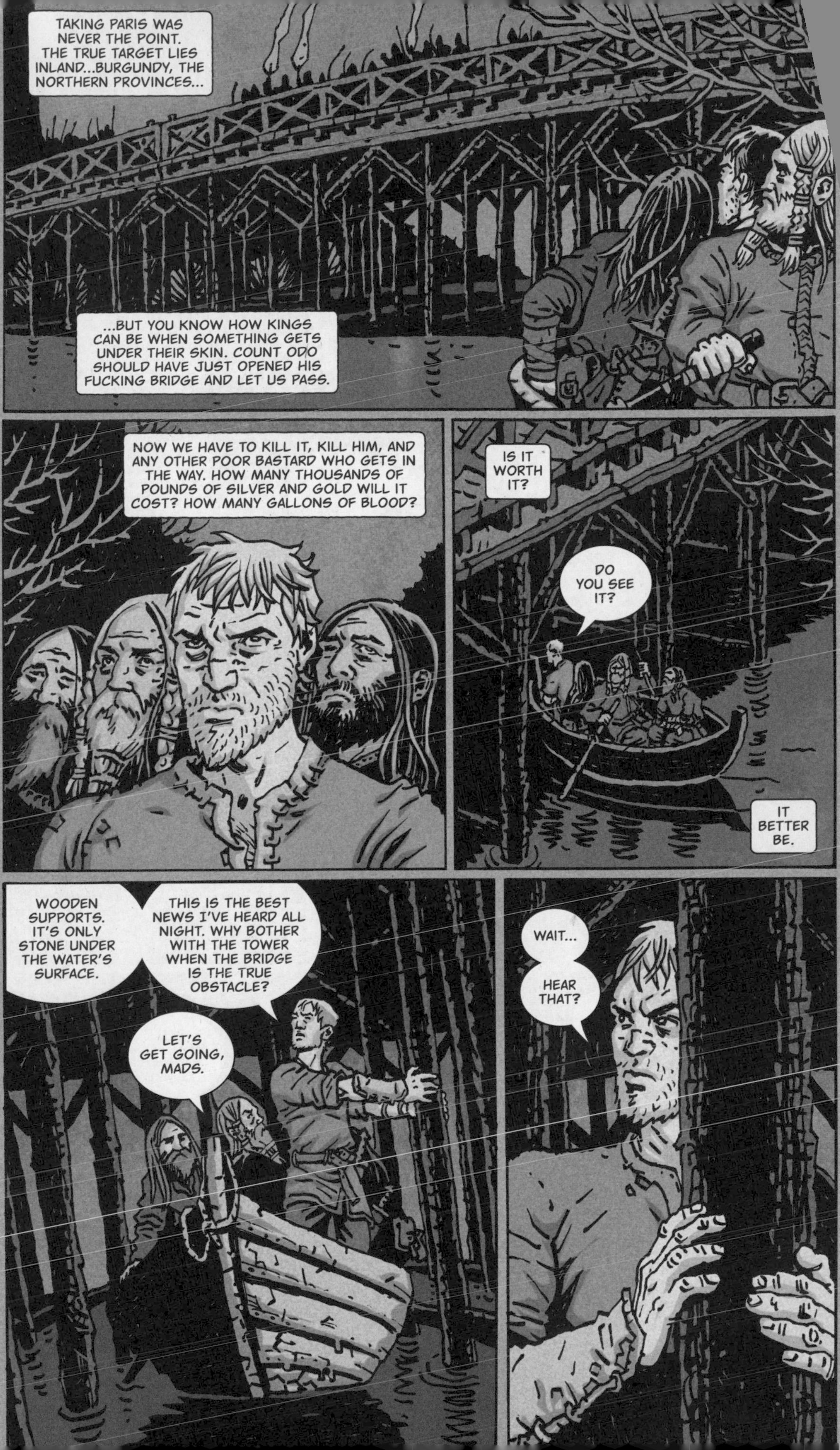
TAKING PARIS WAS NEVER THE POINT. THE TRUE TARGET LIES INLAND...BURGUNDY, THE NORTHERN PROVINCES...
...BUT YOU KNOW HOW KINGS CAN BE WHEN SOMETHING GETS UNDER THEIR SKIN. COUNT ODO SHOULD HAVE JUST OPENED HIS FUCKING BRIDGE AND LET US PASS.
NOW WE HAVE TO KILL IT, KILL HIM, AND ANY OTHER POOR BASTARD WHO GETS IN THE WAY. HOW MANY THOUSANDS OF POUNDS OF SILVER AND GOLD WILL IT COST? HOW MANY GALLONS OF BLOOD?
IS IT WORTH IT?
DO YOU SEE IT?
IT BETTER BE.
WOODEN SUPPORTS. IT'S ONLY STONE UNDER THE WATER'S SURFACE.
THIS IS THE BEST NEWS I'VE HEARD ALL NIGHT. WHY BOTHER WITH THE TOWER WHEN THE BRIDGE IS THE TRUE OBSTACLE?
LET'S GET GOING, MADS.
WAIT...
HEAR THAT?

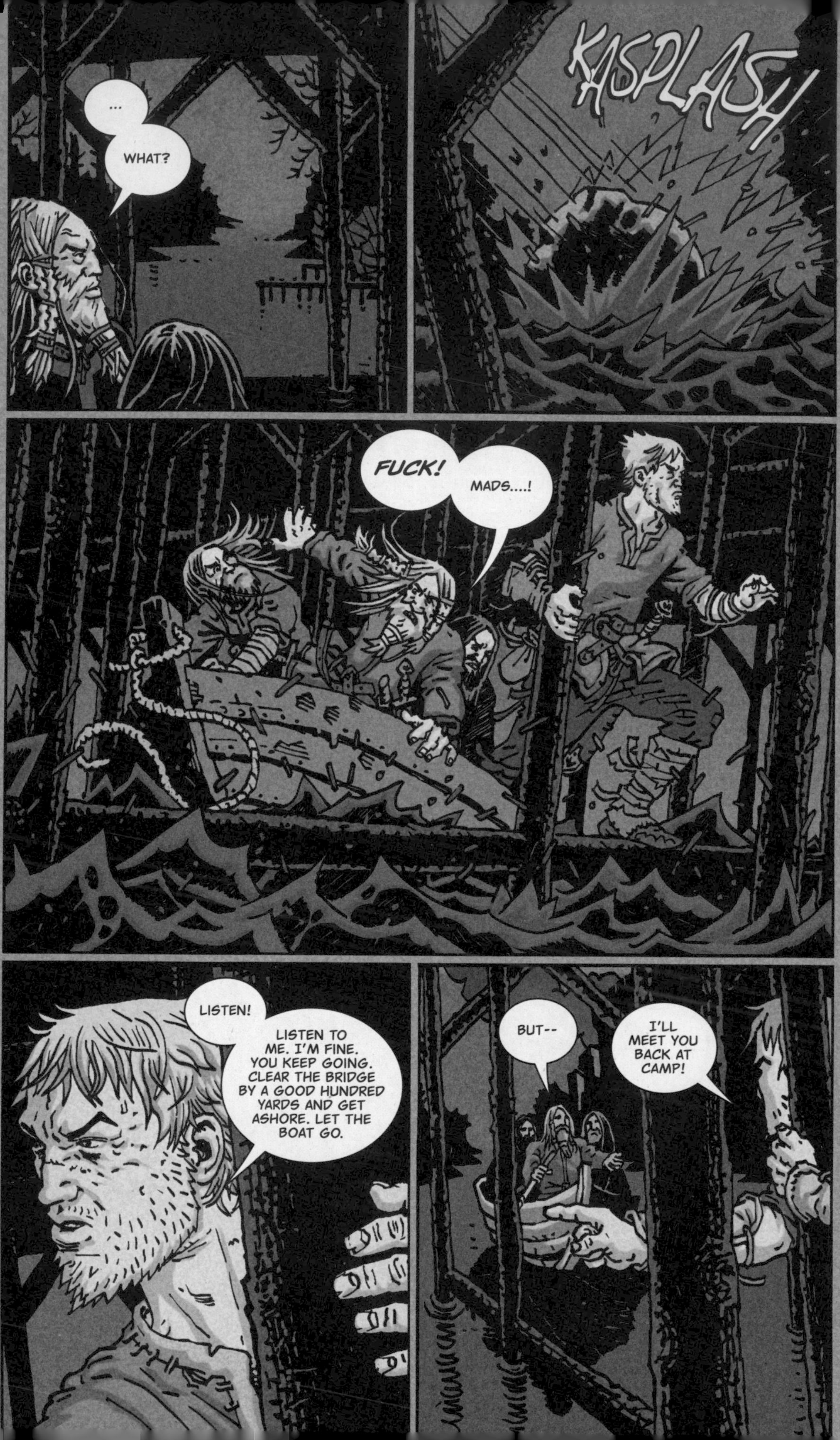

...
WHAT?
KASPLASH
FUCK!
MADS....!
LISTEN!
LISTEN TO ME. I'M FINE. YOU KEEP GOING. CLEAR THE BRIDGE BY A GOOD HUNDRED YARDS AND GET ASHORE. LET THE BOAT GO.
BUT--
I'LL MEET YOU BACK AT CAMP!

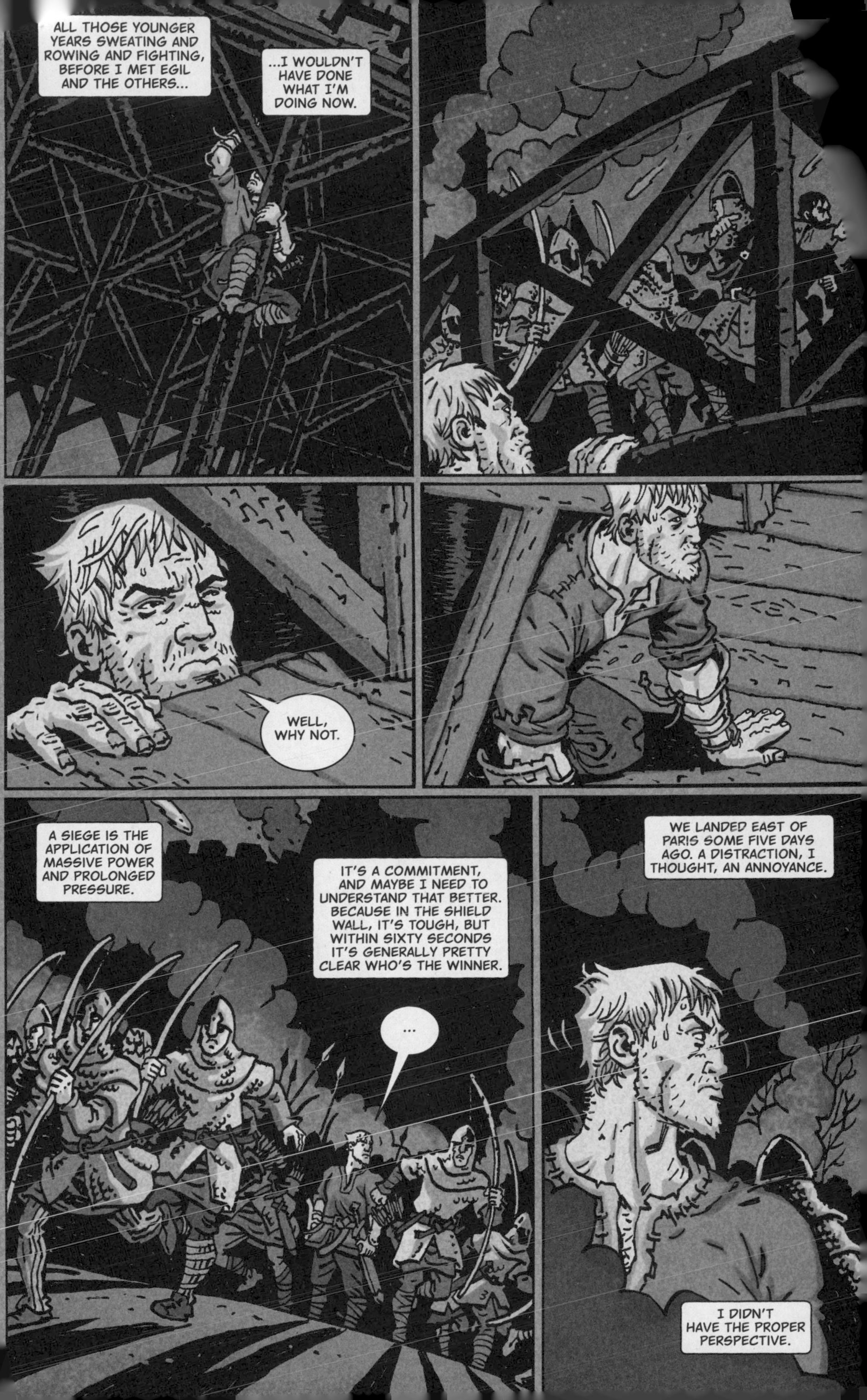
ALL THOSE YOUNGER YEARS SWEATING AND ROWING AND FIGHTING, BEFORE I MET EGIL AND THE OTHERS...
...I WOULDN'T HAVE DONE WHAT I'M DOING NOW.
WELL, WHY NOT.
A SIEGE IS THE APPLICATION OF MASSIVE POWER AND PROLONGED PRESSURE.
IT'S A COMMITMENT, AND MAYBE I NEED TO UNDERSTAND THAT BETTER. BECAUSE IN THE SHIELD WALL, IT'S TOUGH, BUT WITHIN SIXTY SECONDS IT'S GENERALLY PRETTY CLEAR WHO'S THE WINNER.
...
WE LANDED EAST OF PARIS SOME FIVE DAYS AGO. A DISTRACTION, I THOUGHT, AN ANNOYANCE.
I DIDN'T HAVE THE PROPER PERSPECTIVE.

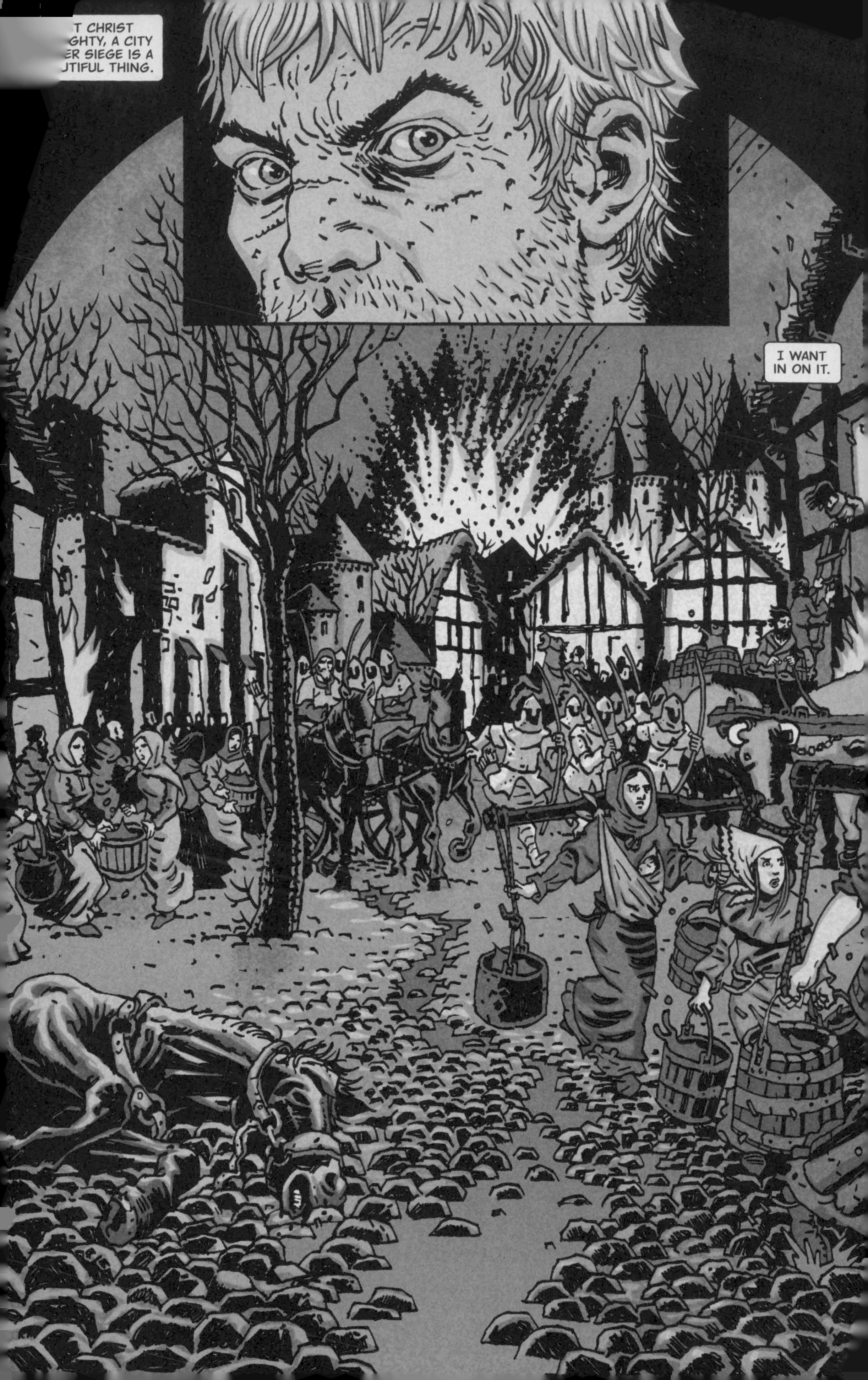
T CHRIST
GHTY, A CITY
ER SIEGE IS A
UTIFUL THING.
I WANT
IN ON IT.

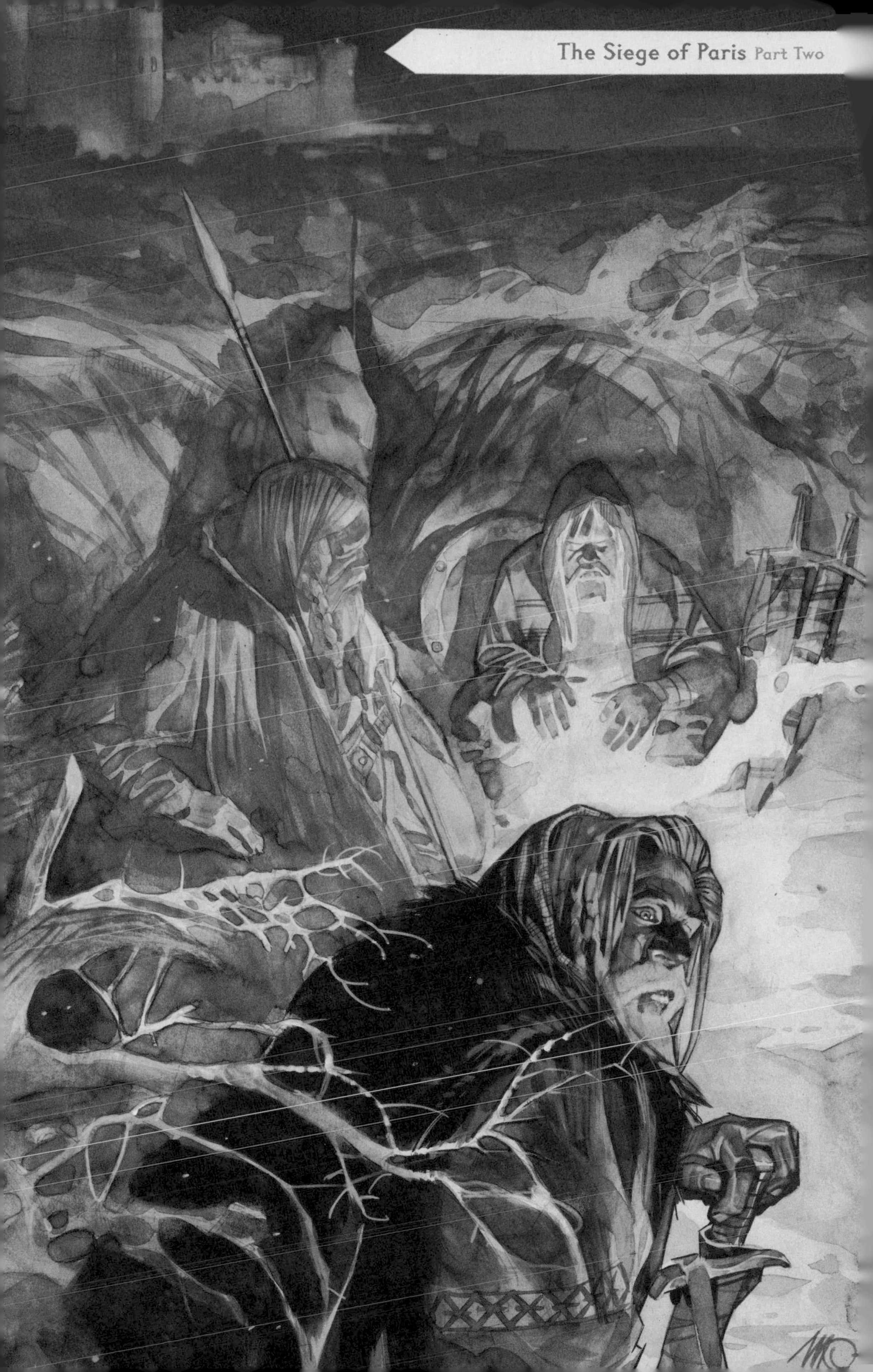

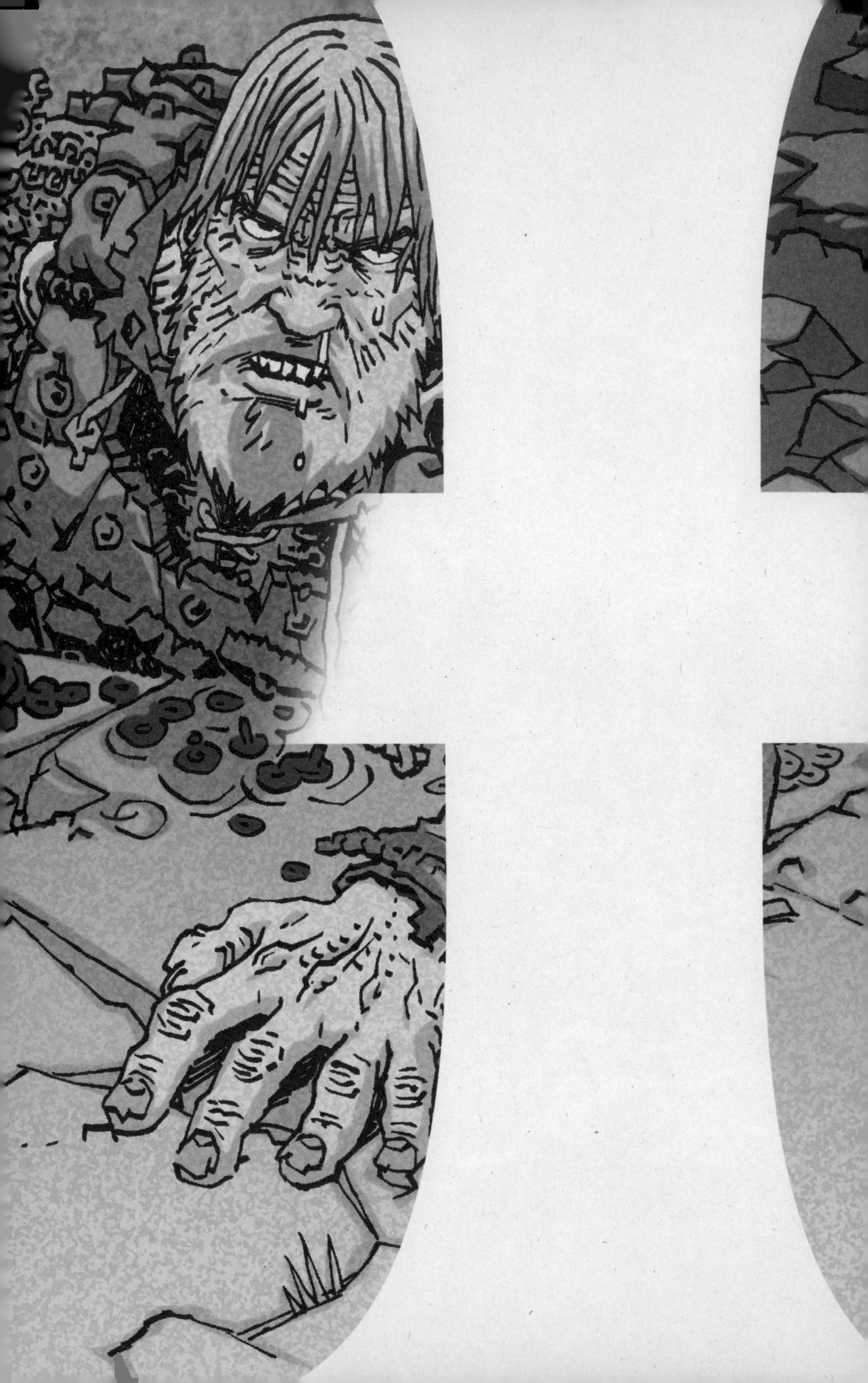

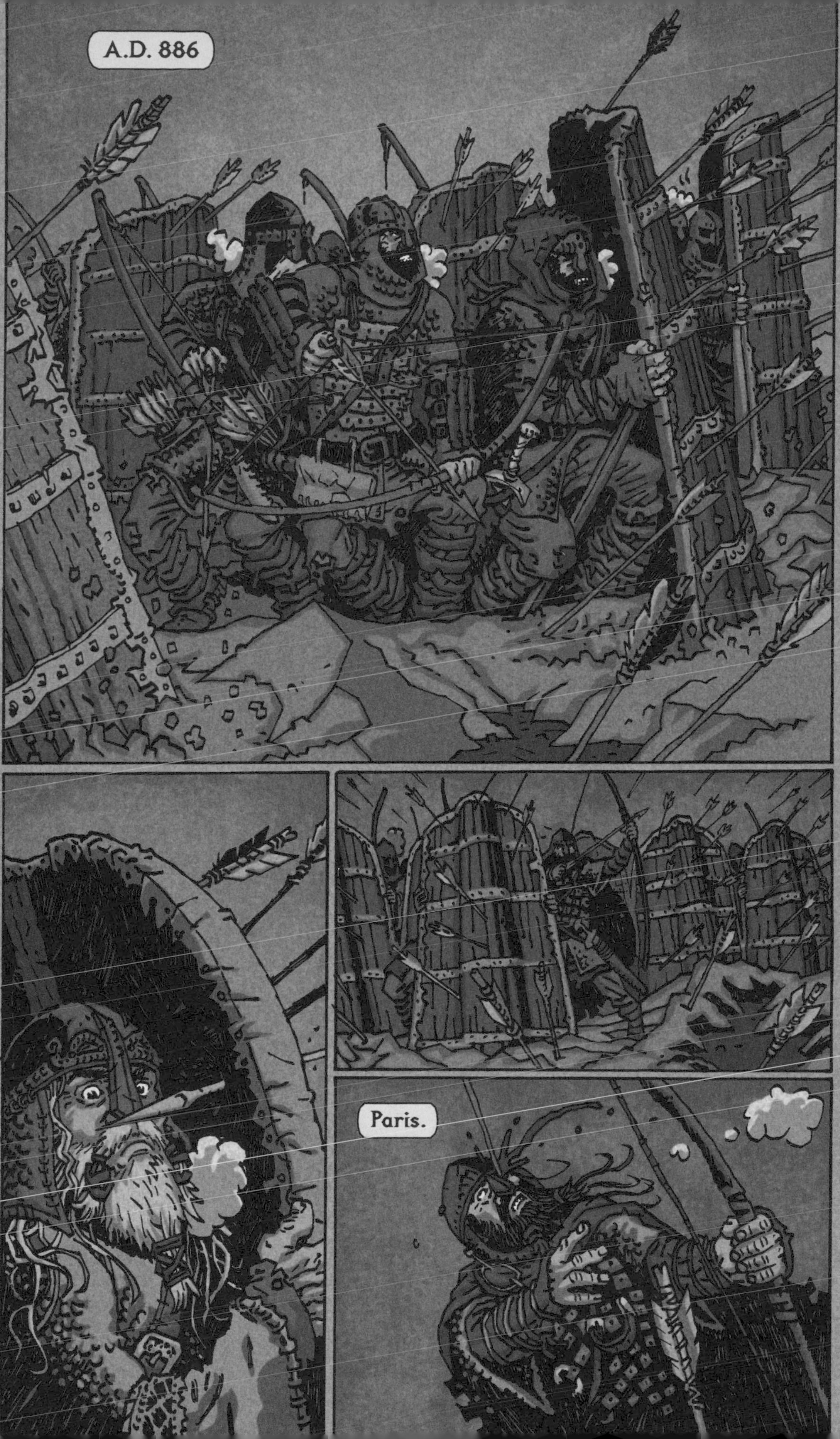
A.D. 886
Paris.

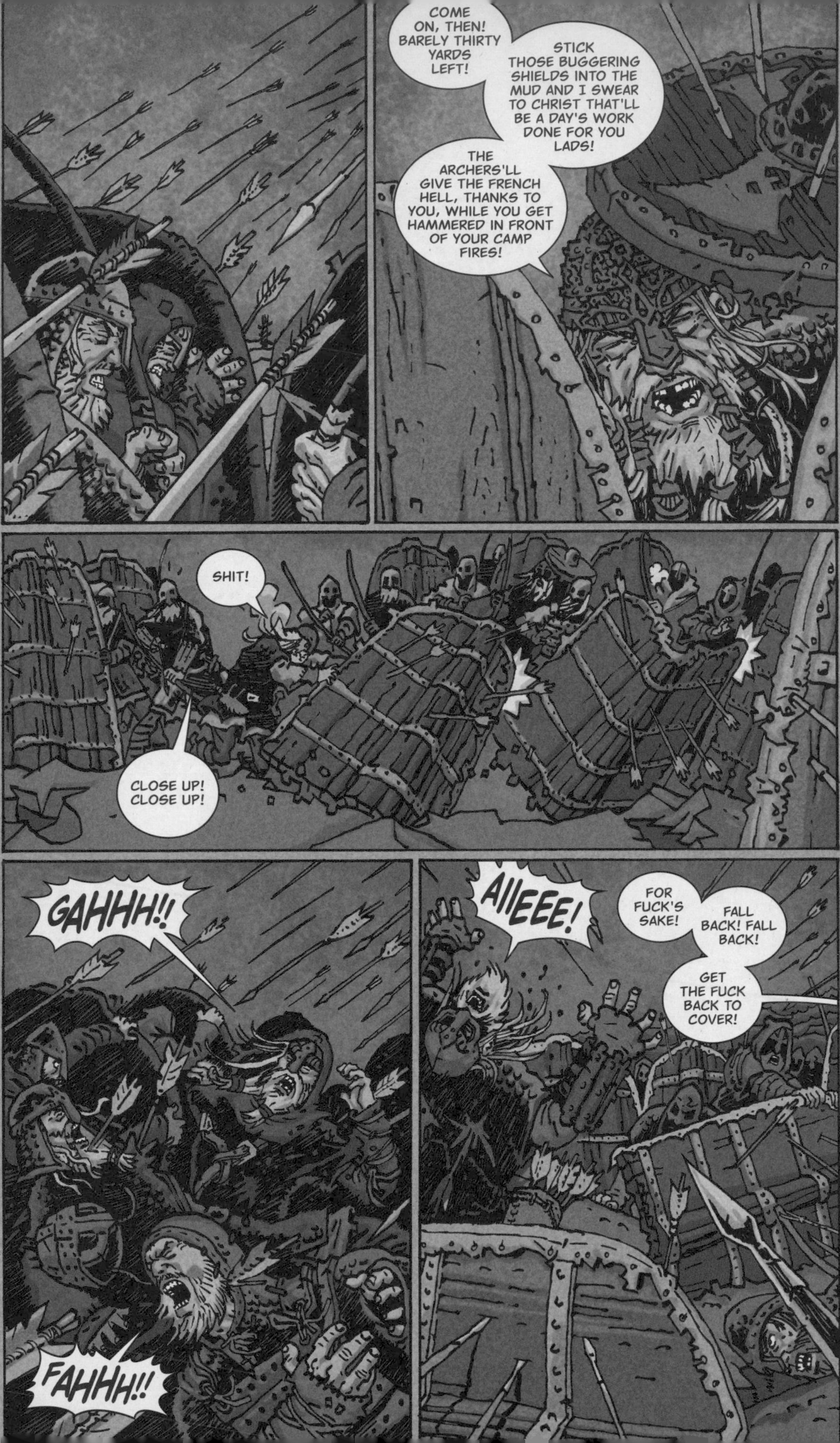
COME ON, THEN! BARELY THIRTY YARDS LEFT!
STICK THOSE BUGGERING SHIELDS INTO THE MUD AND I SWEAR TO CHRIST THAT'LL BE A DAY'S WORK DONE FOR YOU LADS!
THE ARCHERS'LL GIVE THE FRENCH HELL, THANKS TO YOU, WHILE YOU GET HAMMERED IN FRONT OF YOUR CAMP FIRES!
SHIT!
CLOSE UP! CLOSE UP!
GAHHH!!
FAHHH!!
AIIEEE!
FOR FUCK'S SAKE!
FALL BACK! FALL BACK!
GET THE FUCK BACK TO COVER!

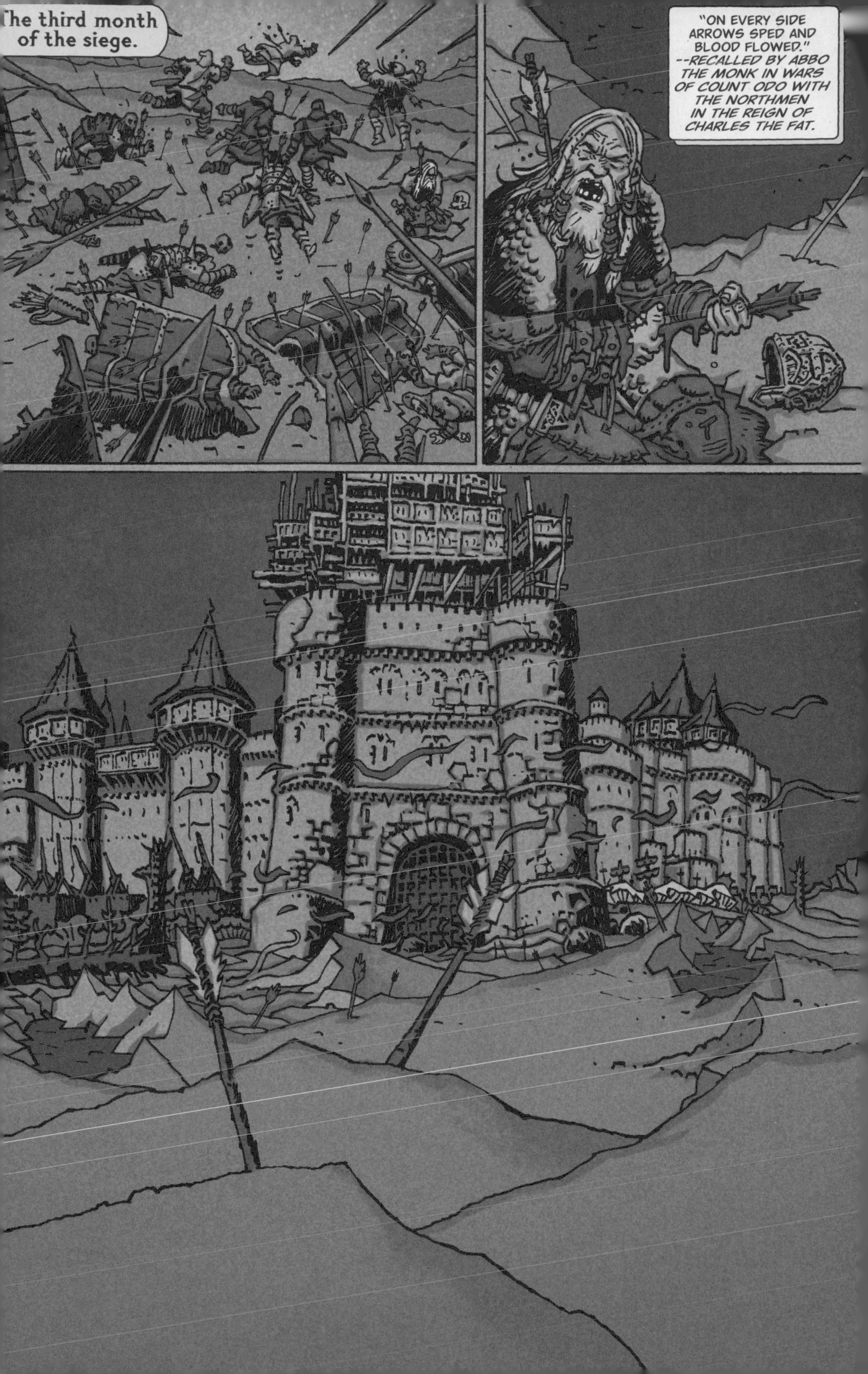
The third month of the siege.
"ON EVERY SIDE ARROWS SPED AND BLOOD FLOWED."
--RECALLED BY ABBO THE MONK IN WARS OF COUNT ODO WITH THE NORTHMEN IN THE REIGN OF CHARLES THE FAT.

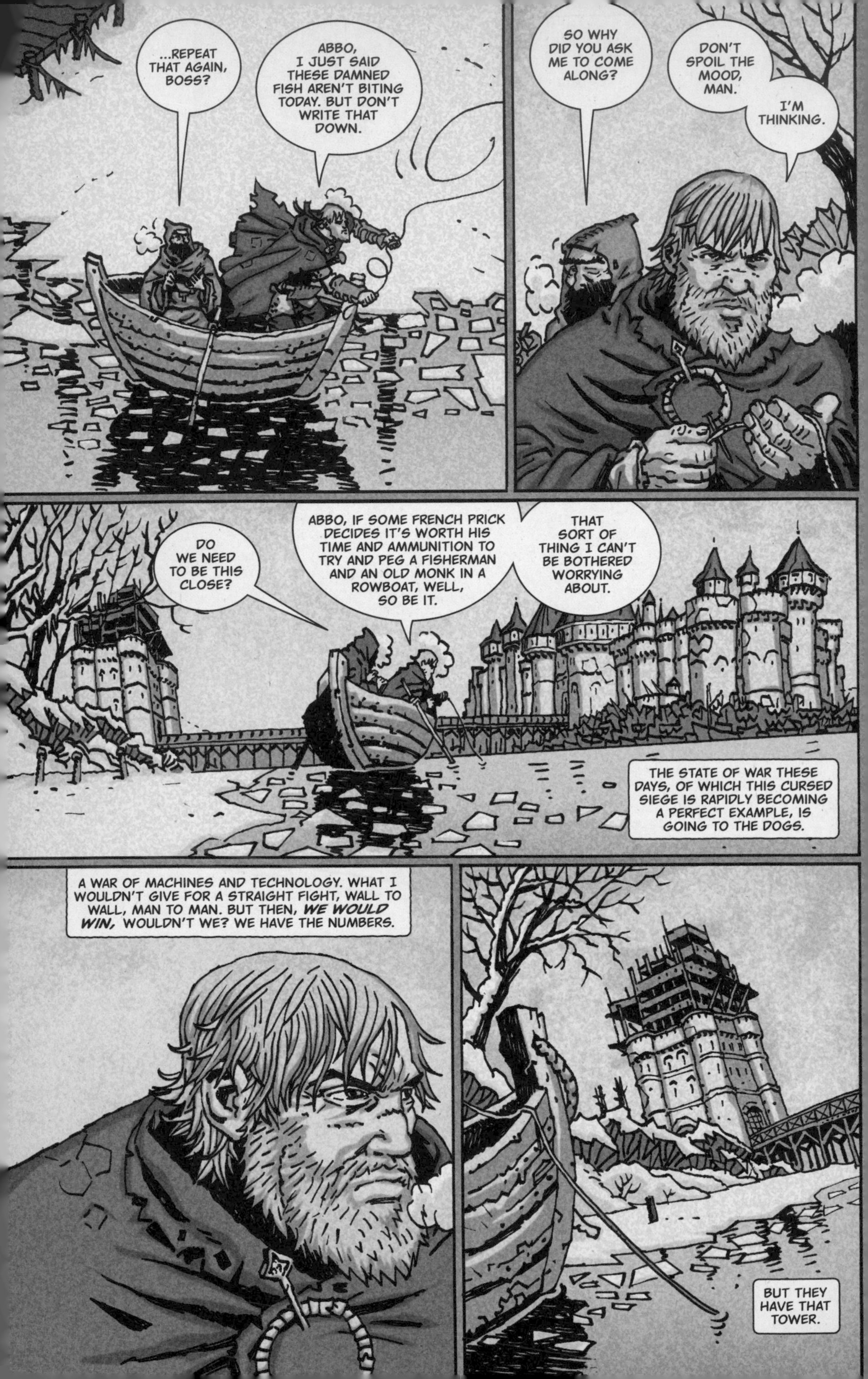
...REPEAT THAT AGAIN, BOSS?
ABBO, I JUST SAID THESE DAMNED FISH AREN'T BITING TODAY. BUT DON'T WRITE THAT DOWN.
SO WHY DID YOU ASK ME TO COME ALONG?
DON'T SPOIL THE MOOD, MAN.
I'M THINKING.
DO WE NEED TO BE THIS CLOSE?
ABBO, IF SOME FRENCH PRICK DECIDES IT'S WORTH HIS TIME AND AMMUNITION TO TRY AND PEG A FISHERMAN AND AN OLD MONK IN A ROWBOAT, WELL, SO BE IT.
THAT SORT OF THING I CAN'T BE BOTHERED WORRYING ABOUT.
THE STATE OF WAR THESE DAYS, OF WHICH THIS CURSED SIEGE IS RAPIDLY BECOMING A PERFECT EXAMPLE, IS GOING TO THE DOGS.
A WAR OF MACHINES AND TECHNOLOGY. WHAT I WOULDN'T GIVE FOR A STRAIGHT FIGHT, WALL TO WALL, MAN TO MAN. BUT THEN, *WE WOULD WIN,* WOULDN'T WE? WE HAVE THE NUMBERS.
BUT THEY HAVE THAT TOWER.

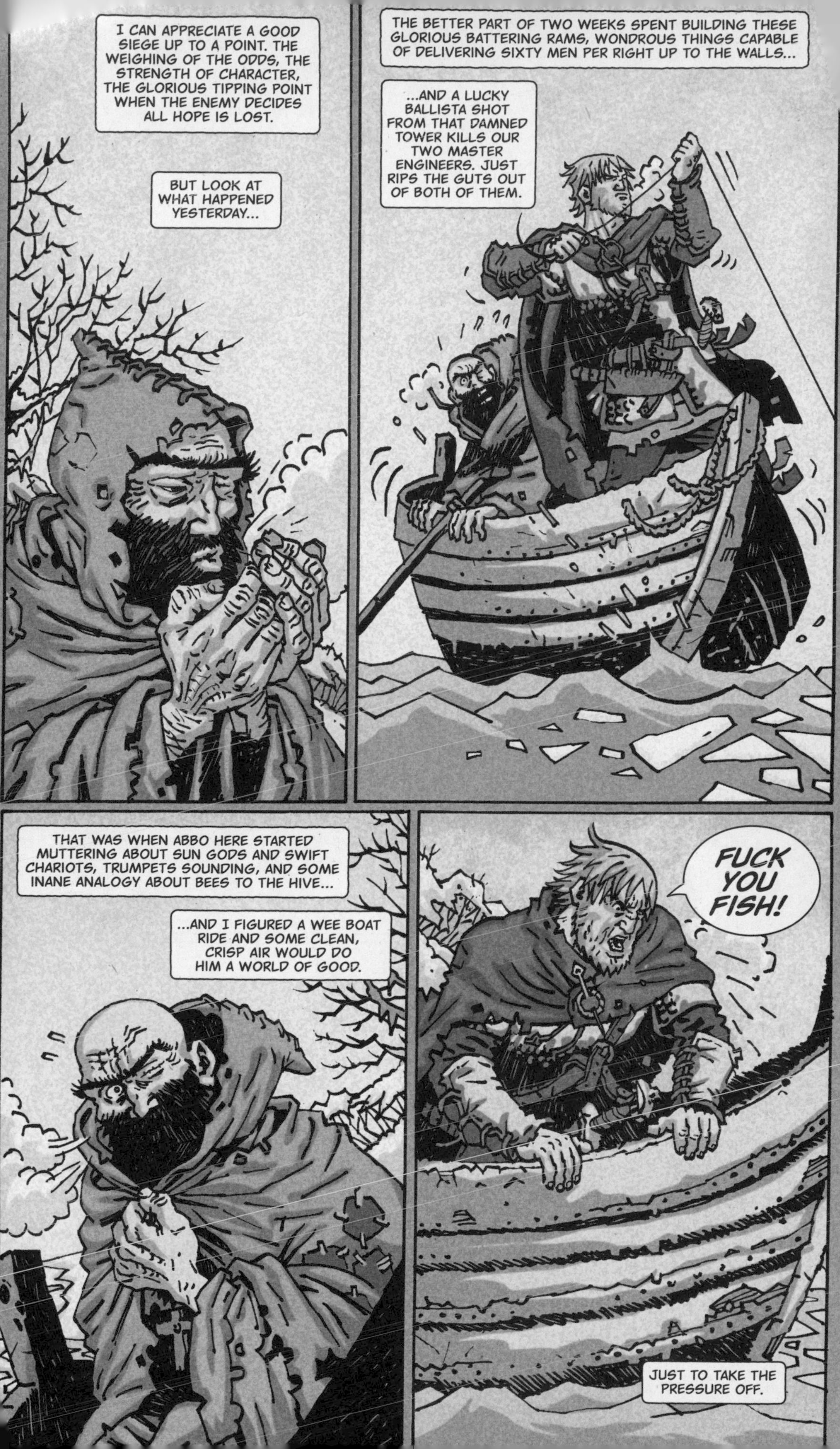
I CAN APPRECIATE A GOOD SIEGE UP TO A POINT. THE WEIGHING OF THE ODDS, THE STRENGTH OF CHARACTER, THE GLORIOUS TIPPING POINT WHEN THE ENEMY DECIDES ALL HOPE IS LOST.
BUT LOOK AT WHAT HAPPENED YESTERDAY...
THE BETTER PART OF TWO WEEKS SPENT BUILDING THESE GLORIOUS BATTERING RAMS, WONDROUS THINGS CAPABLE OF DELIVERING SIXTY MEN PER RIGHT UP TO THE WALLS...
...AND A LUCKY BALLISTA SHOT FROM THAT DAMNED TOWER KILLS OUR TWO MASTER ENGINEERS. JUST RIPS THE GUTS OUT OF BOTH OF THEM.
THAT WAS WHEN ABBO HERE STARTED MUTTERING ABOUT SUN GODS AND SWIFT CHARIOTS, TRUMPETS SOUNDING, AND SOME INANE ANALOGY ABOUT BEES TO THE HIVE...
...AND I FIGURED A WEE BOAT RIDE AND SOME CLEAN, CRISP AIR WOULD DO HIM A WORLD OF GOOD.
FUCK YOU FISH!
JUST TO TAKE THE PRESSURE OFF.

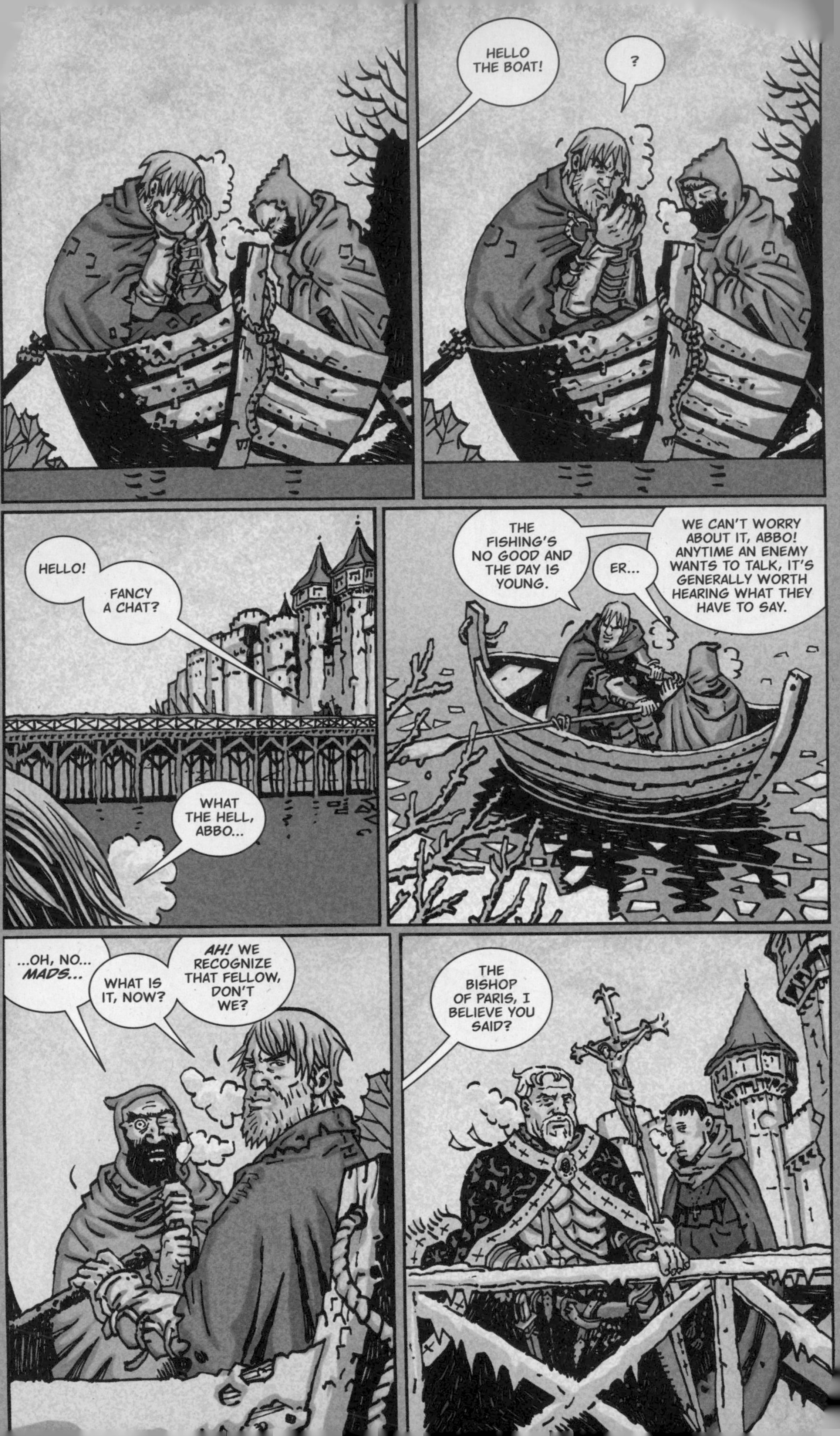
HELLO THE BOAT!
?
HELLO!
FANCY A CHAT?
WHAT THE HELL, ABBO...
THE FISHING'S NO GOOD AND THE DAY IS YOUNG.
ER...
WE CAN'T WORRY ABOUT IT, ABBO! ANYTIME AN ENEMY WANTS TO TALK, IT'S GENERALLY WORTH HEARING WHAT THEY HAVE TO SAY.
...OH, NO... *MADS*...
WHAT IS IT, NOW?
AH! WE RECOGNIZE THAT FELLOW, DON'T WE?
THE BISHOP OF PARIS, I BELIEVE YOU SAID?

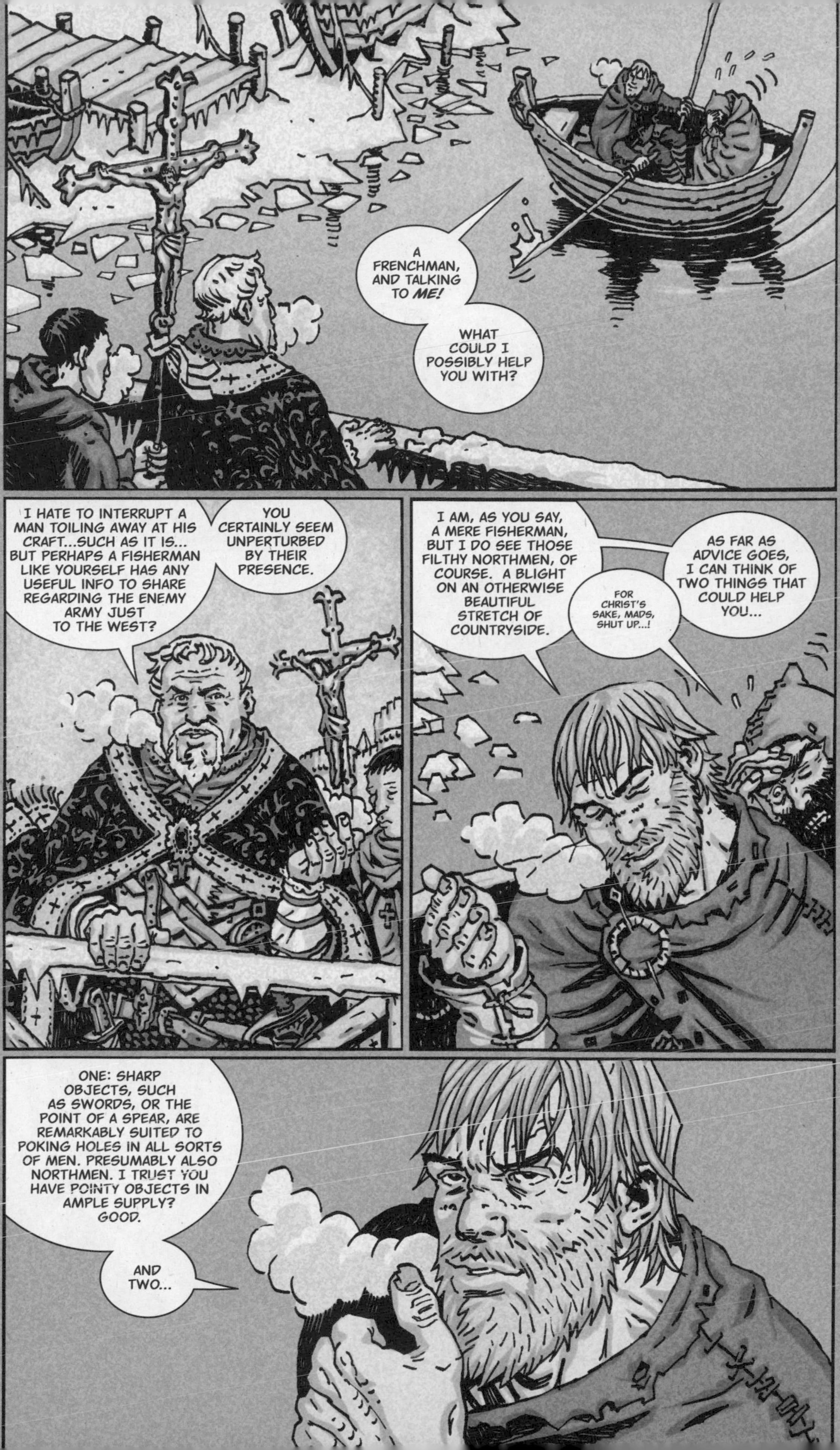

A FRENCHMAN, AND TALKING TO *ME!*
WHAT COULD I POSSIBLY HELP YOU WITH?
I HATE TO INTERRUPT A MAN TOILING AWAY AT HIS CRAFT...SUCH AS IT IS... BUT PERHAPS A FISHERMAN LIKE YOURSELF HAS ANY USEFUL INFO TO SHARE REGARDING THE ENEMY ARMY JUST TO THE WEST?
YOU CERTAINLY SEEM UNPERTURBED BY THEIR PRESENCE.
I AM, AS YOU SAY, A MERE FISHERMAN, BUT I DO SEE THOSE FILTHY NORTHMEN, OF COURSE. A BLIGHT ON AN OTHERWISE BEAUTIFUL STRETCH OF COUNTRYSIDE.
AS FAR AS ADVICE GOES, I CAN THINK OF TWO THINGS THAT COULD HELP YOU...
FOR CHRIST'S SAKE, MADS, SHUT UP...!
ONE: SHARP OBJECTS, SUCH AS SWORDS, OR THE POINT OF A SPEAR, ARE REMARKABLY SUITED TO POKING HOLES IN ALL SORTS OF MEN. PRESUMABLY ALSO NORTHMEN. I TRUST YOU HAVE POINTY OBJECTS IN AMPLE SUPPLY? GOOD.
AND TWO...

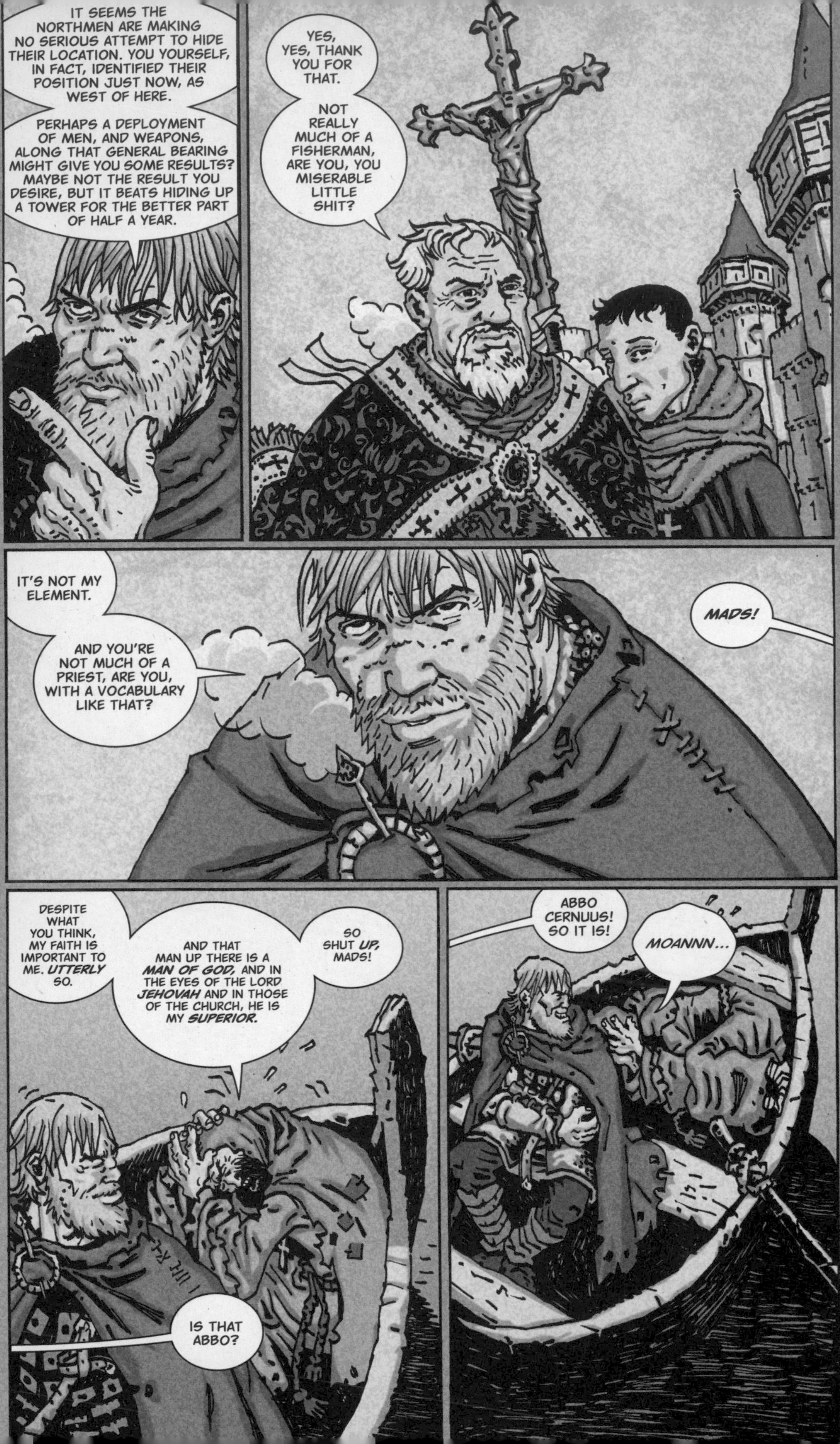

IT SEEMS THE NORTHMEN ARE MAKING NO SERIOUS ATTEMPT TO HIDE THEIR LOCATION. YOU YOURSELF, IN FACT, IDENTIFIED THEIR POSITION JUST NOW, AS WEST OF HERE.
PERHAPS A DEPLOYMENT OF MEN, AND WEAPONS, ALONG THAT GENERAL BEARING MIGHT GIVE YOU SOME RESULTS? MAYBE NOT THE RESULT YOU DESIRE, BUT IT BEATS HIDING UP A TOWER FOR THE BETTER PART OF HALF A YEAR.
YES, YES, THANK YOU FOR THAT.
NOT REALLY MUCH OF A FISHERMAN, ARE YOU, YOU MISERABLE LITTLE SHIT?
IT'S NOT MY ELEMENT.
AND YOU'RE NOT MUCH OF A PRIEST, ARE YOU, WITH A VOCABULARY LIKE THAT?
MADS!
DESPITE WHAT YOU THINK, MY FAITH IS IMPORTANT TO ME. *UTTERLY* SO.
AND THAT MAN UP THERE IS A *MAN OF GOD,* AND IN THE EYES OF THE LORD *JEHOVAH* AND IN THOSE OF THE CHURCH, HE IS MY *SUPERIOR.*
SO SHUT *UP,* MADS!
IS THAT ABBO?
ABBO CERNUUS! SO IT IS!
MOANNN...

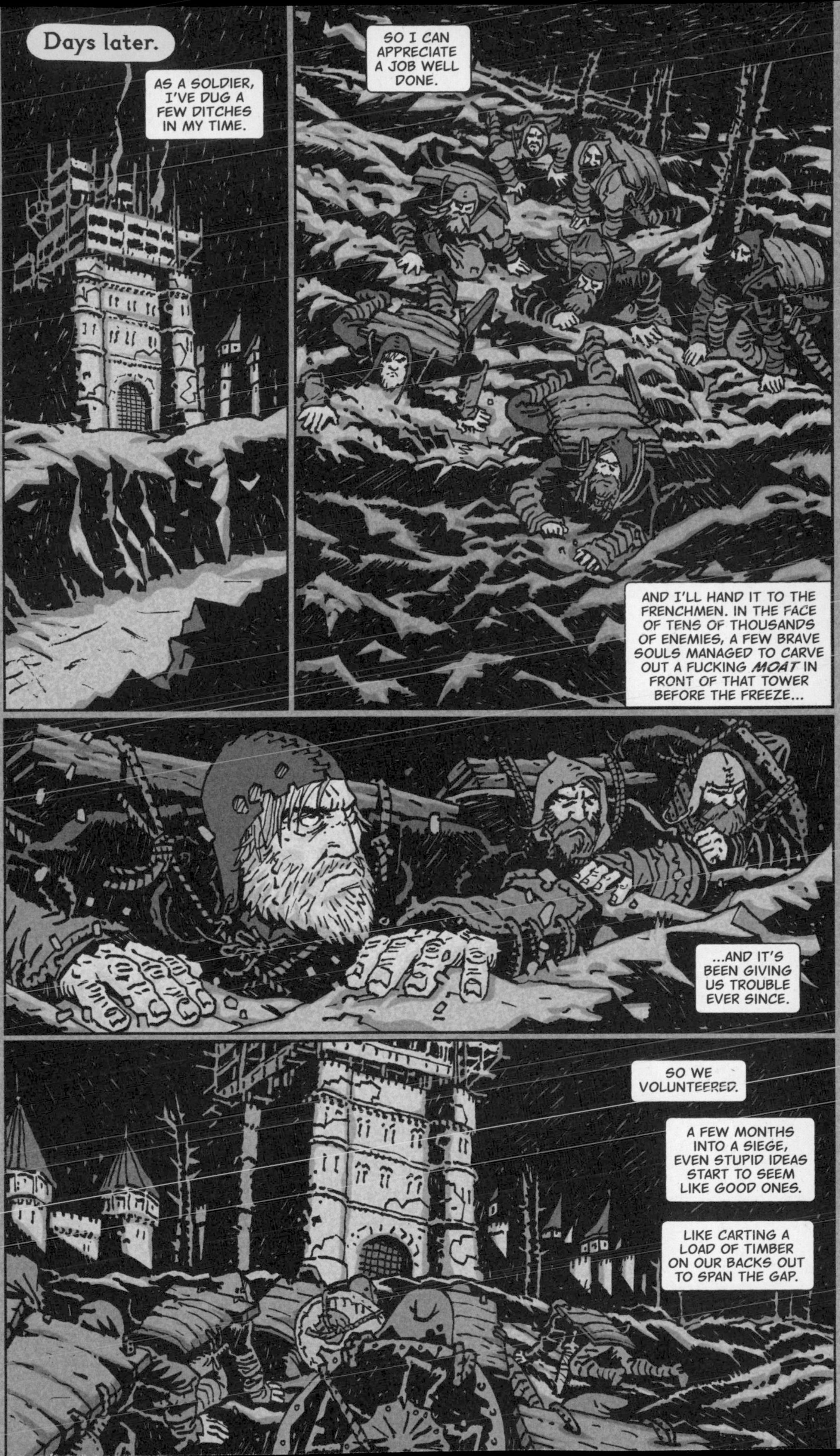
Days later.
AS A SOLDIER, I'VE DUG A FEW DITCHES IN MY TIME.
SO I CAN APPRECIATE A JOB WELL DONE.
AND I'LL HAND IT TO THE FRENCHMEN. IN THE FACE OF TENS OF THOUSANDS OF ENEMIES, A FEW BRAVE SOULS MANAGED TO CARVE OUT A FUCKING *MOAT* IN FRONT OF THAT TOWER BEFORE THE FREEZE...
...AND IT'S BEEN GIVING US TROUBLE EVER SINCE.
SO WE VOLUNTEERED.
A FEW MONTHS INTO A SIEGE, EVEN STUPID IDEAS START TO SEEM LIKE GOOD ONES.
LIKE CARTING A LOAD OF TIMBER ON OUR BACKS OUT TO SPAN THE GAP.

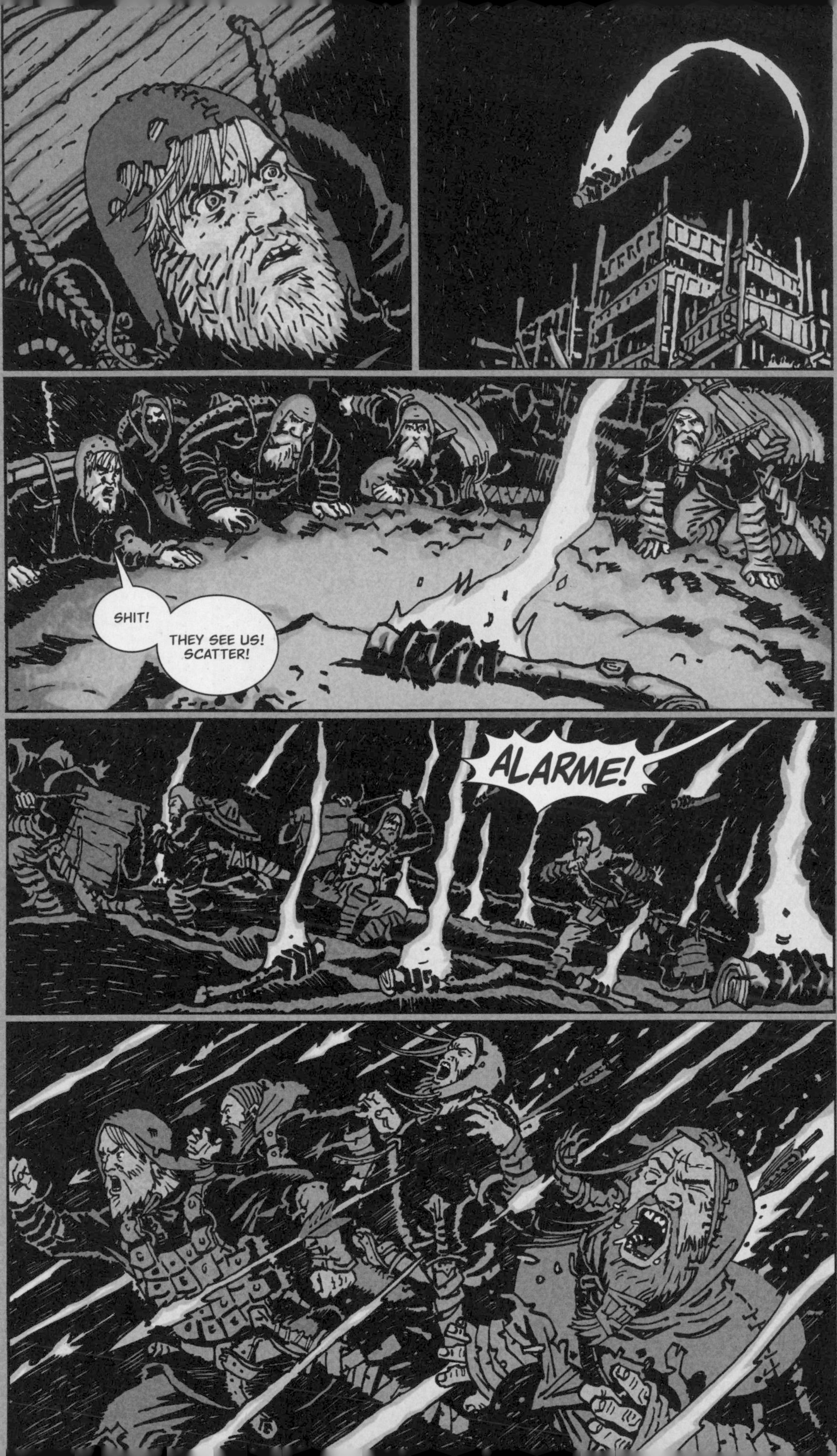
SHIT!
THEY SEE US! SCATTER!
ALARME!

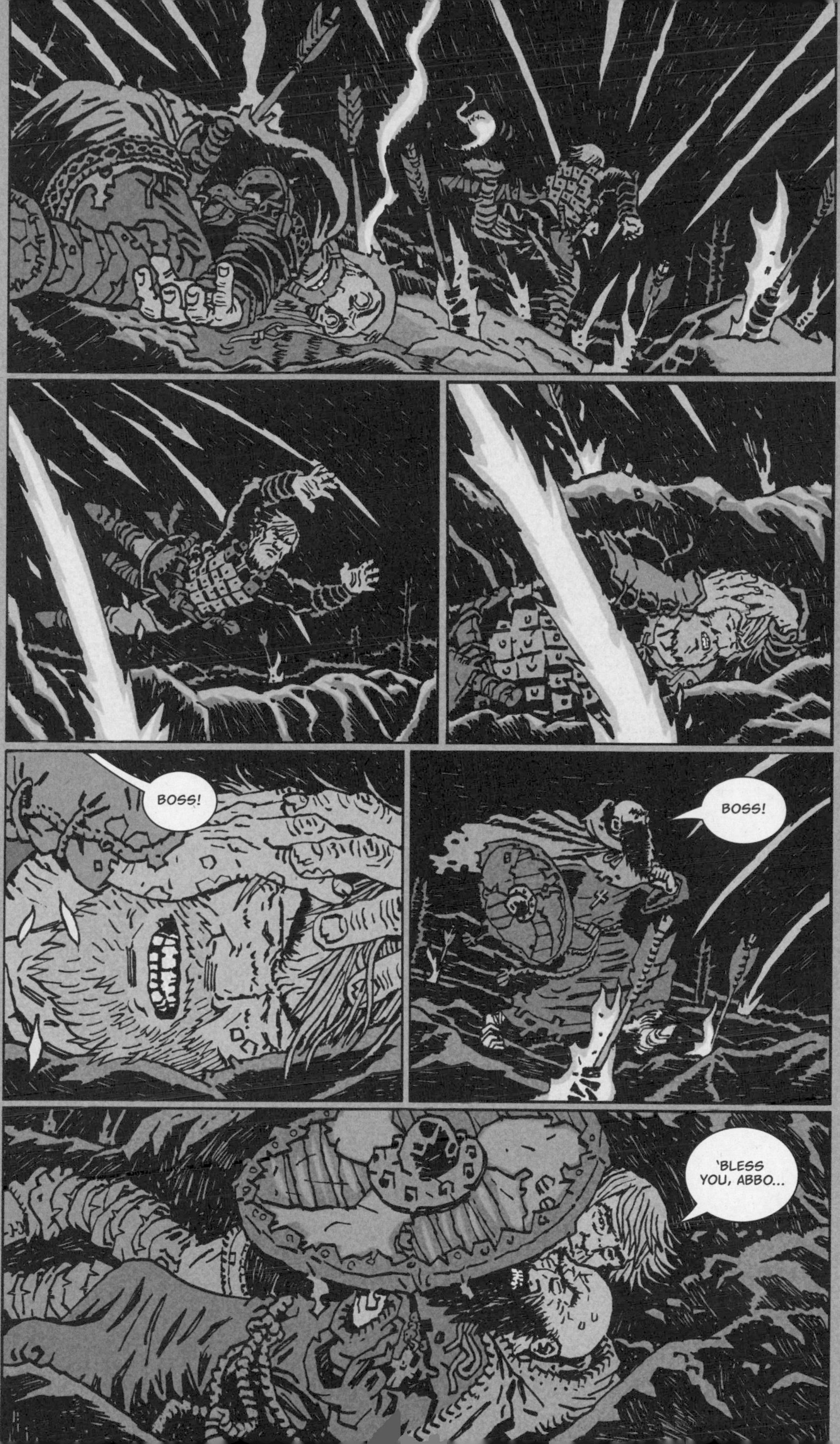
BOSS!
BOSS!
'BLESS YOU, ABBO...

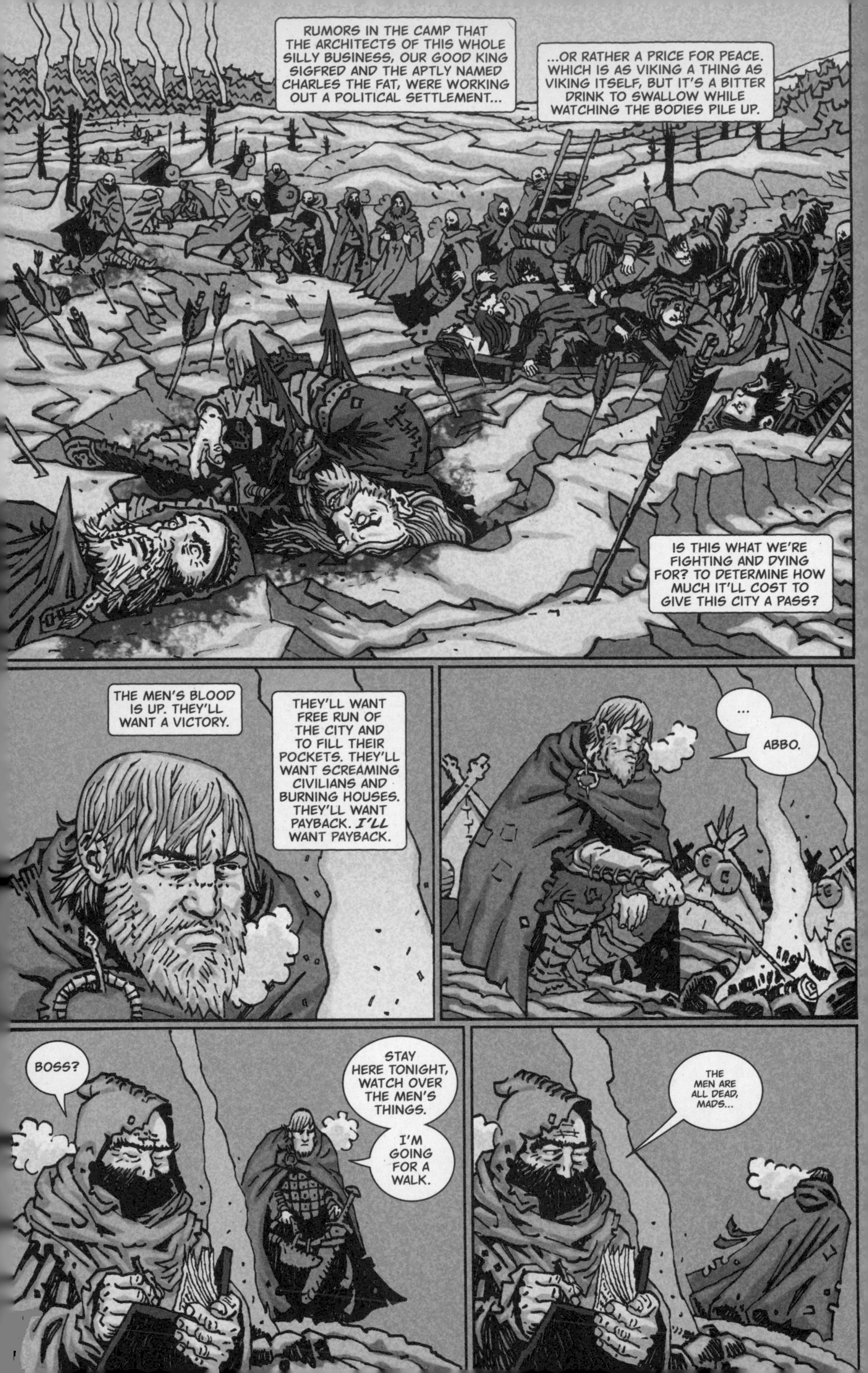
RUMORS IN THE CAMP THAT THE ARCHITECTS OF THIS WHOLE SILLY BUSINESS, OUR GOOD KING SIGFRED AND THE APTLY NAMED CHARLES THE FAT, WERE WORKING OUT A POLITICAL SETTLEMENT...
...OR RATHER A PRICE FOR PEACE. WHICH IS AS VIKING A THING AS VIKING ITSELF, BUT IT'S A BITTER DRINK TO SWALLOW WHILE WATCHING THE BODIES PILE UP.
IS THIS WHAT WE'RE FIGHTING AND DYING FOR? TO DETERMINE HOW MUCH IT'LL COST TO GIVE THIS CITY A PASS?
THE MEN'S BLOOD IS UP. THEY'LL WANT A VICTORY.
THEY'LL WANT FREE RUN OF THE CITY AND TO FILL THEIR POCKETS. THEY'LL WANT SCREAMING CIVILIANS AND BURNING HOUSES. THEY'LL WANT PAYBACK. *I'LL* WANT PAYBACK.
...
ABBO.
BOSS?
STAY HERE TONIGHT, WATCH OVER THE MEN'S THINGS.
I'M GOING FOR A WALK.
THE MEN ARE ALL DEAD, MADS...

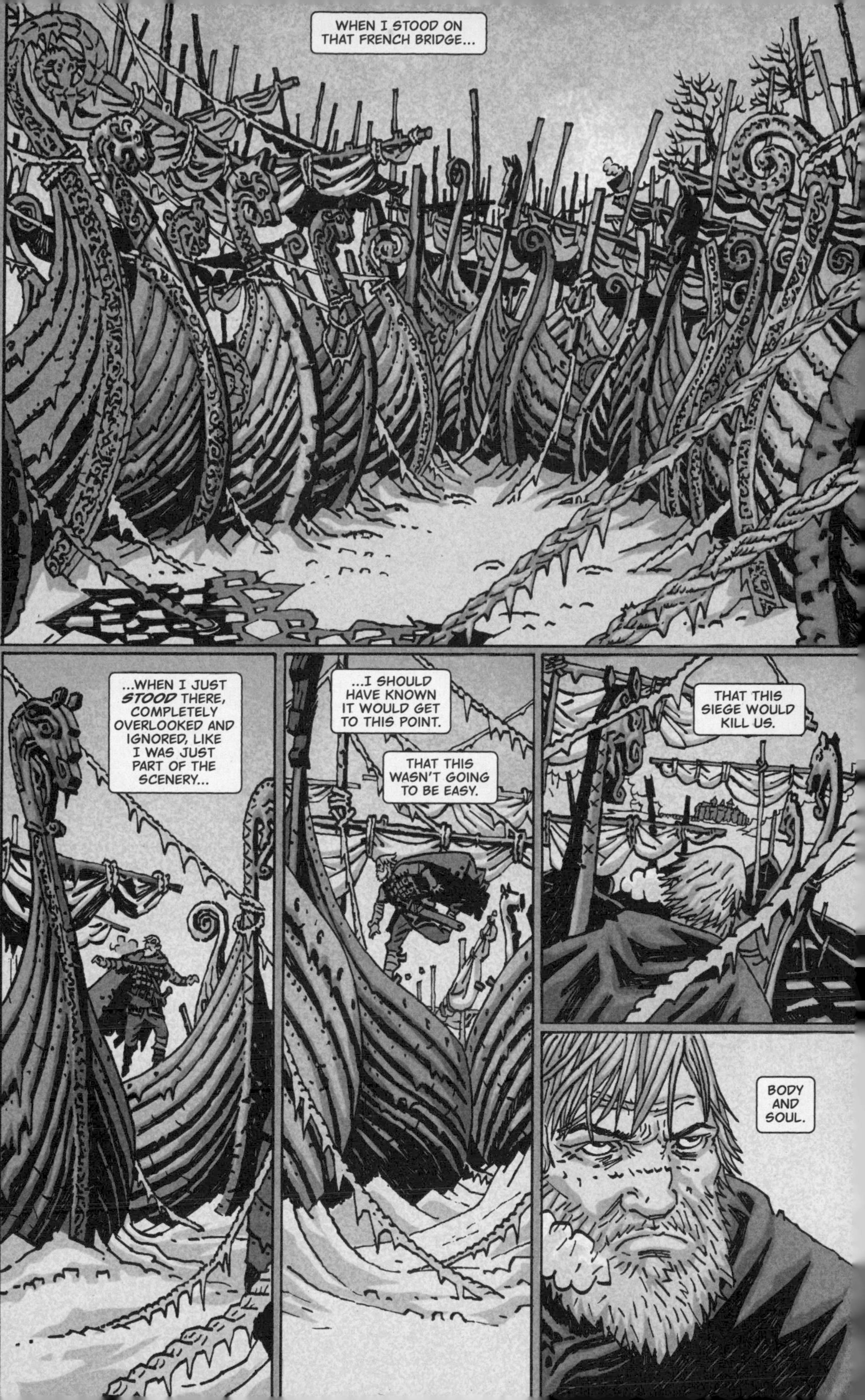
WHEN I STOOD ON THAT FRENCH BRIDGE...
...WHEN I JUST *STOOD* THERE, COMPLETELY OVERLOOKED AND IGNORED, LIKE I WAS JUST PART OF THE SCENERY...
...I SHOULD HAVE KNOWN IT WOULD GET TO THIS POINT.
THAT THIS WASN'T GOING TO BE EASY.
THAT THIS SIEGE WOULD KILL US.
BODY AND SOUL.

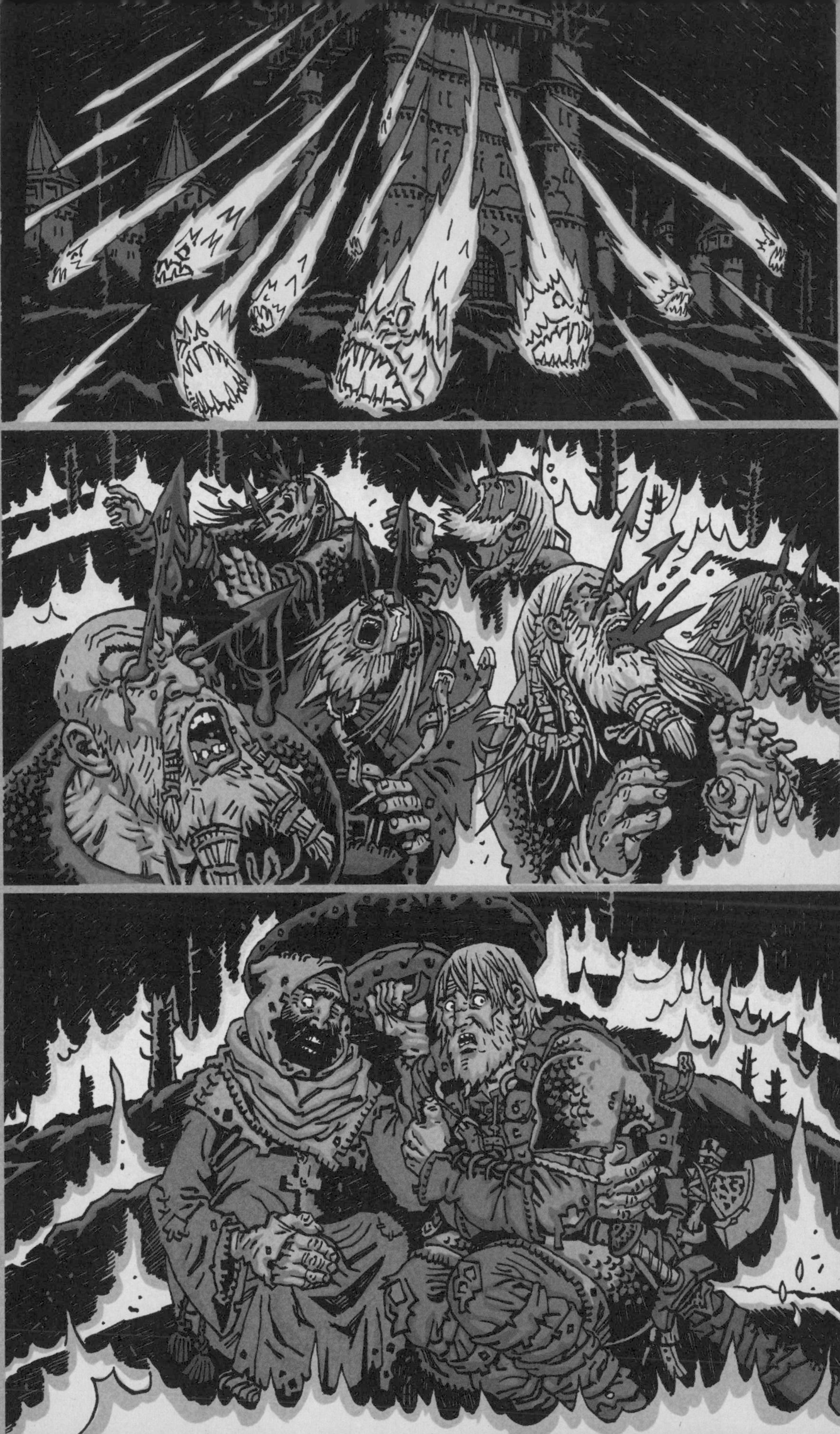

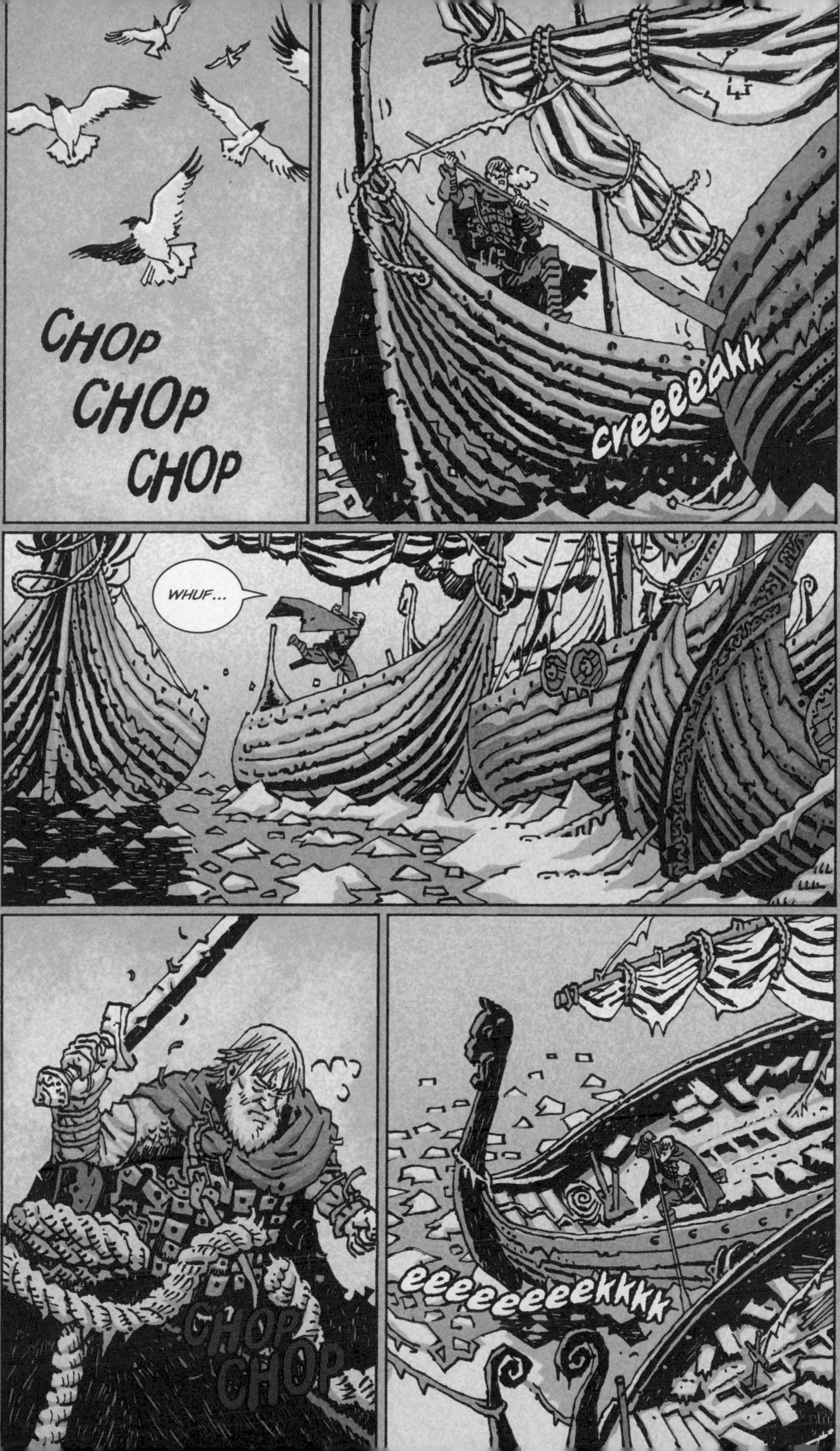
CHOP
CHOP
CHOP
creeeeakk
WHUF...
CHOP
CHOP
eeeeeeeeekkkk

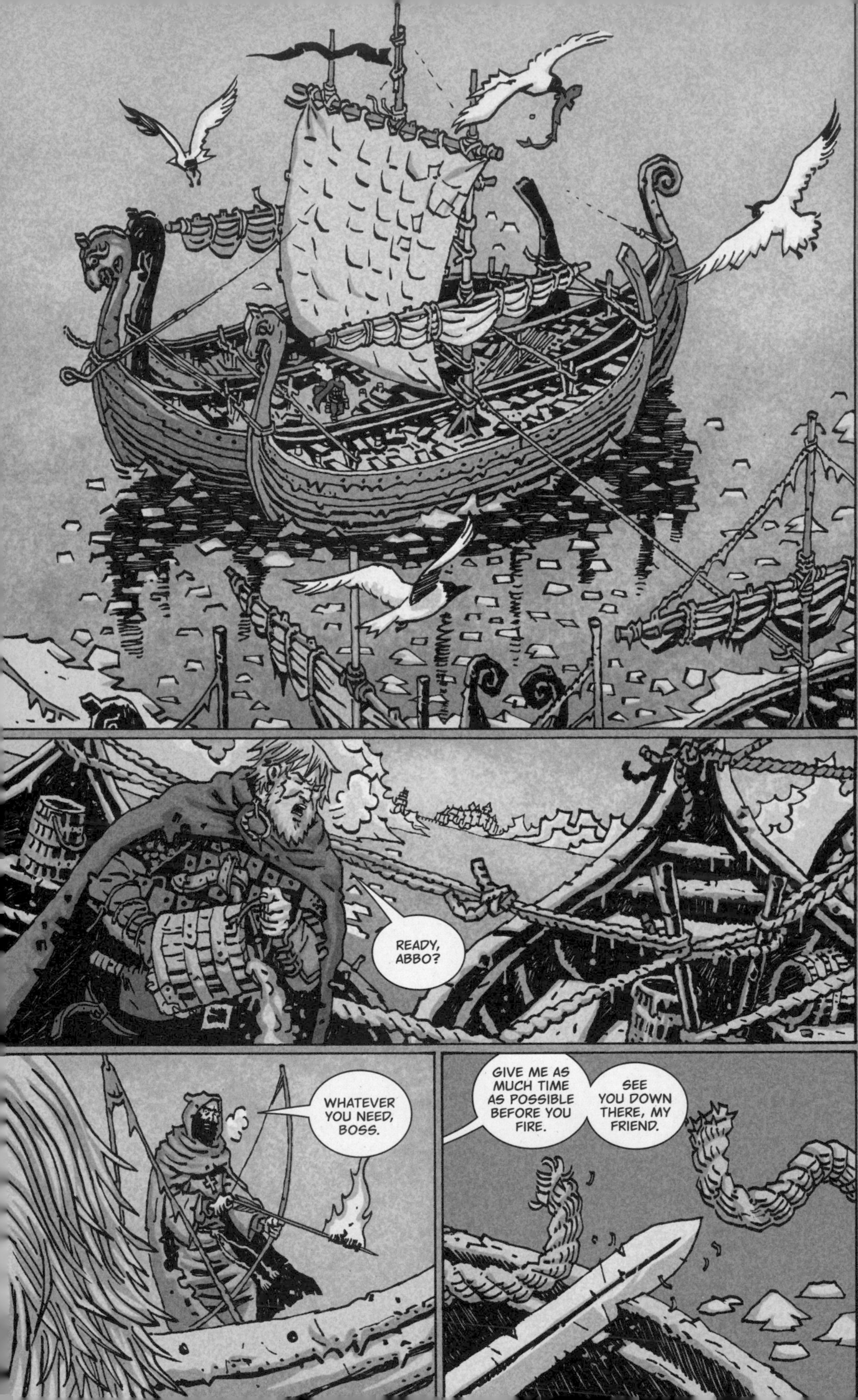
READY, ABBO?
WHATEVER YOU NEED, BOSS.
GIVE ME AS MUCH TIME AS POSSIBLE BEFORE YOU FIRE.
SEE YOU DOWN THERE, MY FRIEND.

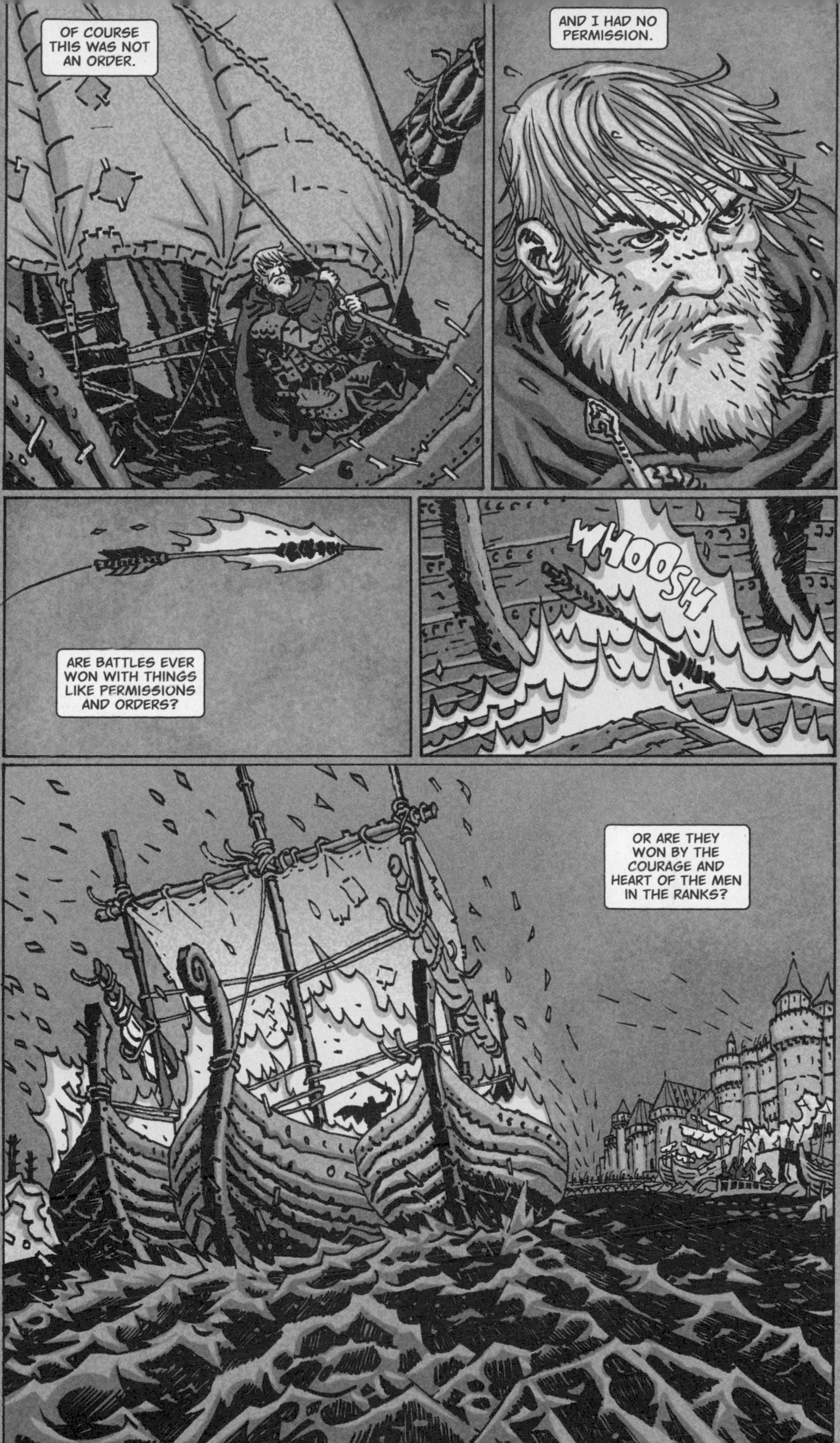
OF COURSE THIS WAS NOT AN ORDER.
AND I HAD NO PERMISSION.
ARE BATTLES EVER WON WITH THINGS LIKE PERMISSIONS AND ORDERS?
WHOOSH
OR ARE THEY WON BY THE COURAGE AND HEART OF THE MEN IN THE RANKS?

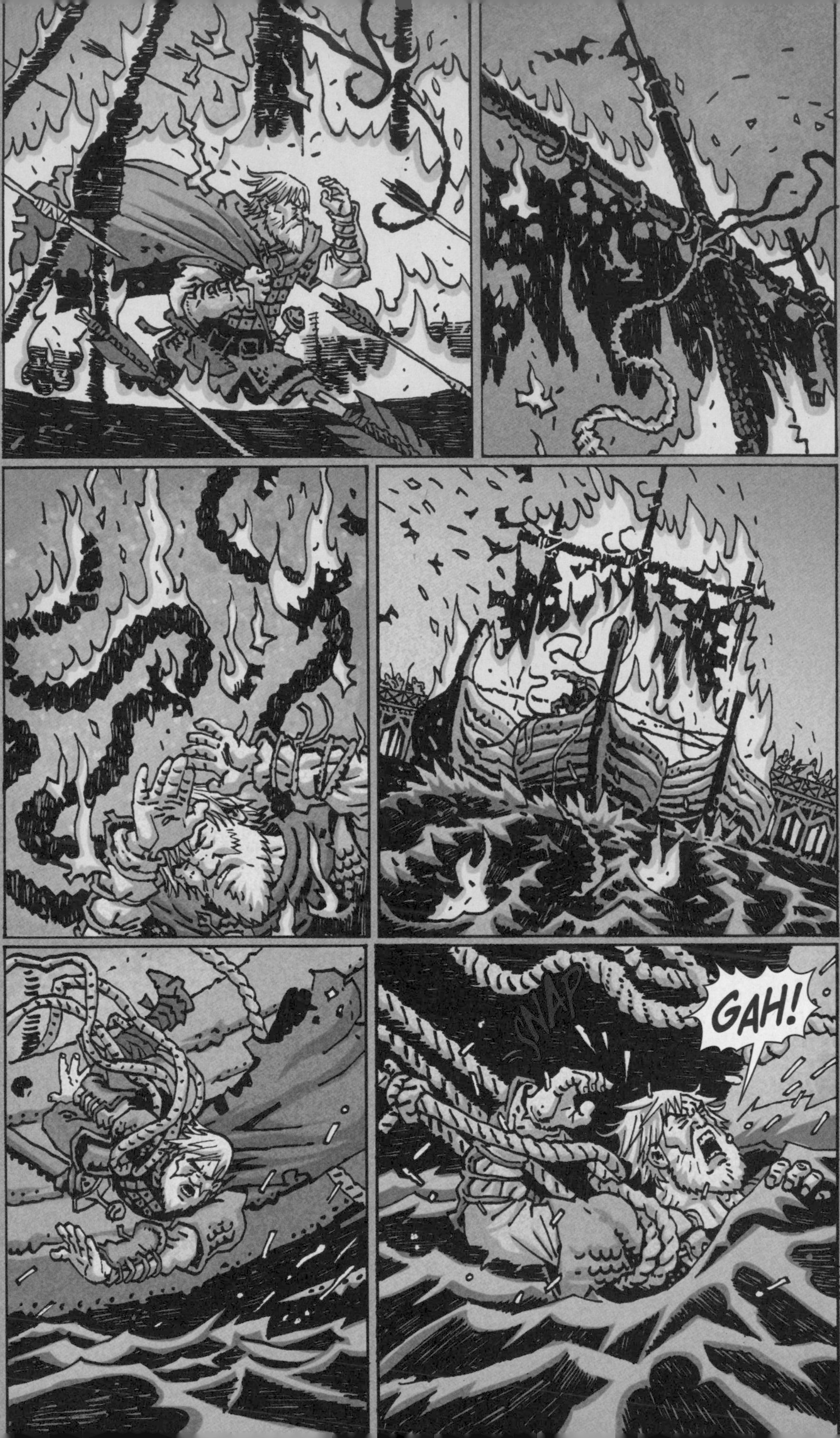
SNAP
GAH!

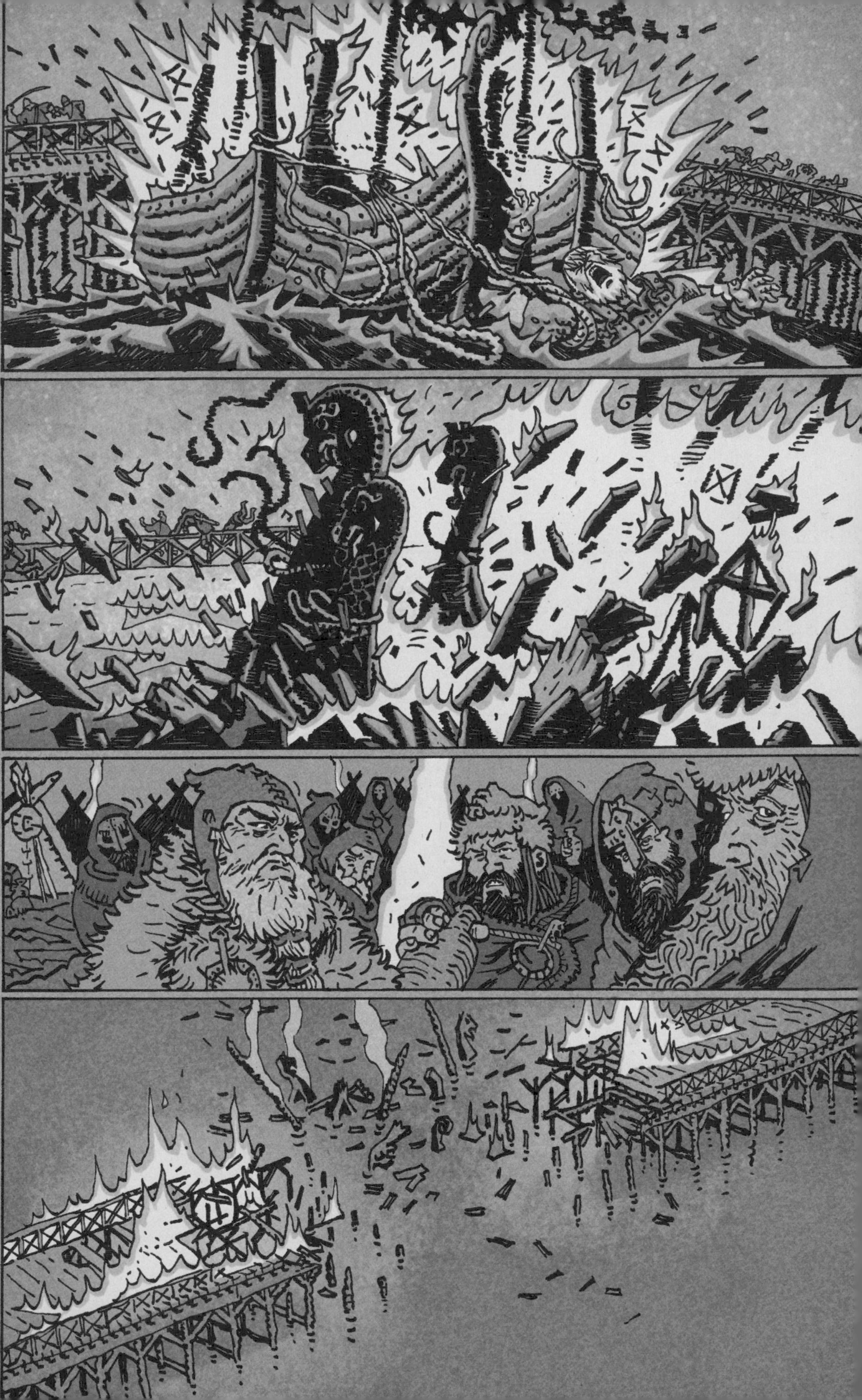

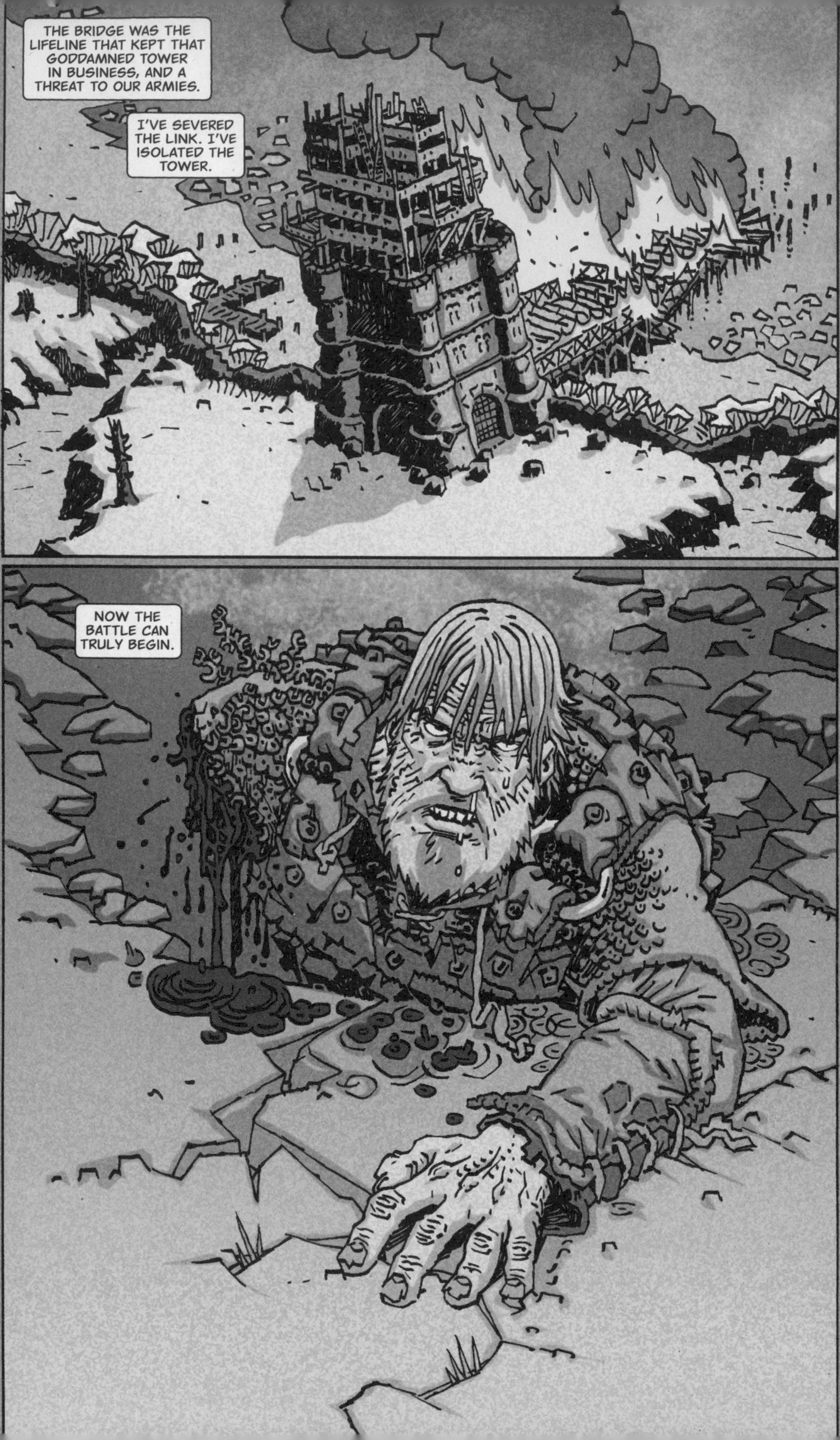
THE BRIDGE WAS THE LIFELINE THAT KEPT THAT GODDAMNED TOWER IN BUSINESS, AND A THREAT TO OUR ARMIES.
I'VE SEVERED THE LINK. I'VE ISOLATED THE TOWER.
NOW THE BATTLE CAN TRULY BEGIN.

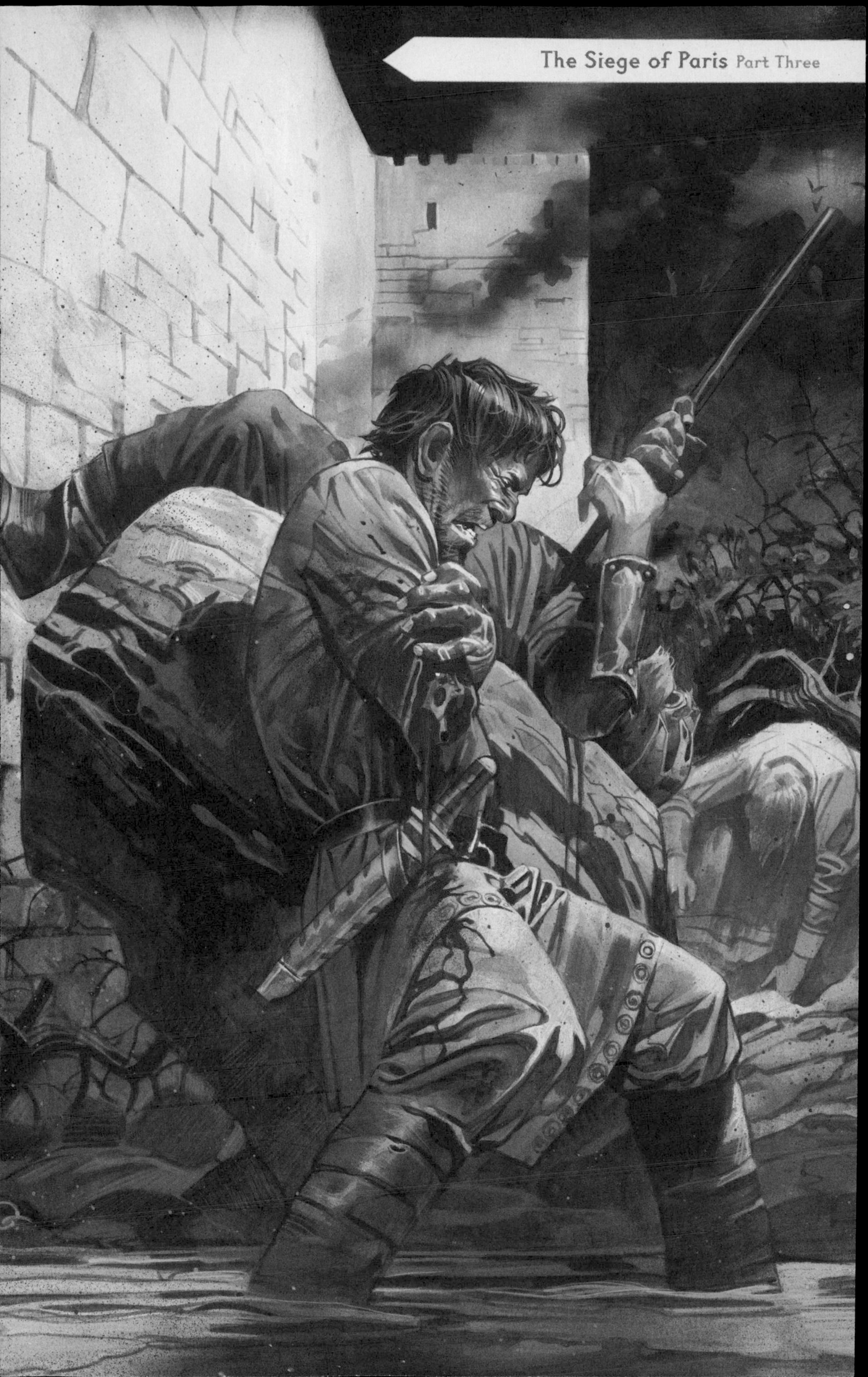
The Siege of Paris Part Three

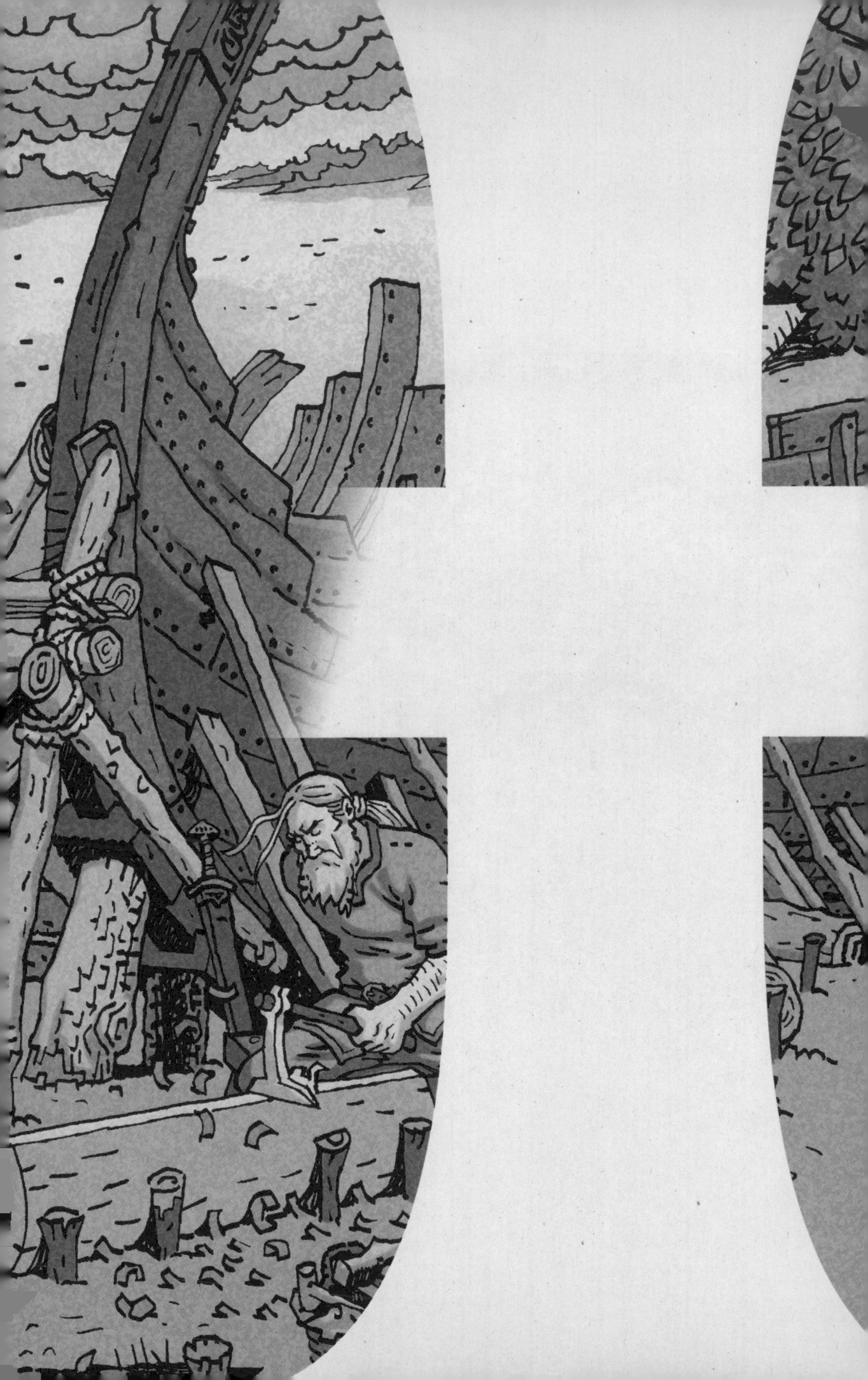

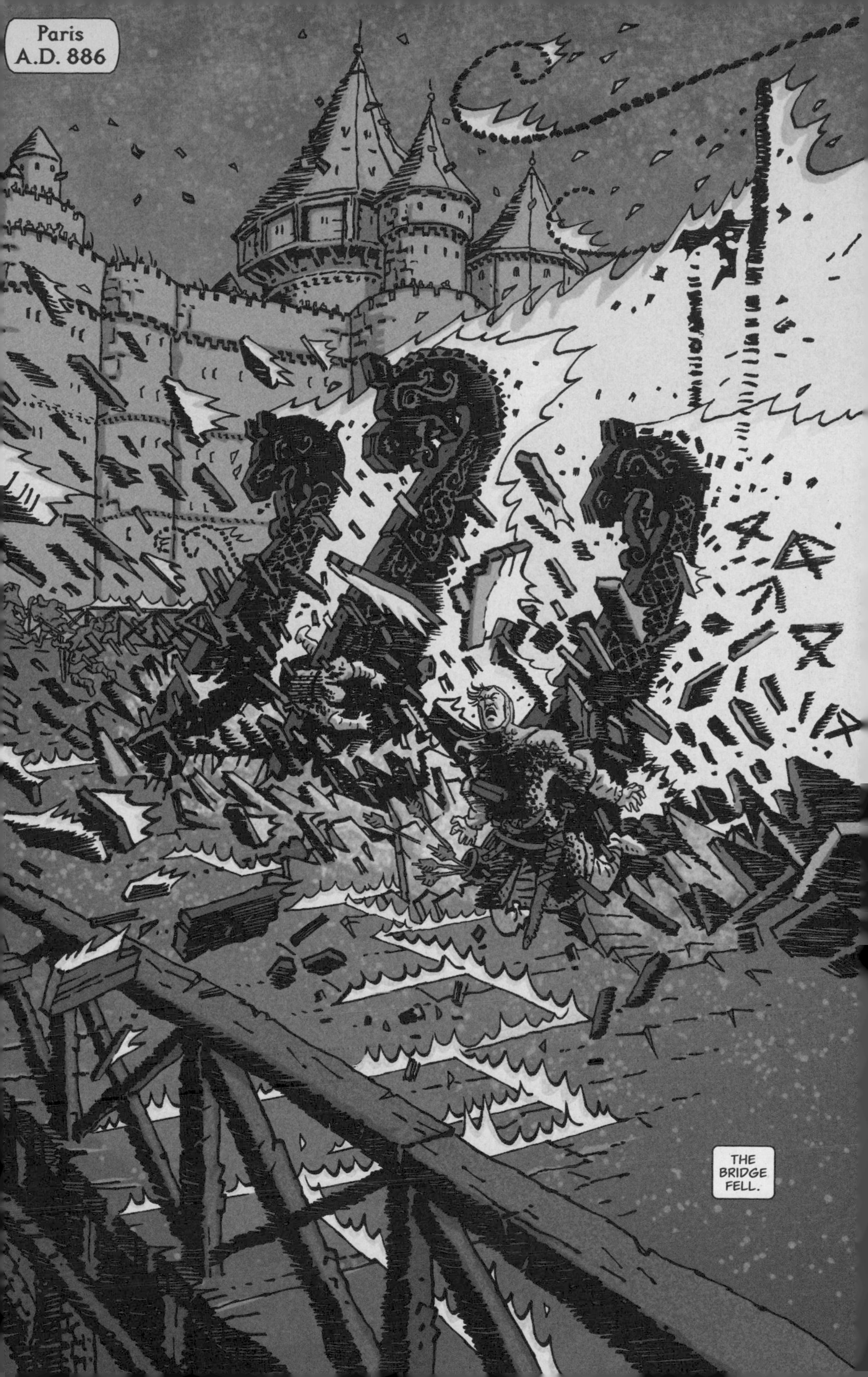
Paris
A.D. 886
THE BRIDGE FELL.

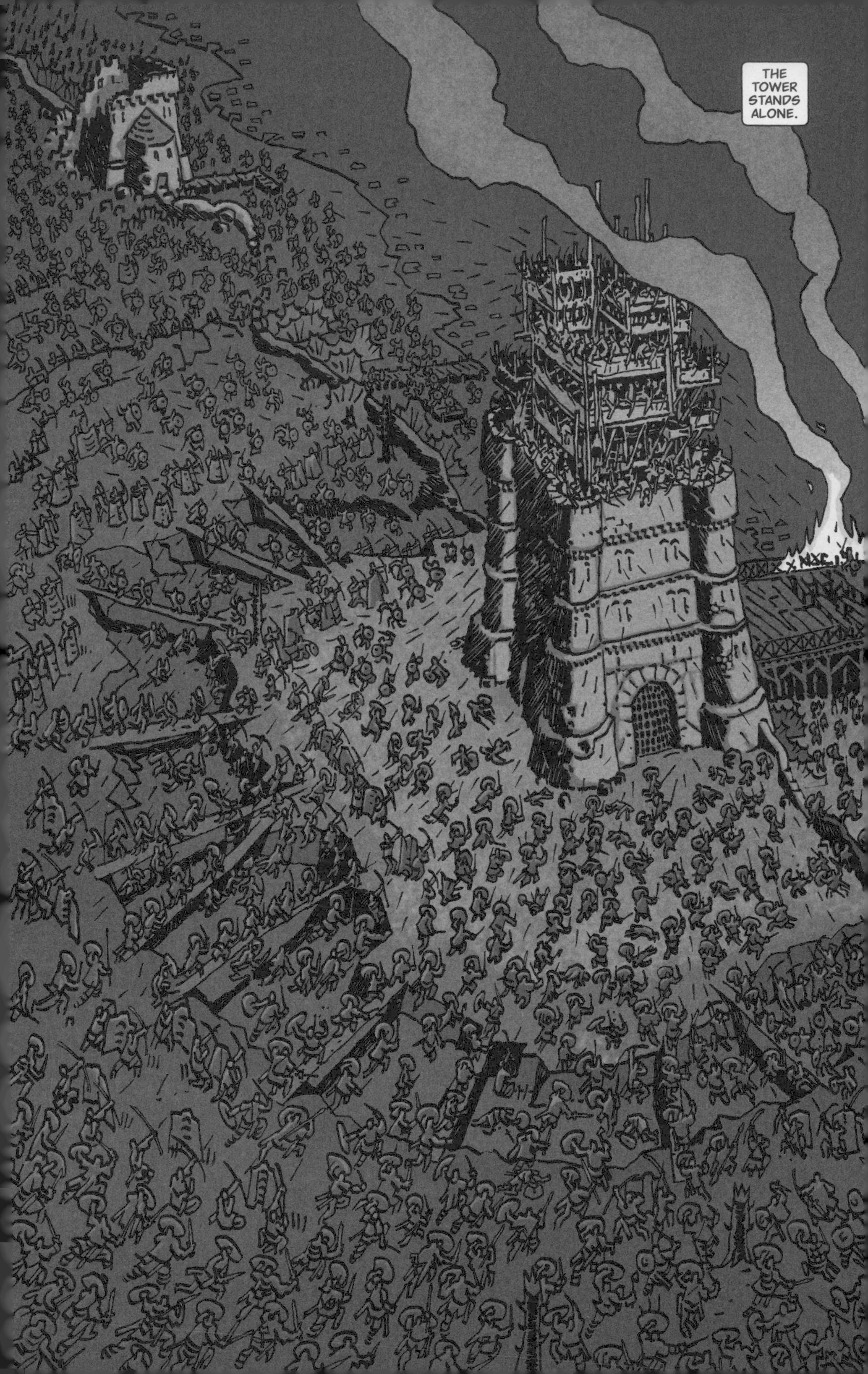
THE TOWER STANDS ALONE.

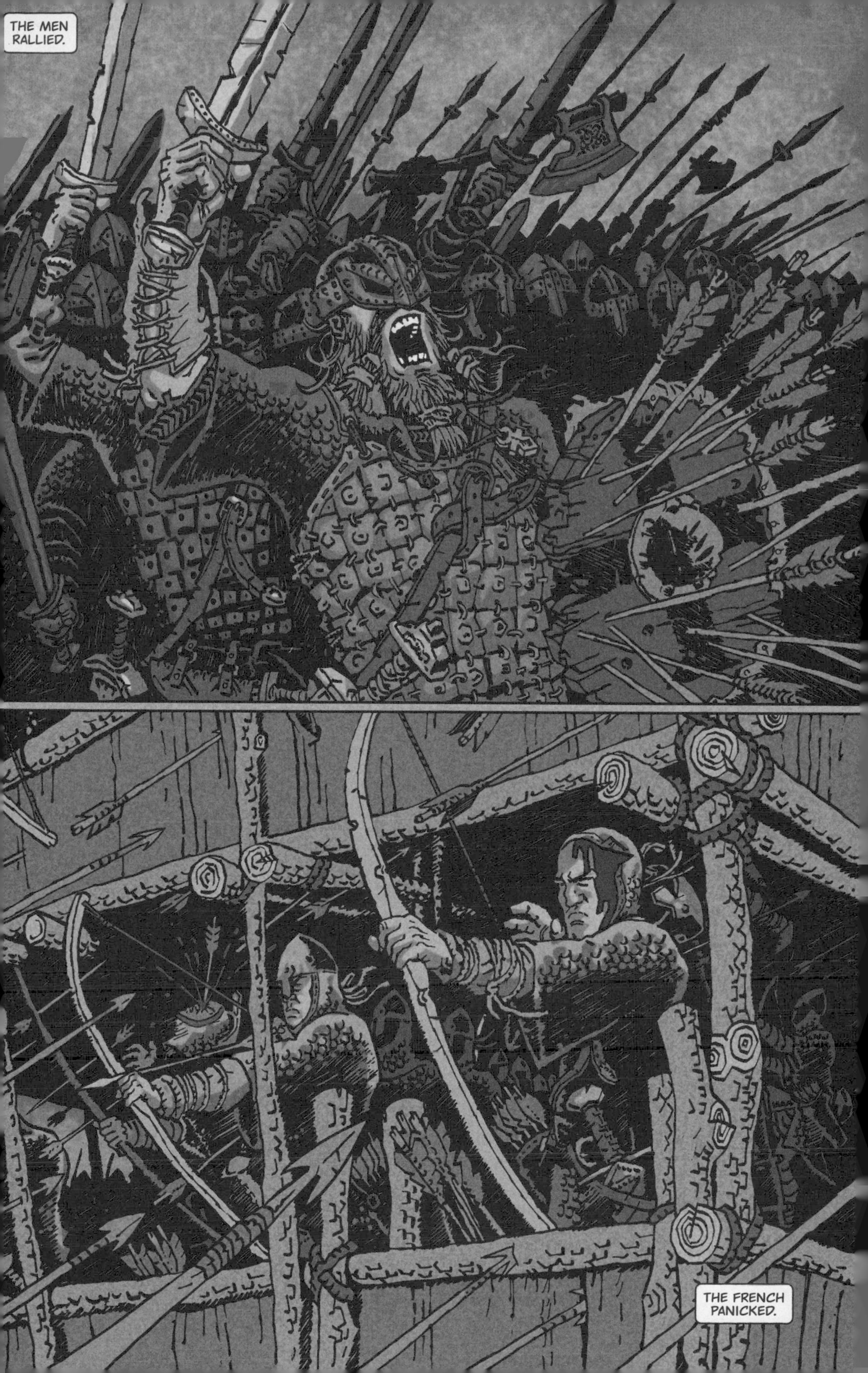
THE MEN RALLIED.
THE FRENCH PANICKED.

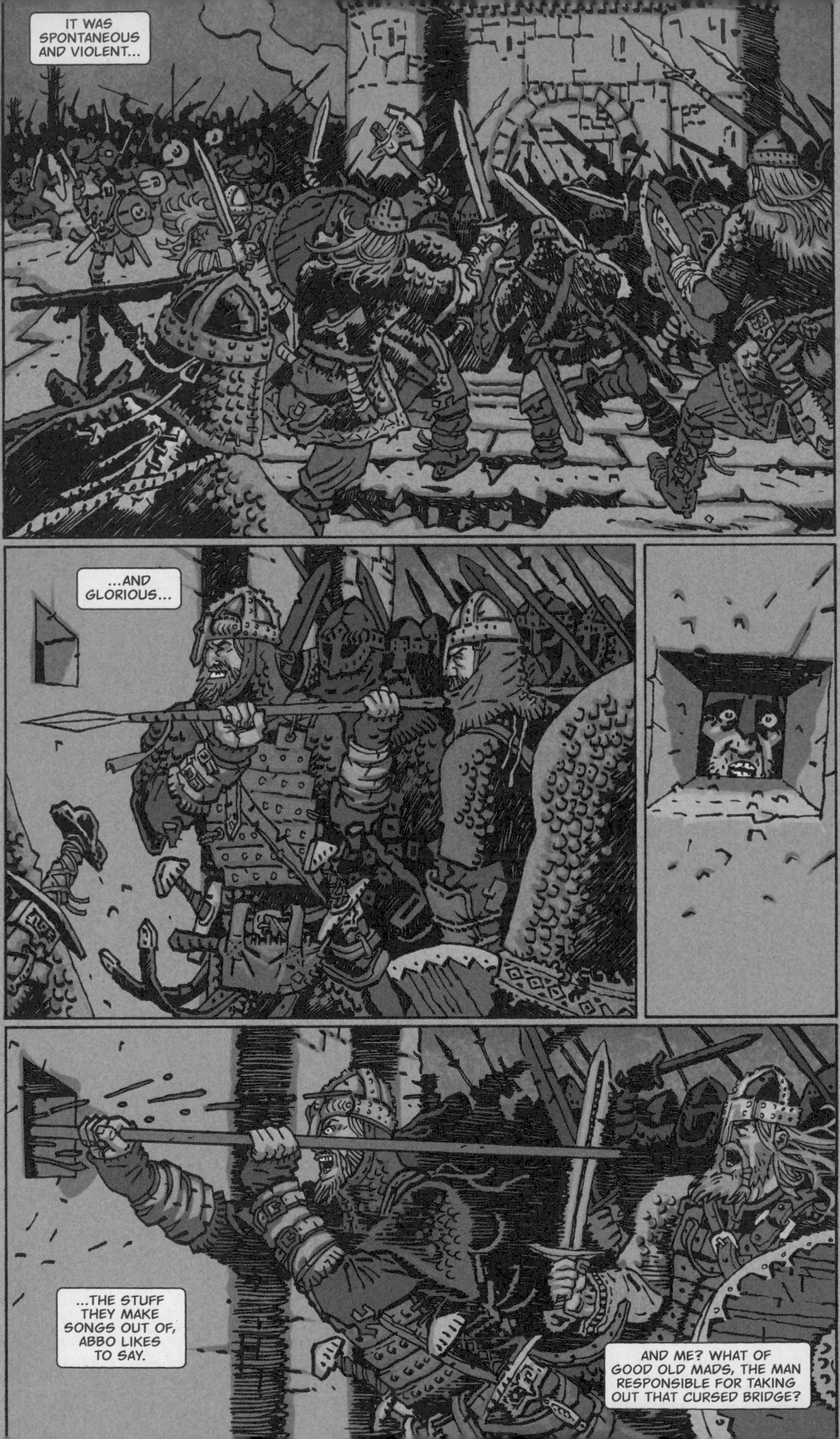
IT WAS SPONTANEOUS AND VIOLENT...
...AND GLORIOUS...
...THE STUFF THEY MAKE SONGS OUT OF, ABBO LIKES TO SAY.
AND ME? WHAT OF GOOD OLD MADS, THE MAN RESPONSIBLE FOR TAKING OUT THAT CURSED BRIDGE?

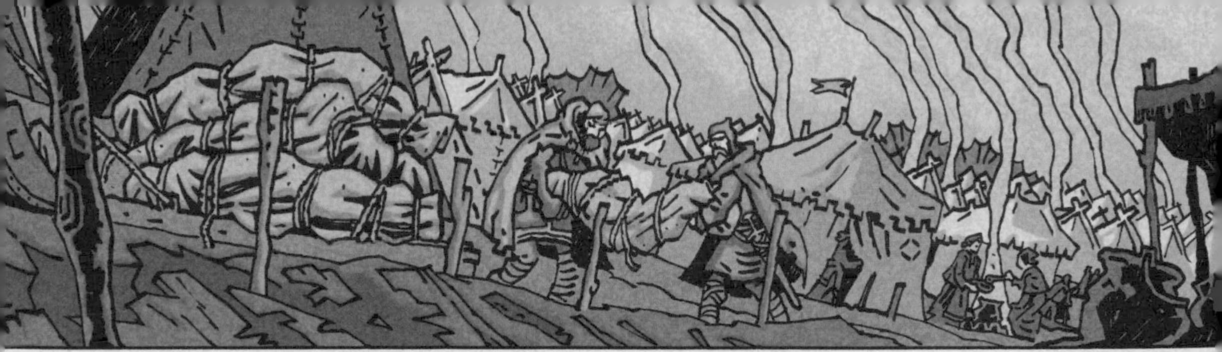

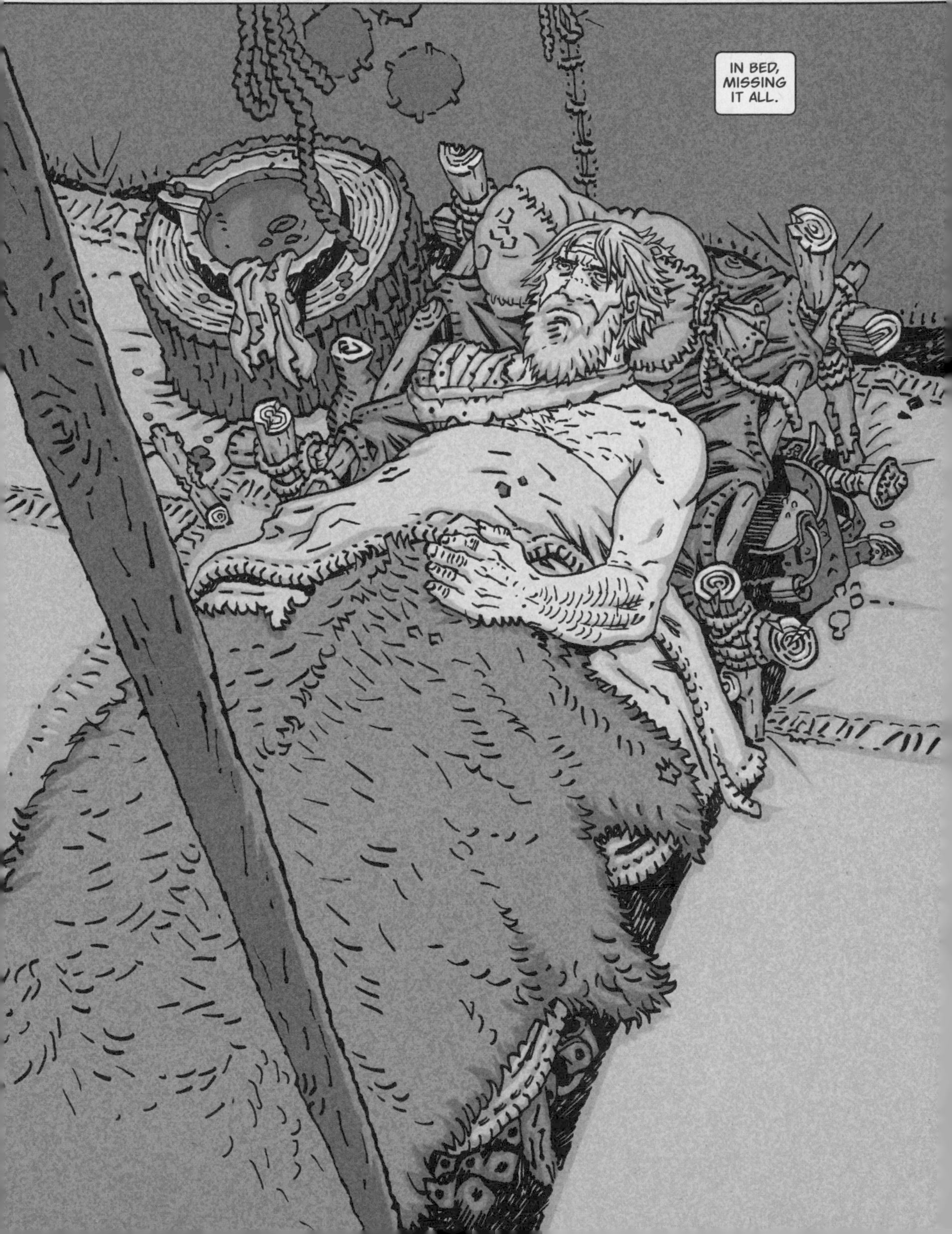
IN BED, MISSING IT ALL.

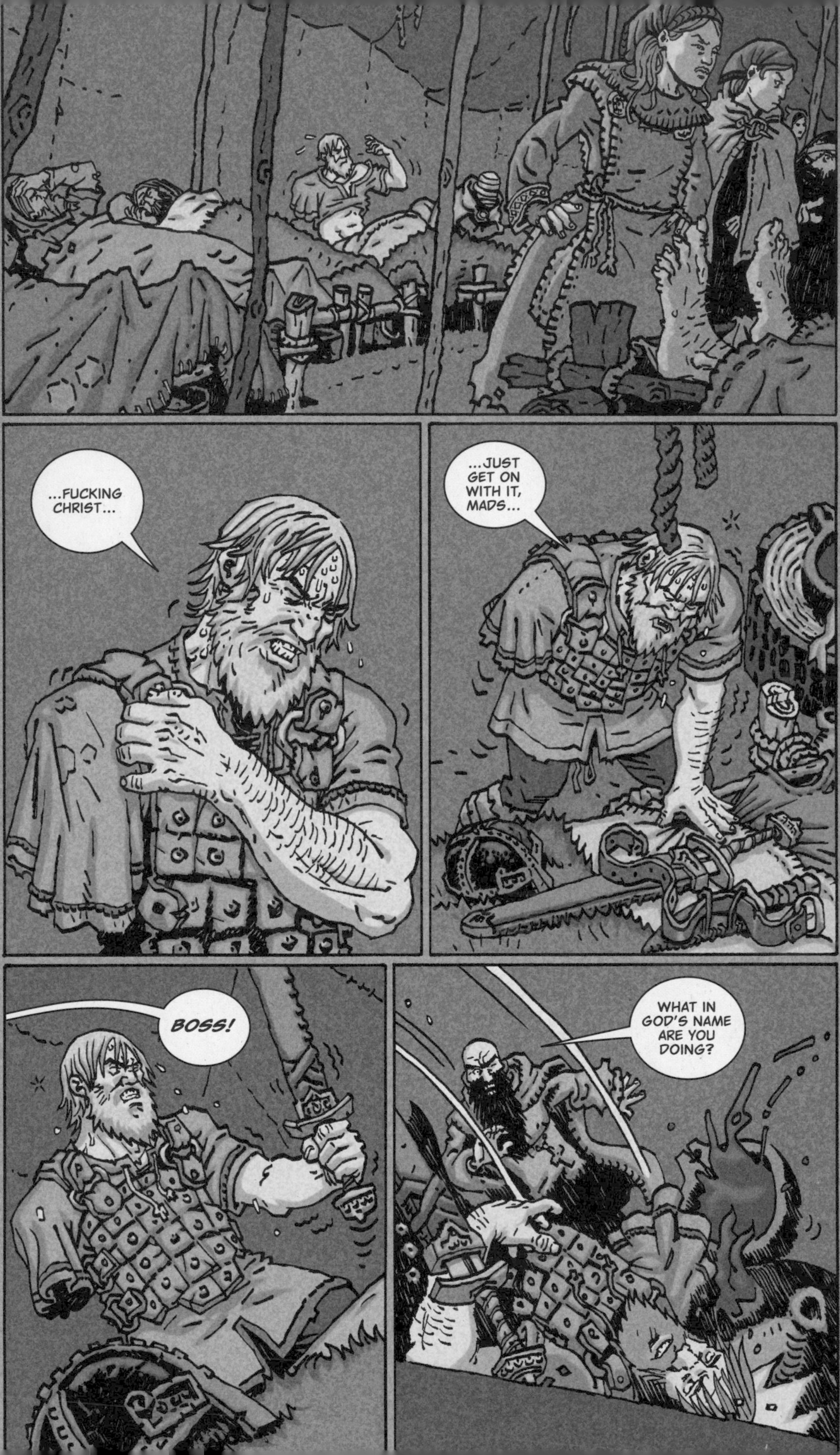
...FUCKING CHRIST...
...JUST GET ON WITH IT, MADS...
BOSS!
WHAT IN GOD'S NAME ARE YOU DOING?

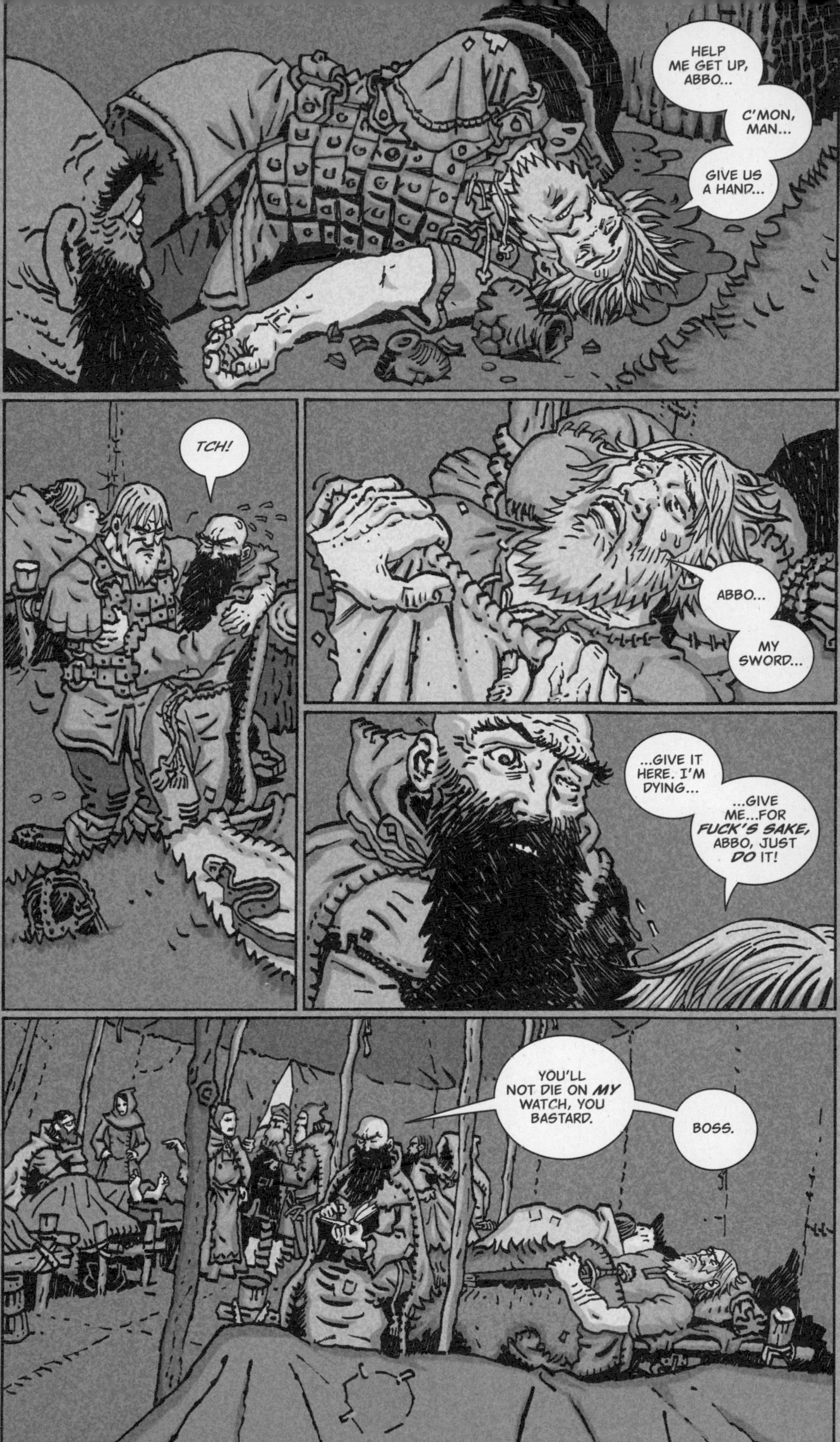

HELP ME GET UP, ABBO...
C'MON, MAN...
GIVE US A HAND...
TCH!
ABBO...
MY SWORD...
...GIVE IT HERE. I'M DYING...
...GIVE ME...FOR FUCK'S SAKE, ABBO, JUST DO IT!
YOU'LL NOT DIE ON MY WATCH, YOU BASTARD.
BOSS.

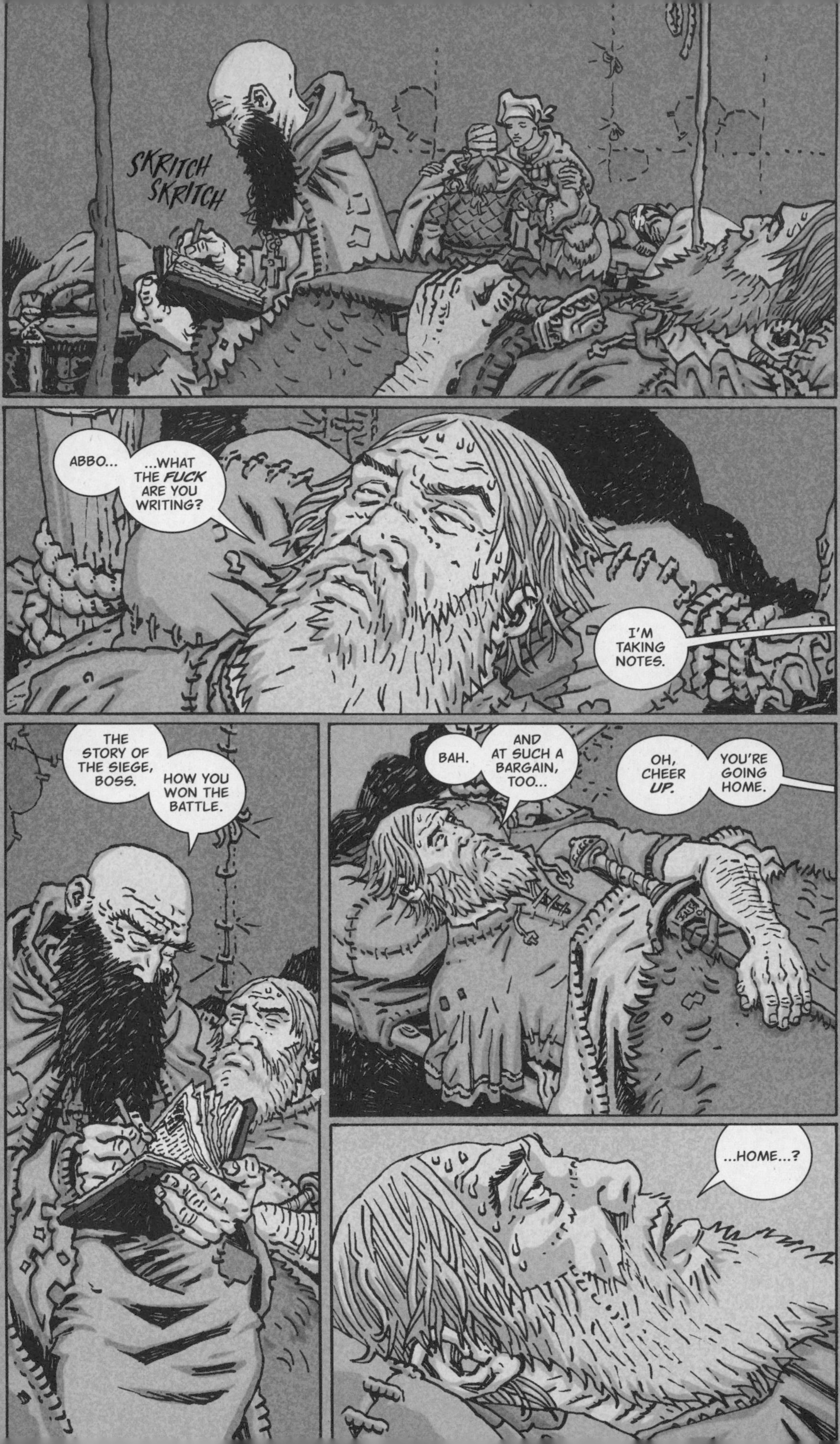
SKRITCH SKRITCH
ABBO...
...WHAT THE FUCK ARE YOU WRITING?
I'M TAKING NOTES.
THE STORY OF THE SIEGE, BOSS.
HOW YOU WON THE BATTLE.
BAH.
AND AT SUCH A BARGAIN, TOO...
OH, CHEER UP.
YOU'RE GOING HOME.
...HOME...?

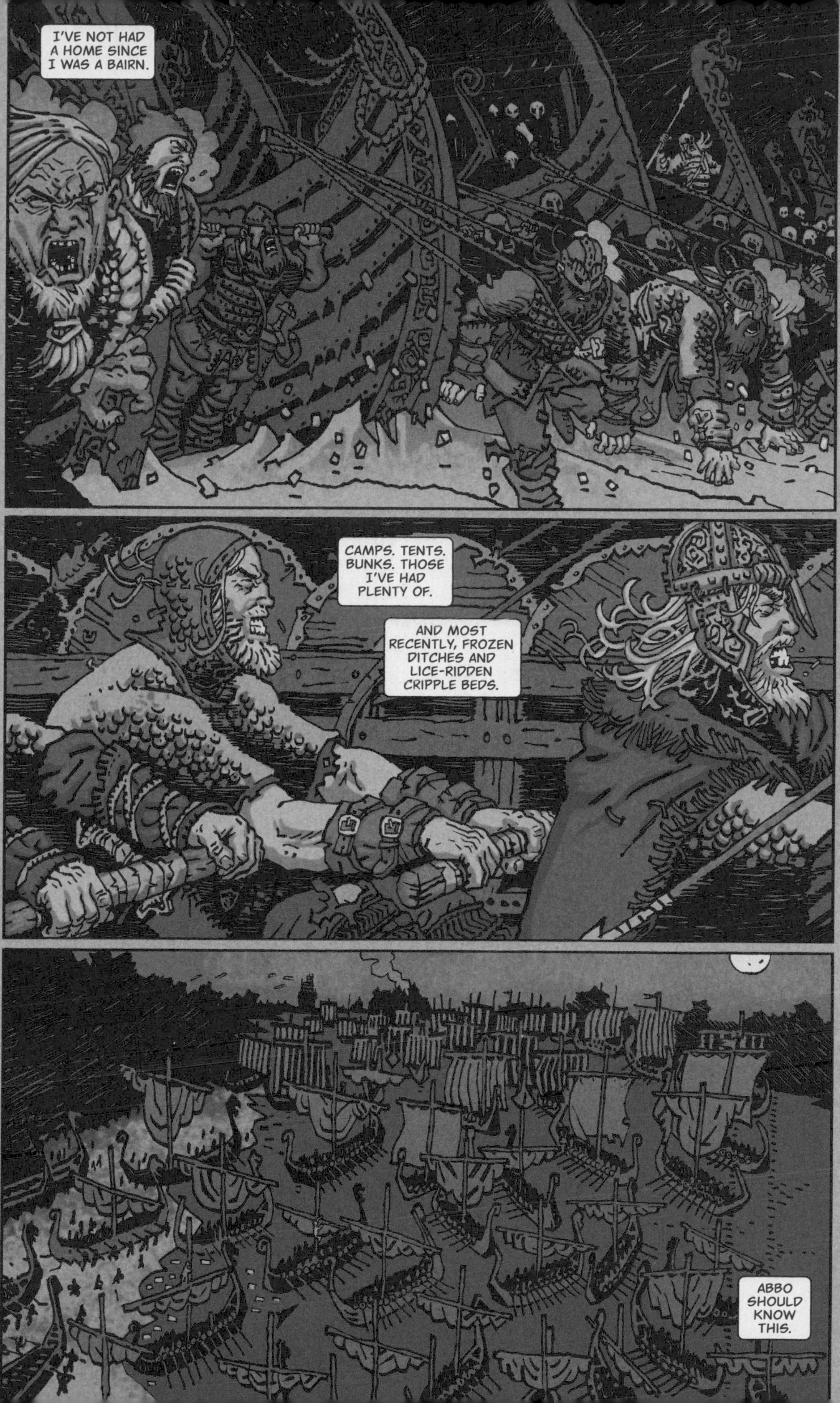
I'VE NOT HAD A HOME SINCE I WAS A BAIRN.
CAMPS. TENTS. BUNKS. THOSE I'VE HAD PLENTY OF.
AND MOST RECENTLY, FROZEN DITCHES AND LICE-RIDDEN CRIPPLE BEDS.
ABBO SHOULD KNOW THIS.

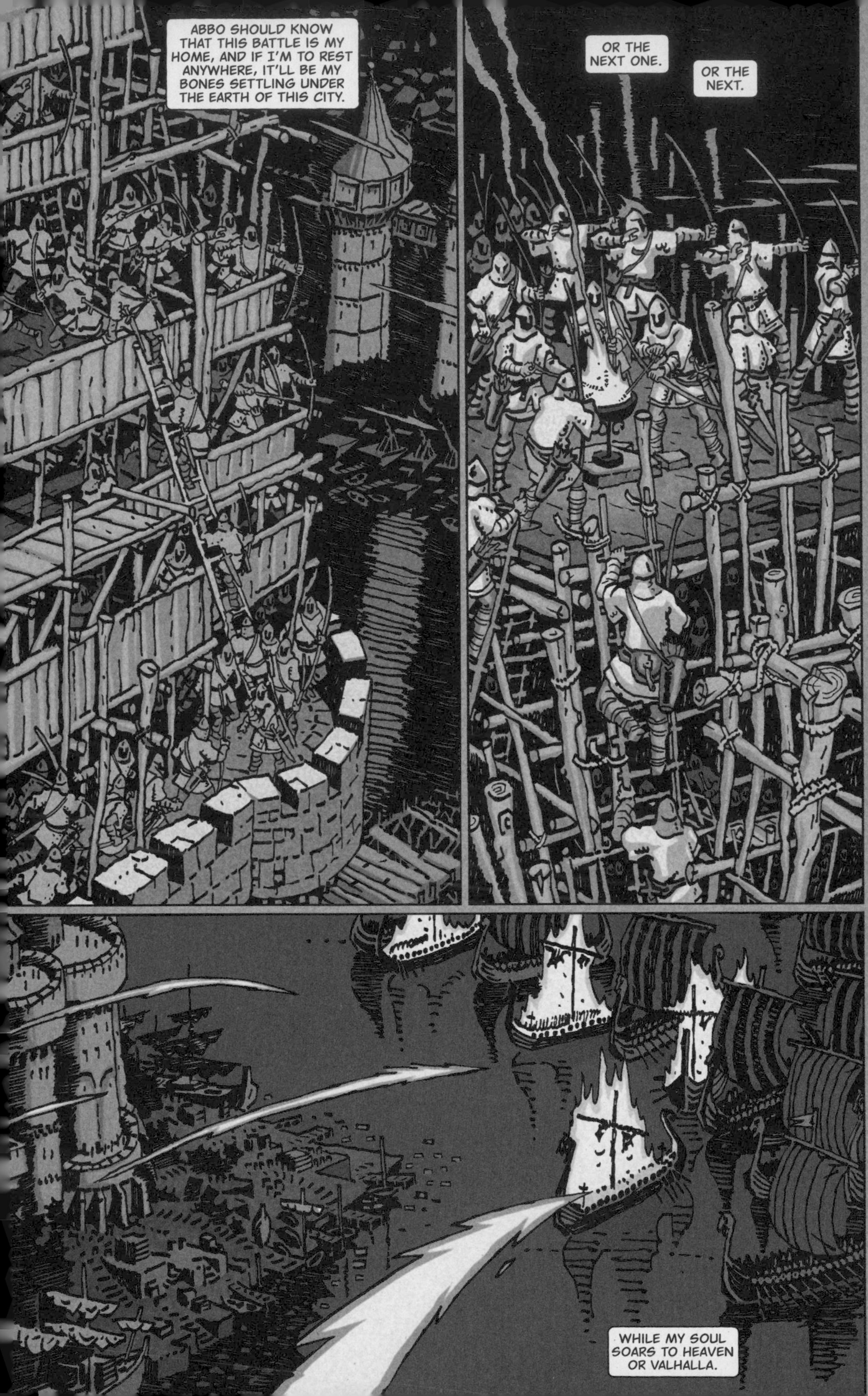
ABBO SHOULD KNOW THAT THIS BATTLE IS MY HOME, AND IF I'M TO REST ANYWHERE, IT'LL BE MY BONES SETTLING UNDER THE EARTH OF THIS CITY.
OR THE NEXT ONE.
OR THE NEXT.
WHILE MY SOUL SOARS TO HEAVEN OR VALHALLA.

CLANG
CLANG
CLANG

CLANG

KRIK
KRACK

GRRAAAHH!

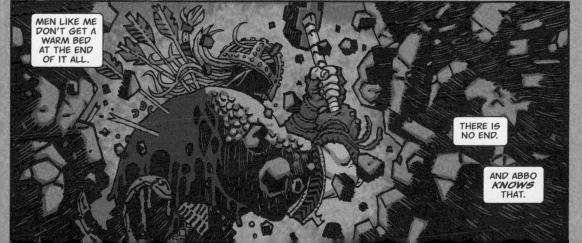

MEN LIKE ME
DON'T GET A
WARM BED
AT THE END
OF IT ALL.

THERE IS
NO END.

AND ABBO
KNOWS
THAT.

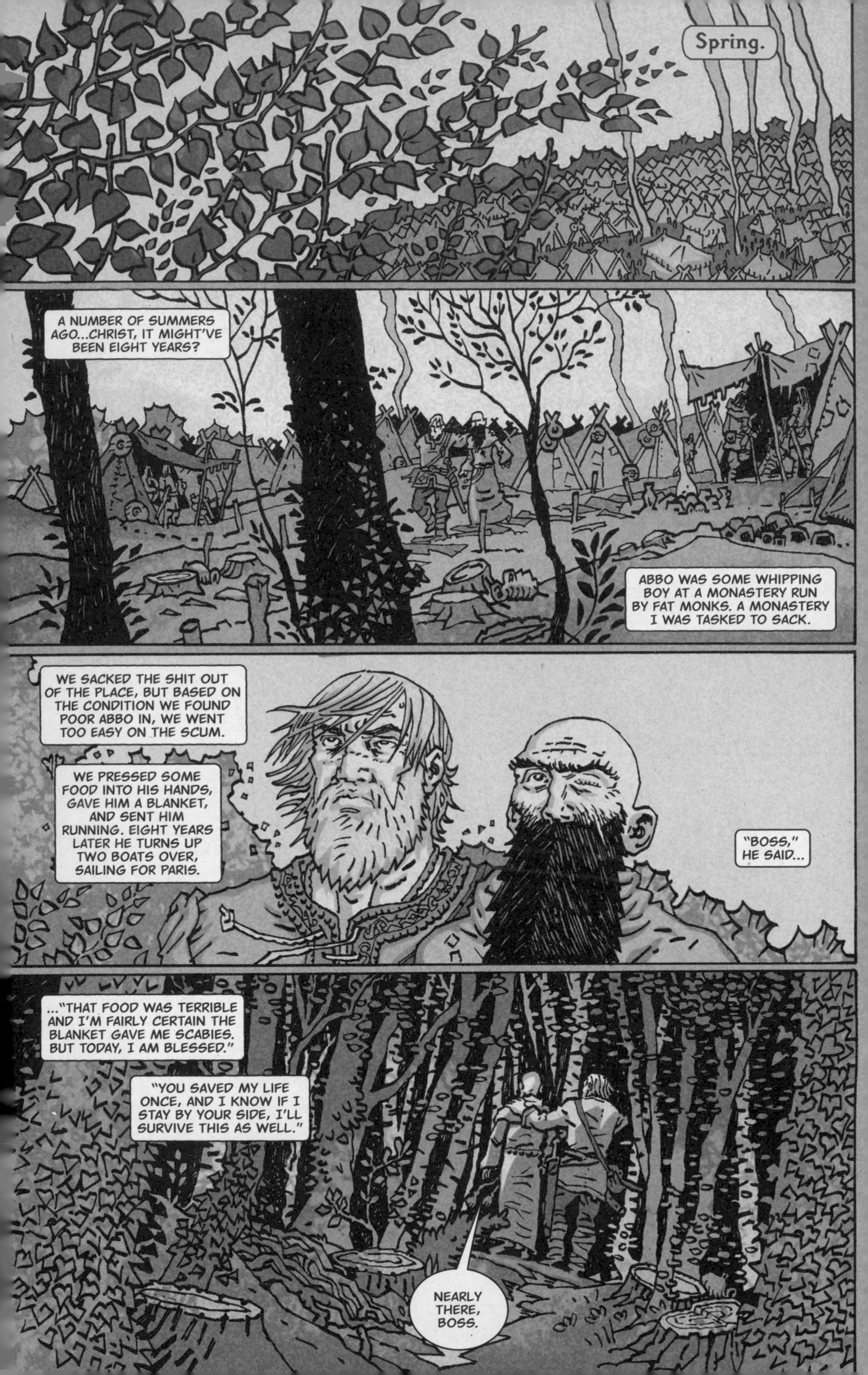
Spring.
A NUMBER OF SUMMERS AGO...CHRIST, IT MIGHT'VE BEEN EIGHT YEARS?
ABBO WAS SOME WHIPPING BOY AT A MONASTERY RUN BY FAT MONKS. A MONASTERY I WAS TASKED TO SACK.
WE SACKED THE SHIT OUT OF THE PLACE, BUT BASED ON THE CONDITION WE FOUND POOR ABBO IN, WE WENT TOO EASY ON THE SCUM.
WE PRESSED SOME FOOD INTO HIS HANDS, GAVE HIM A BLANKET, AND SENT HIM RUNNING. EIGHT YEARS LATER HE TURNS UP TWO BOATS OVER, SAILING FOR PARIS.
"BOSS," HE SAID...
..."THAT FOOD WAS TERRIBLE AND I'M FAIRLY CERTAIN THE BLANKET GAVE ME SCABIES. BUT TODAY, I AM BLESSED."
"YOU SAVED MY LIFE ONCE, AND I KNOW IF I STAY BY YOUR SIDE, I'LL SURVIVE THIS AS WELL."
NEARLY THERE, BOSS.

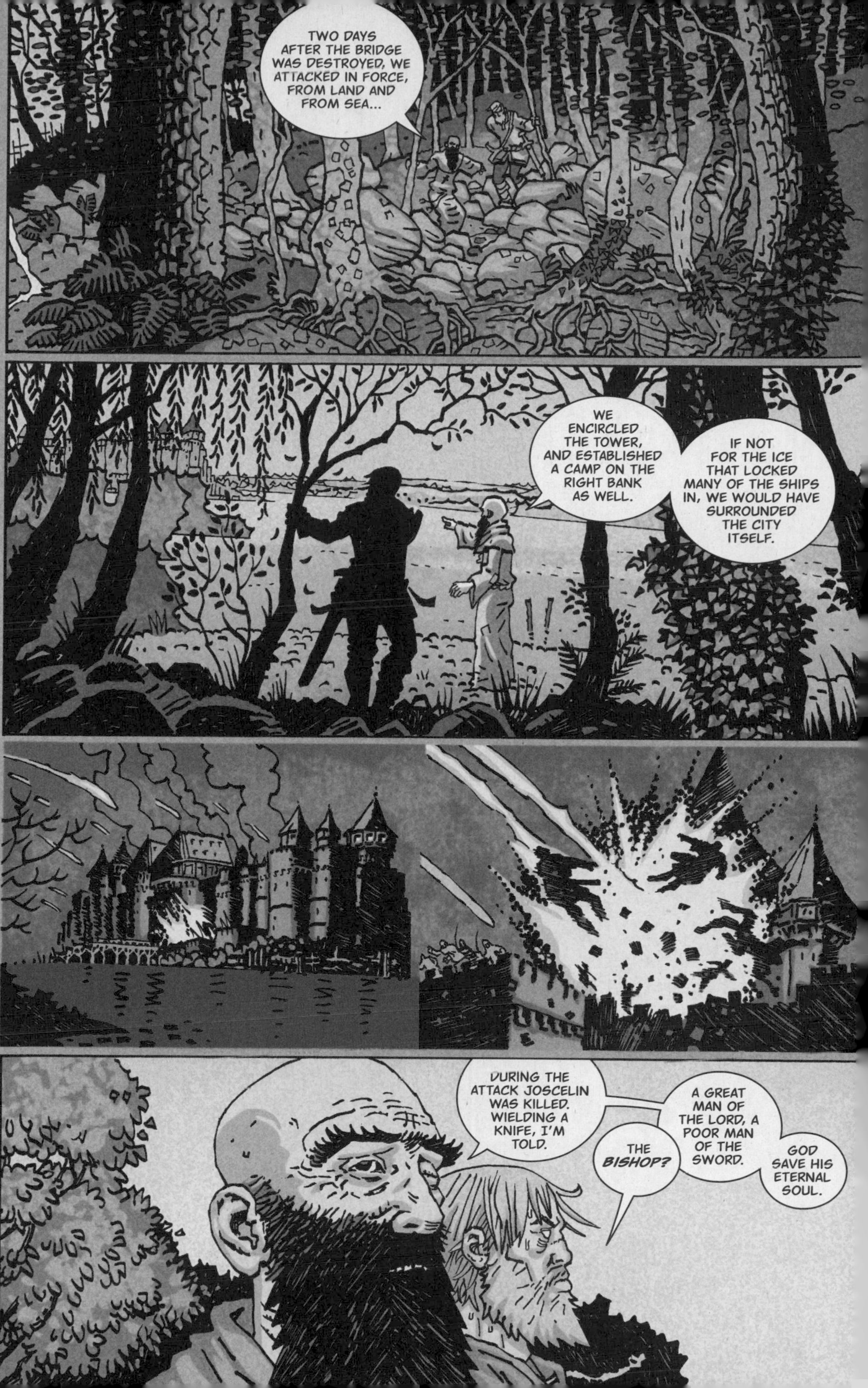
TWO DAYS AFTER THE BRIDGE WAS DESTROYED, WE ATTACKED IN FORCE, FROM LAND AND FROM SEA...
WE ENCIRCLED THE TOWER, AND ESTABLISHED A CAMP ON THE RIGHT BANK AS WELL.
IF NOT FOR THE ICE THAT LOCKED MANY OF THE SHIPS IN, WE WOULD HAVE SURROUNDED THE CITY ITSELF.
DURING THE ATTACK JOSCELIN WAS KILLED. WIELDING A KNIFE, I'M TOLD.
THE *BISHOP?*
A GREAT MAN OF THE LORD, A POOR MAN OF THE SWORD.
GOD SAVE HIS ETERNAL SOUL.

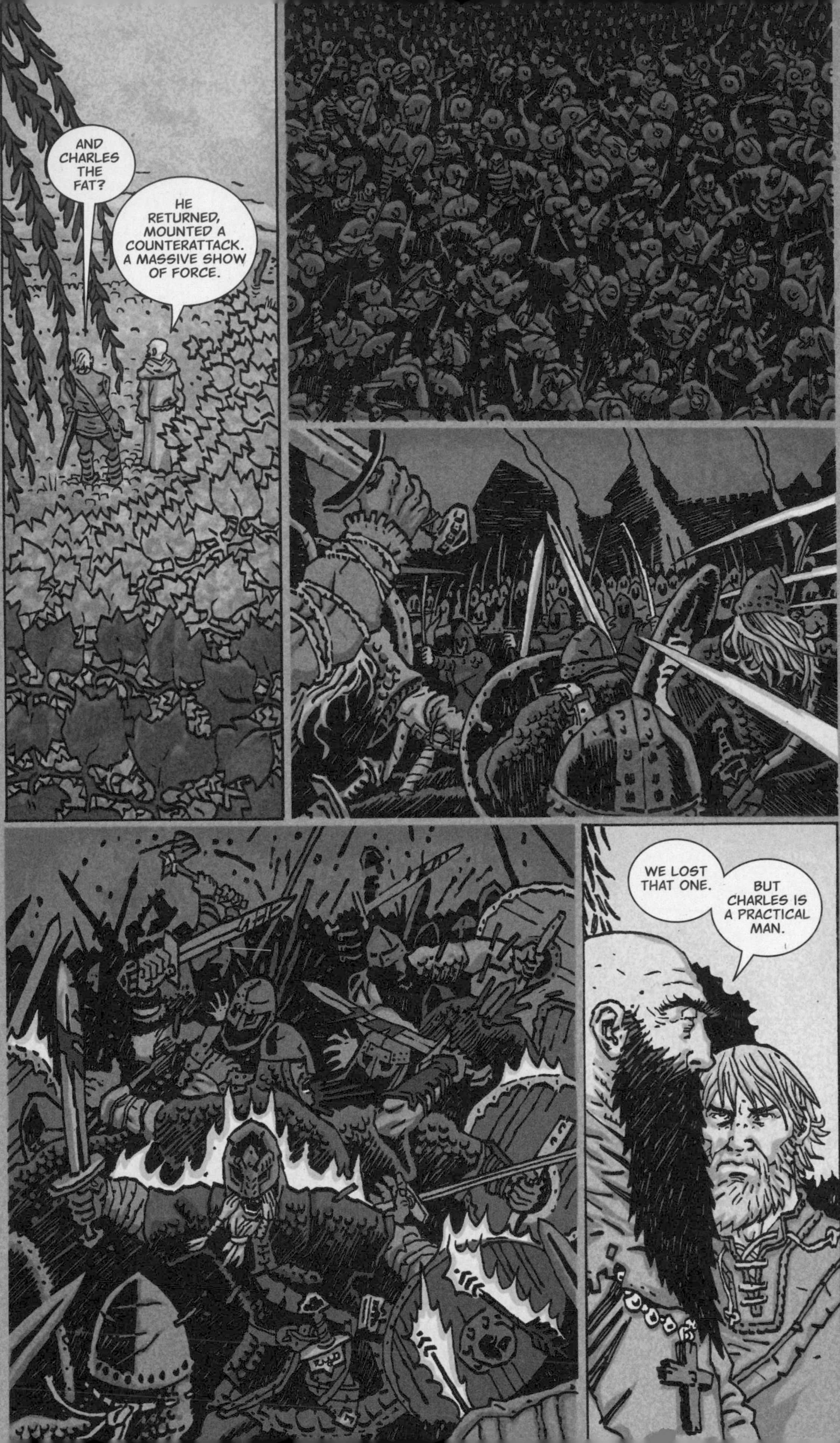
AND CHARLES THE FAT?
HE RETURNED, MOUNTED A COUNTERATTACK. A MASSIVE SHOW OF FORCE.
WE LOST THAT ONE.
BUT CHARLES IS A PRACTICAL MAN.

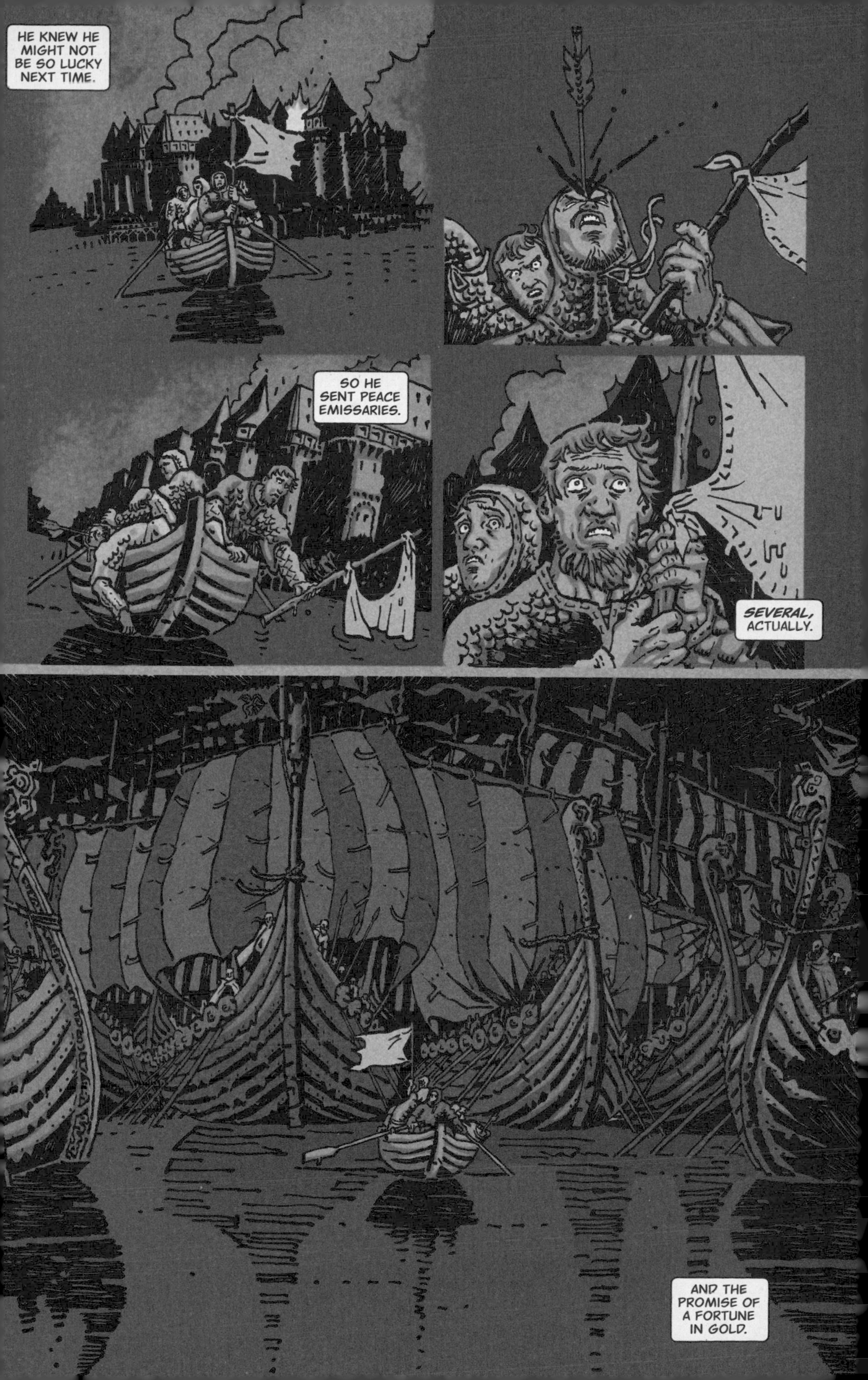
HE KNEW HE MIGHT NOT BE SO LUCKY NEXT TIME.
SO HE SENT PEACE EMISSARIES.
SEVERAL, ACTUALLY.
AND THE PROMISE OF A FORTUNE IN GOLD.

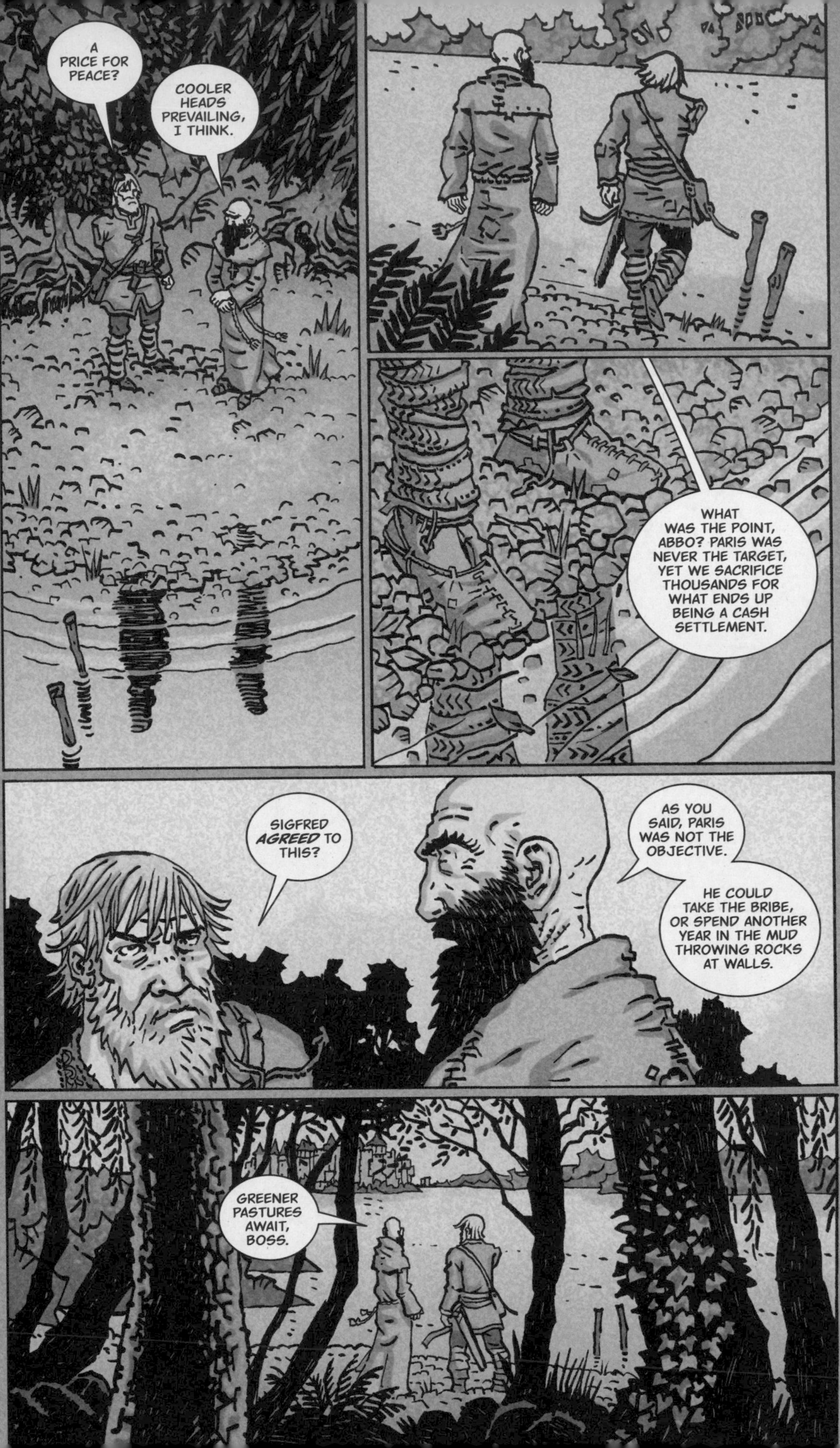
A PRICE FOR PEACE?
COOLER HEADS PREVAILING, I THINK.
WHAT WAS THE POINT, ABBO? PARIS WAS NEVER THE TARGET, YET WE SACRIFICE THOUSANDS FOR WHAT ENDS UP BEING A CASH SETTLEMENT.
SIGFRED *AGREED* TO THIS?
AS YOU SAID, PARIS WAS NOT THE OBJECTIVE.
HE COULD TAKE THE BRIBE, OR SPEND ANOTHER YEAR IN THE MUD THROWING ROCKS AT WALLS.
GREENER PASTURES AWAIT, BOSS.

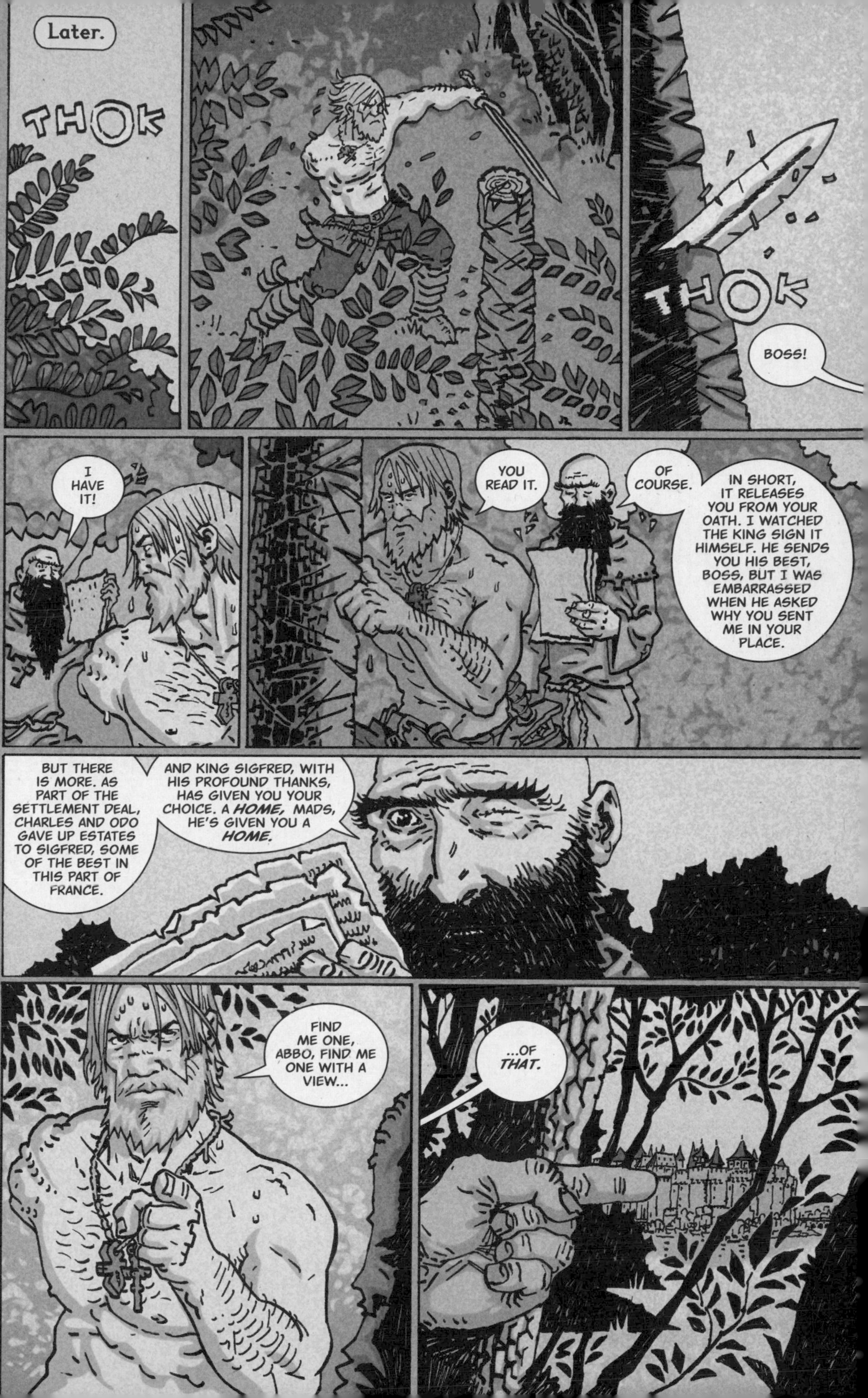
Later.
THOK
THOK
BOSS!
I HAVE IT!
YOU READ IT.
OF COURSE.
IN SHORT, IT RELEASES YOU FROM YOUR OATH. I WATCHED THE KING SIGN IT HIMSELF. HE SENDS YOU HIS BEST, BOSS, BUT I WAS EMBARRASSED WHEN HE ASKED WHY YOU SENT ME IN YOUR PLACE.
BUT THERE IS MORE. AS PART OF THE SETTLEMENT DEAL, CHARLES AND ODO GAVE UP ESTATES TO SIGFRED, SOME OF THE BEST IN THIS PART OF FRANCE.
AND KING SIGFRED, WITH HIS PROFOUND THANKS, HAS GIVEN YOU YOUR CHOICE. A *HOME,* MADS, HE'S GIVEN YOU A *HOME.*
FIND ME ONE, ABBO, FIND ME ONE WITH A VIEW...
...OF *THAT.*

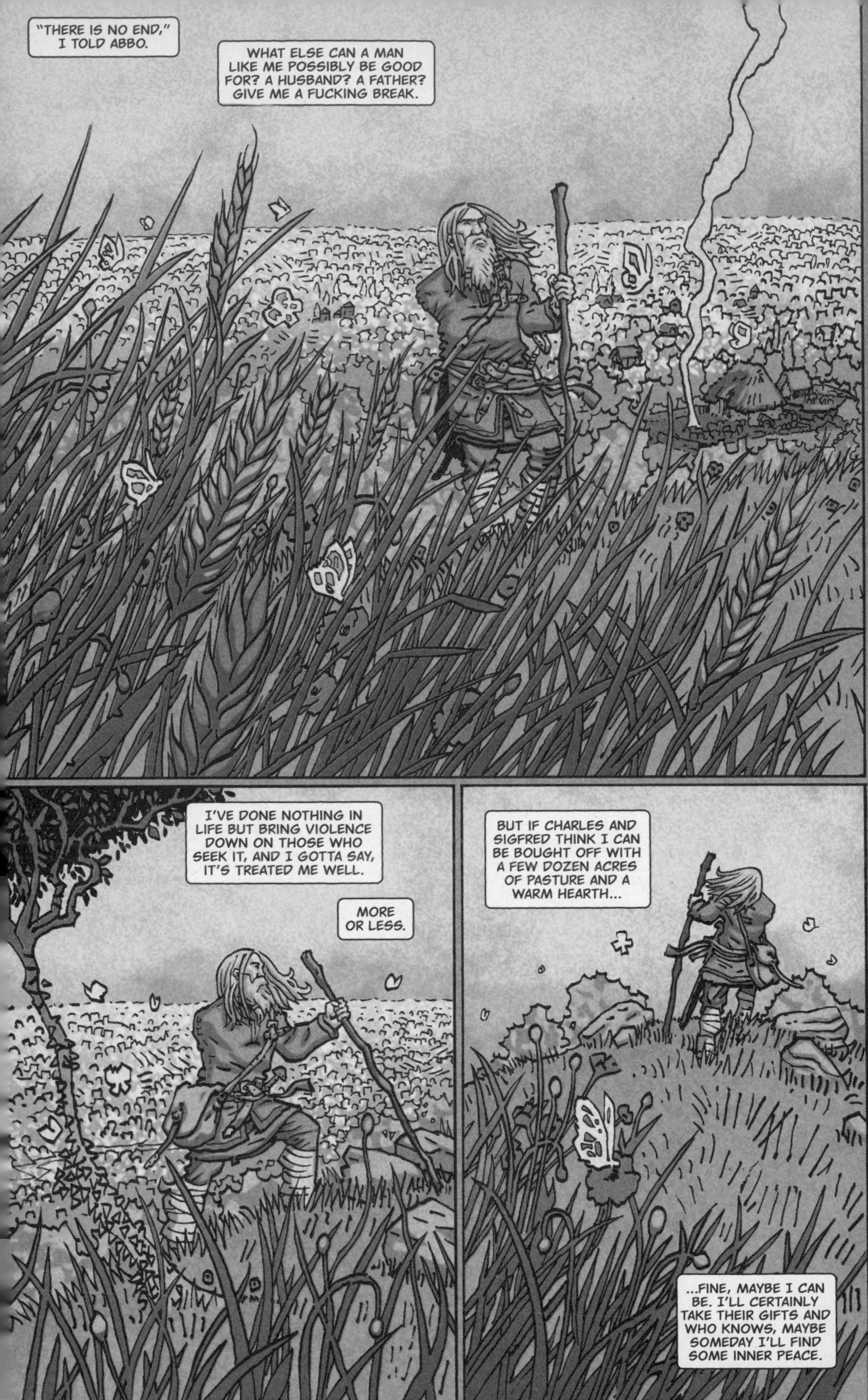
"THERE IS NO END," I TOLD ABBO.
WHAT ELSE CAN A MAN LIKE ME POSSIBLY BE GOOD FOR? A HUSBAND? A FATHER? GIVE ME A FUCKING BREAK.
I'VE DONE NOTHING IN LIFE BUT BRING VIOLENCE DOWN ON THOSE WHO SEEK IT, AND I GOTTA SAY, IT'S TREATED ME WELL.
MORE OR LESS.
BUT IF CHARLES AND SIGFRED THINK I CAN BE BOUGHT OFF WITH A FEW DOZEN ACRES OF PASTURE AND A WARM HEARTH...
...FINE, MAYBE I CAN BE. I'LL CERTAINLY TAKE THEIR GIFTS AND WHO KNOWS, MAYBE SOMEDAY I'LL FIND SOME INNER PEACE.

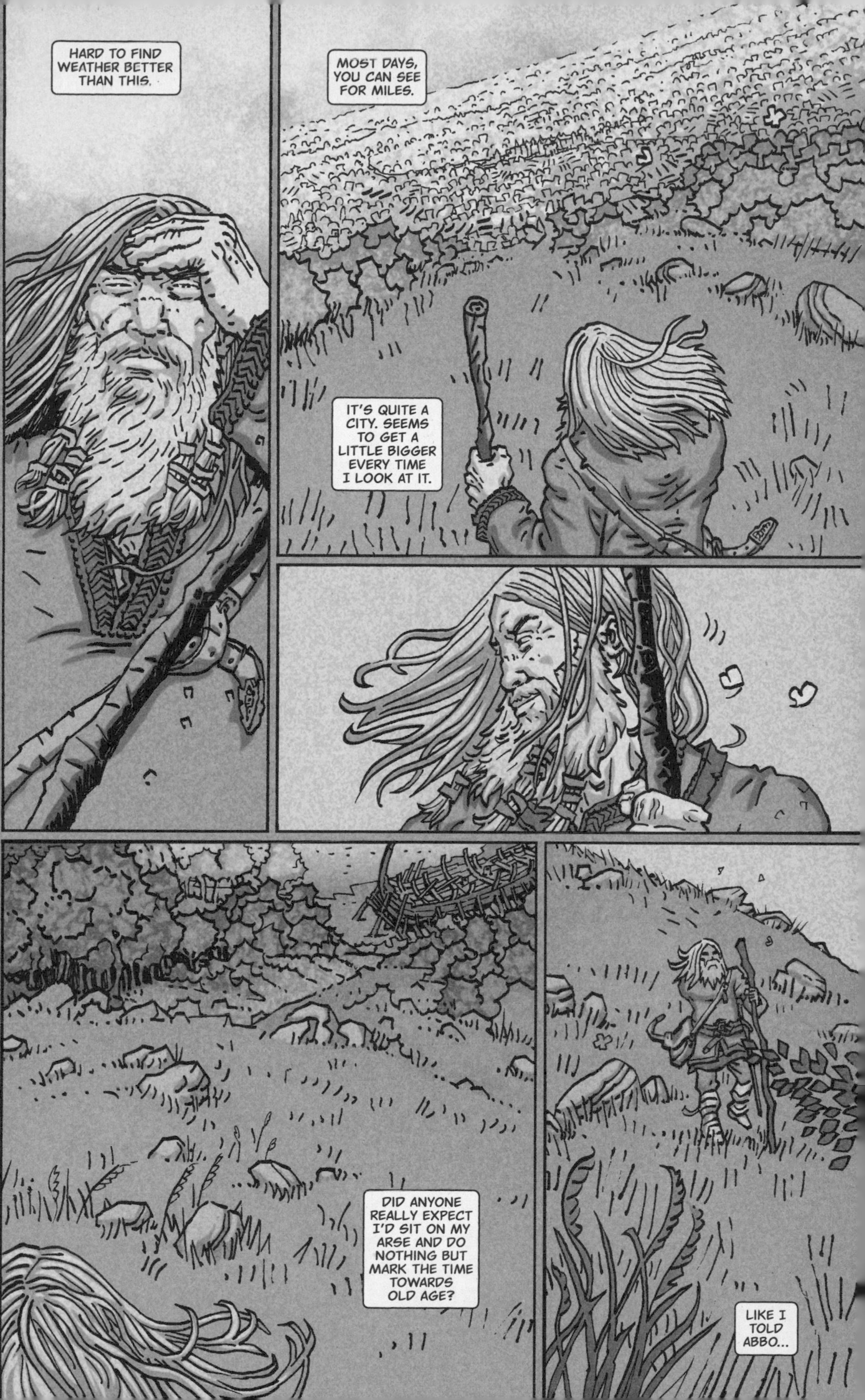
HARD TO FIND WEATHER BETTER THAN THIS.
MOST DAYS, YOU CAN SEE FOR MILES.
IT'S QUITE A CITY. SEEMS TO GET A LITTLE BIGGER EVERY TIME I LOOK AT IT.
DID ANYONE REALLY EXPECT I'D SIT ON MY ARSE AND DO NOTHING BUT MARK THE TIME TOWARDS OLD AGE?
LIKE I TOLD ABBO...

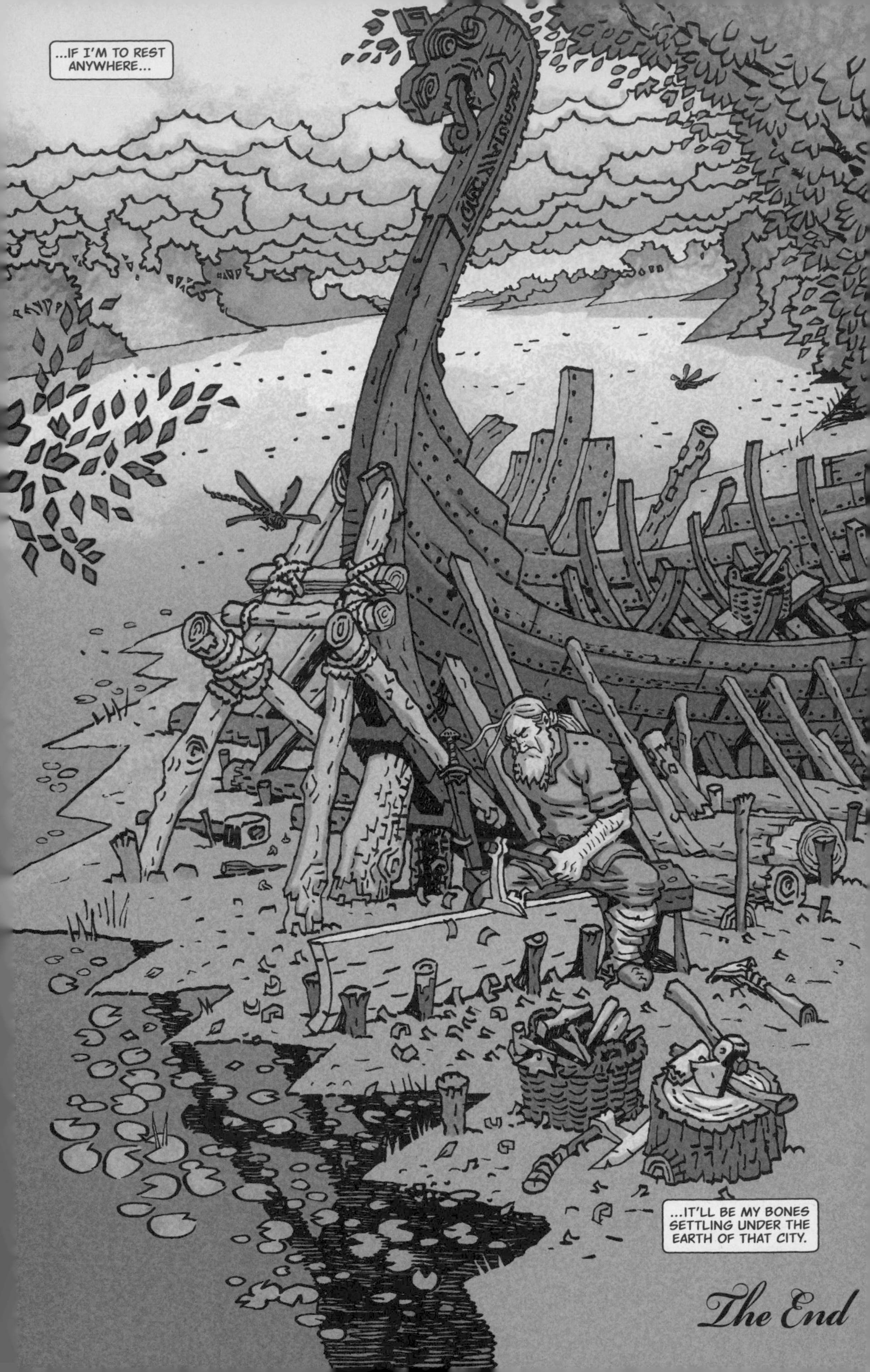
...IF I'M TO REST ANYWHERE...
...IT'LL BE MY BONES SETTLING UNDER THE EARTH OF THAT CITY.
The End

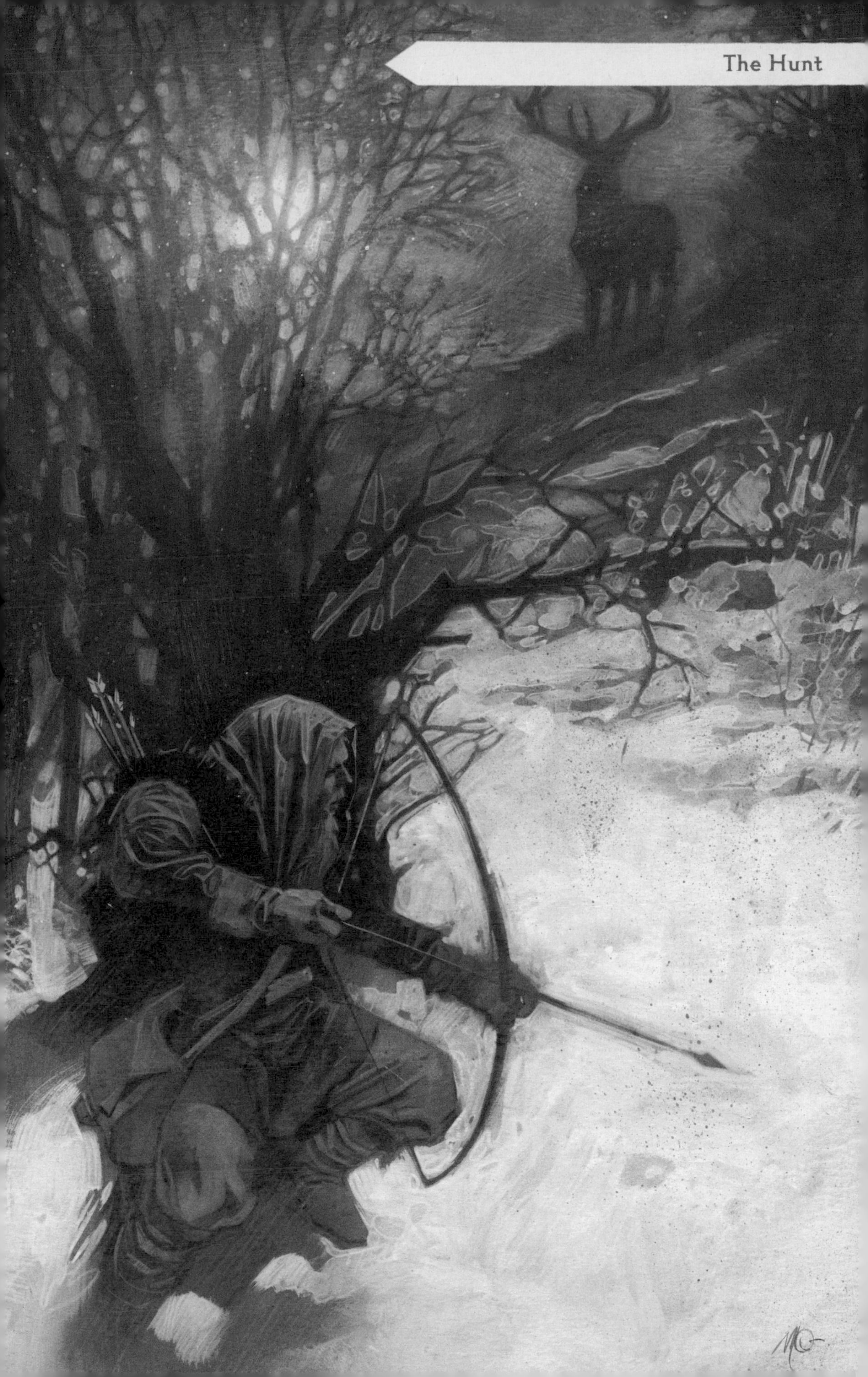

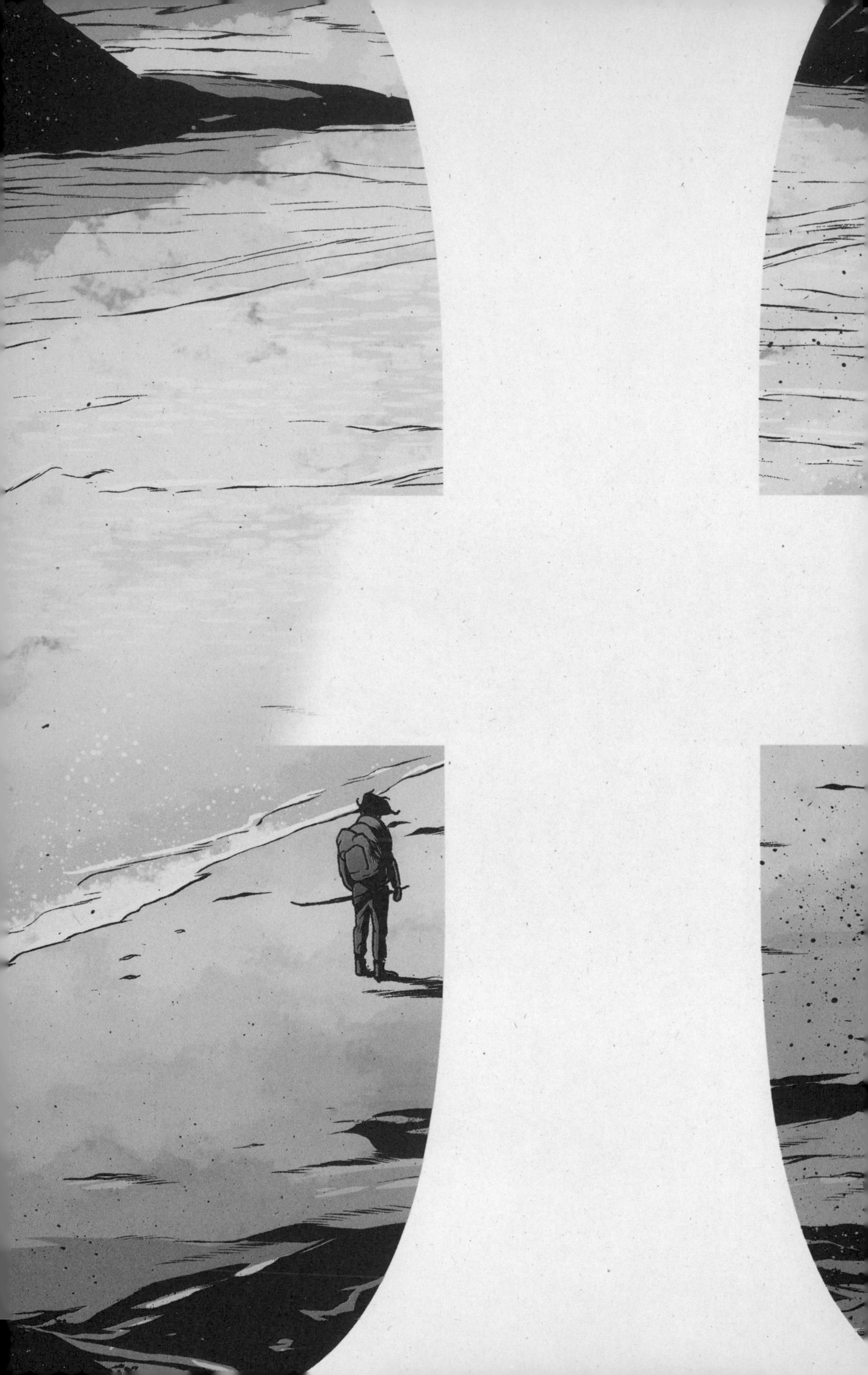

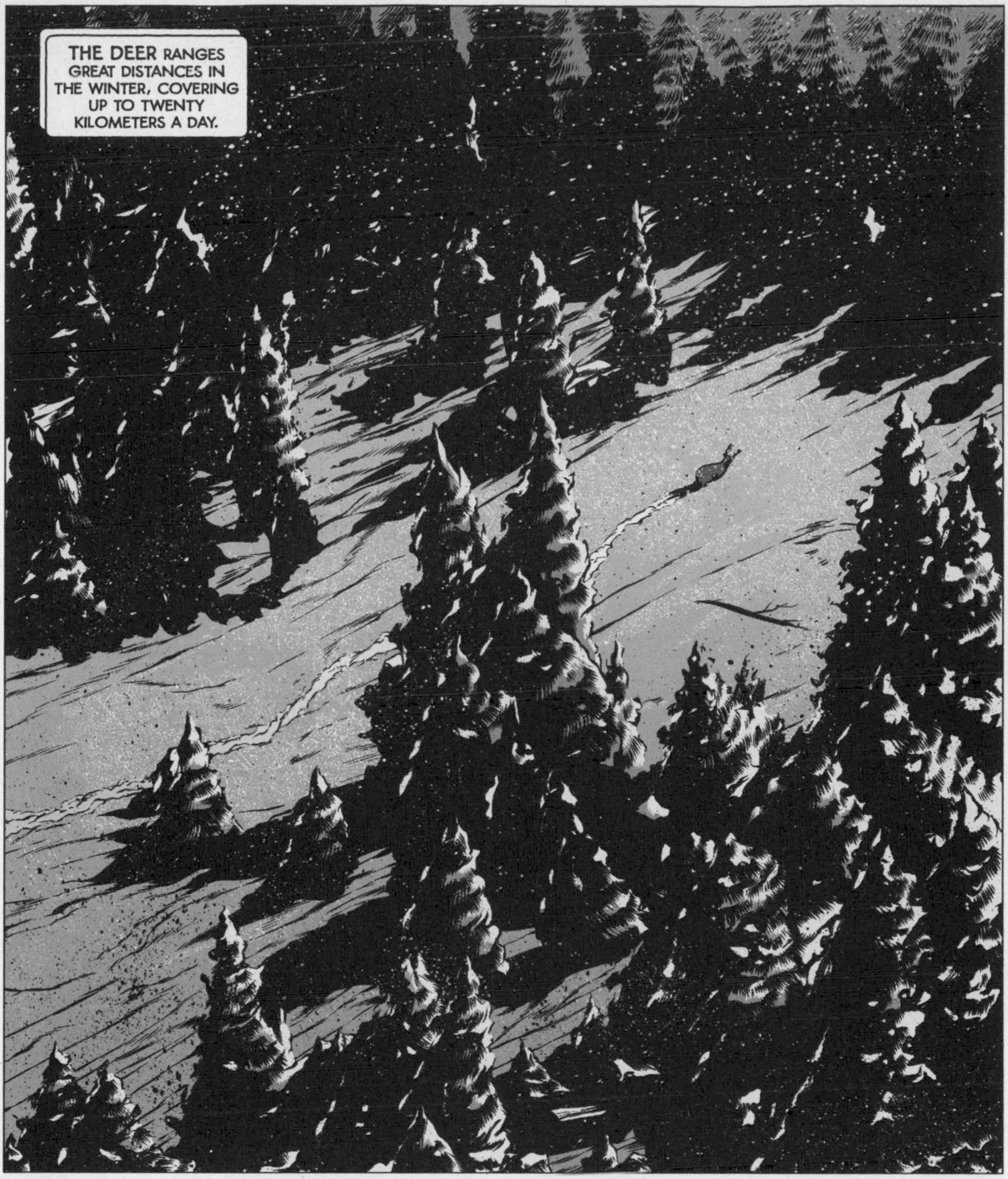
THE DEER RANGES GREAT DISTANCES IN THE WINTER, COVERING UP TO TWENTY KILOMETERS A DAY.

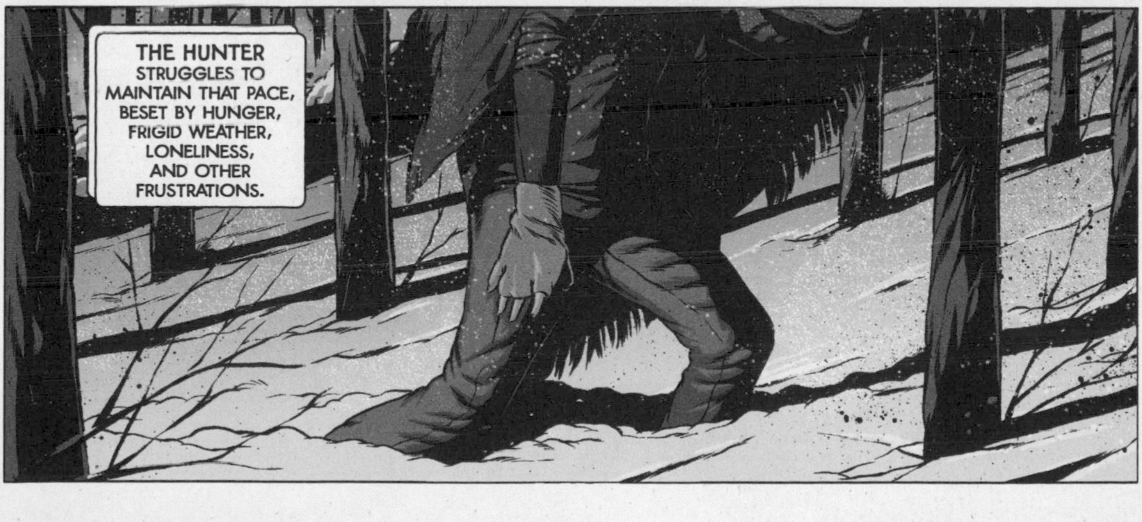
THE HUNTER STRUGGLES TO MAINTAIN THAT PACE, BESET BY HUNGER, FRIGID WEATHER, LONELINESS, AND OTHER FRUSTRATIONS.

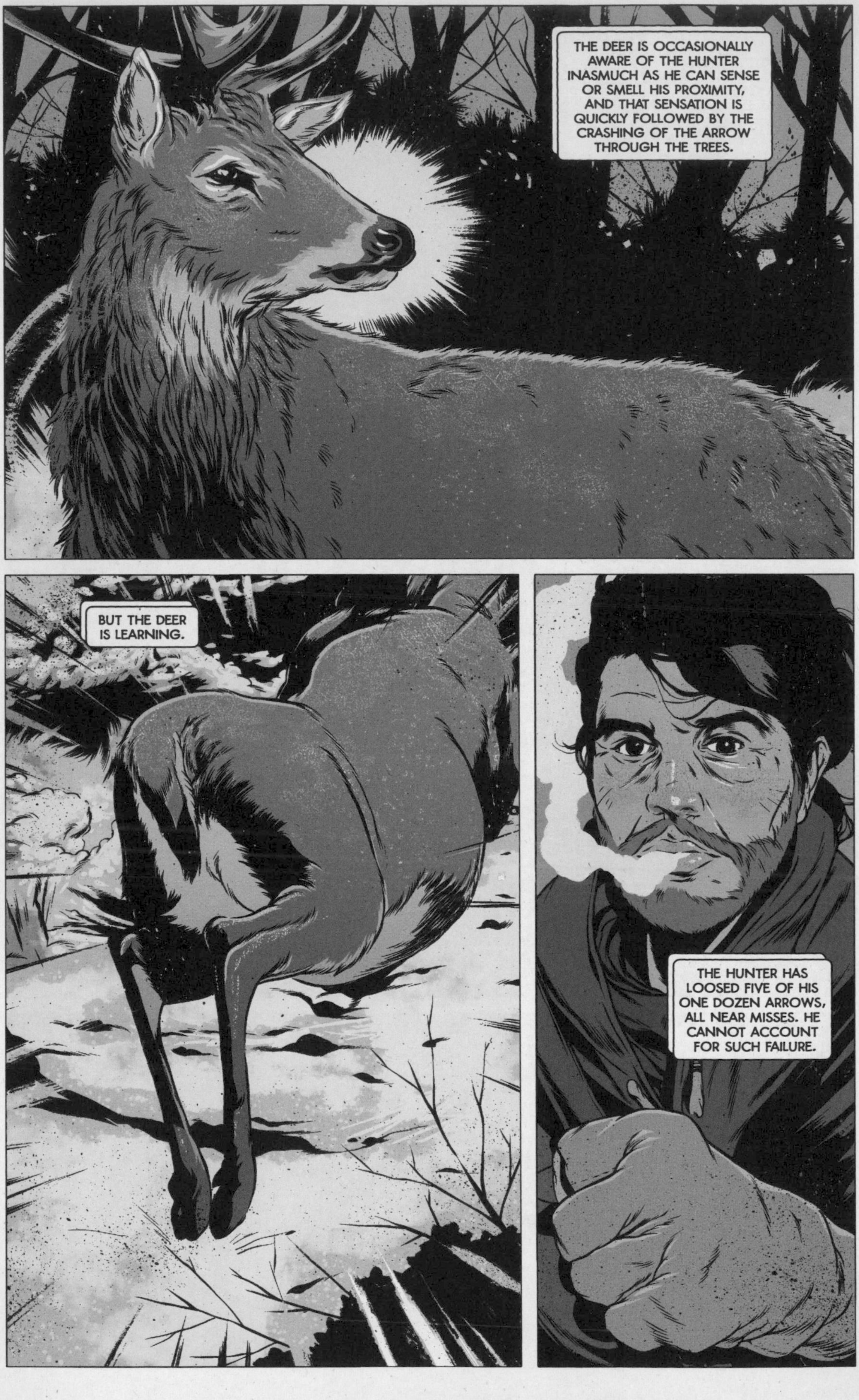
THE DEER IS OCCASIONALLY AWARE OF THE HUNTER INASMUCH AS HE CAN SENSE OR SMELL HIS PROXIMITY, AND THAT SENSATION IS QUICKLY FOLLOWED BY THE CRASHING OF THE ARROW THROUGH THE TREES.
BUT THE DEER IS LEARNING.
THE HUNTER HAS LOOSED FIVE OF HIS ONE DOZEN ARROWS, ALL NEAR MISSES. HE CANNOT ACCOUNT FOR SUCH FAILURE.

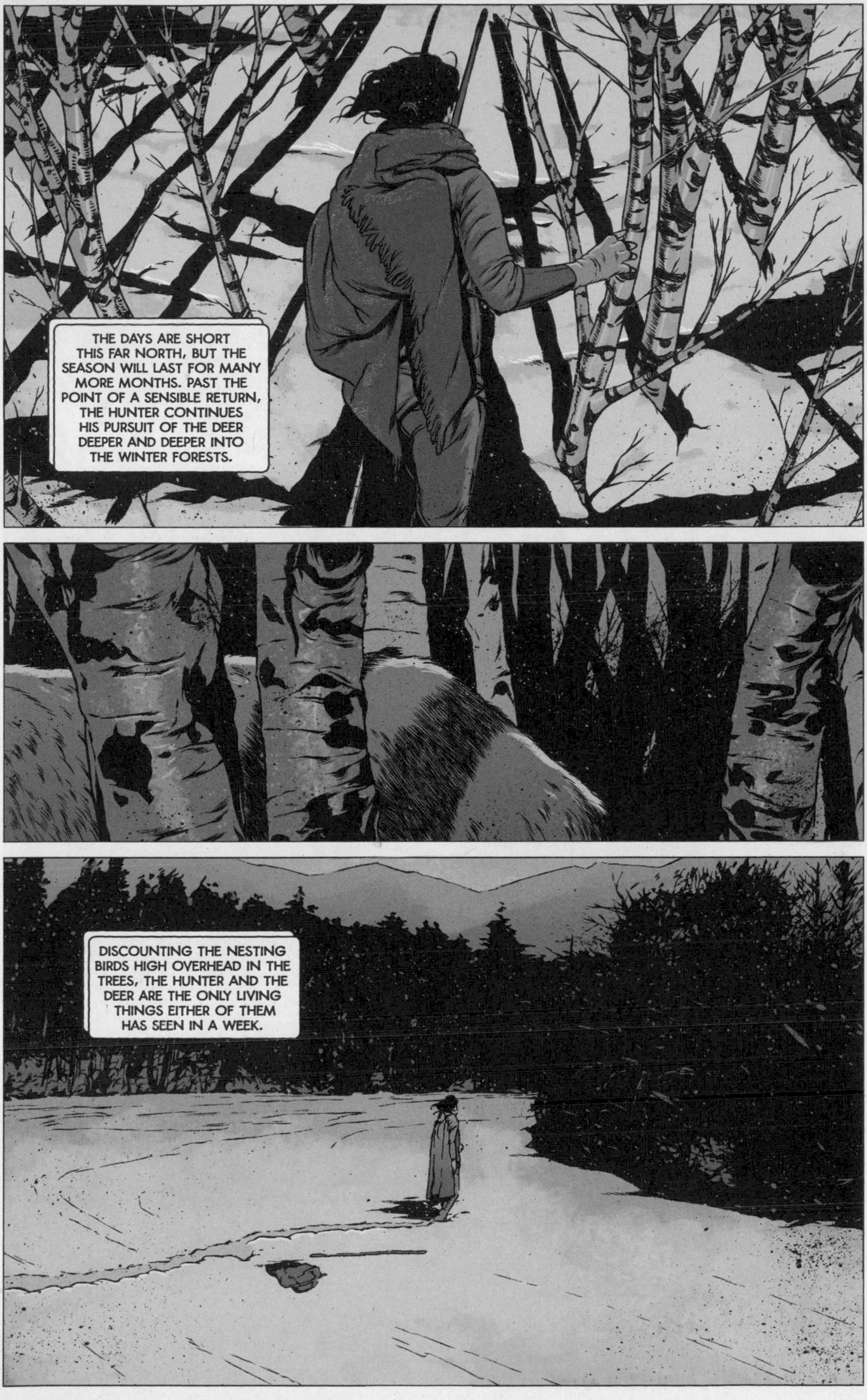
THE DAYS ARE SHORT THIS FAR NORTH, BUT THE SEASON WILL LAST FOR MANY MORE MONTHS. PAST THE POINT OF A SENSIBLE RETURN, THE HUNTER CONTINUES HIS PURSUIT OF THE DEER DEEPER AND DEEPER INTO THE WINTER FORESTS.
DISCOUNTING THE NESTING BIRDS HIGH OVERHEAD IN THE TREES, THE HUNTER AND THE DEER ARE THE ONLY LIVING THINGS EITHER OF THEM HAS SEEN IN A WEEK.

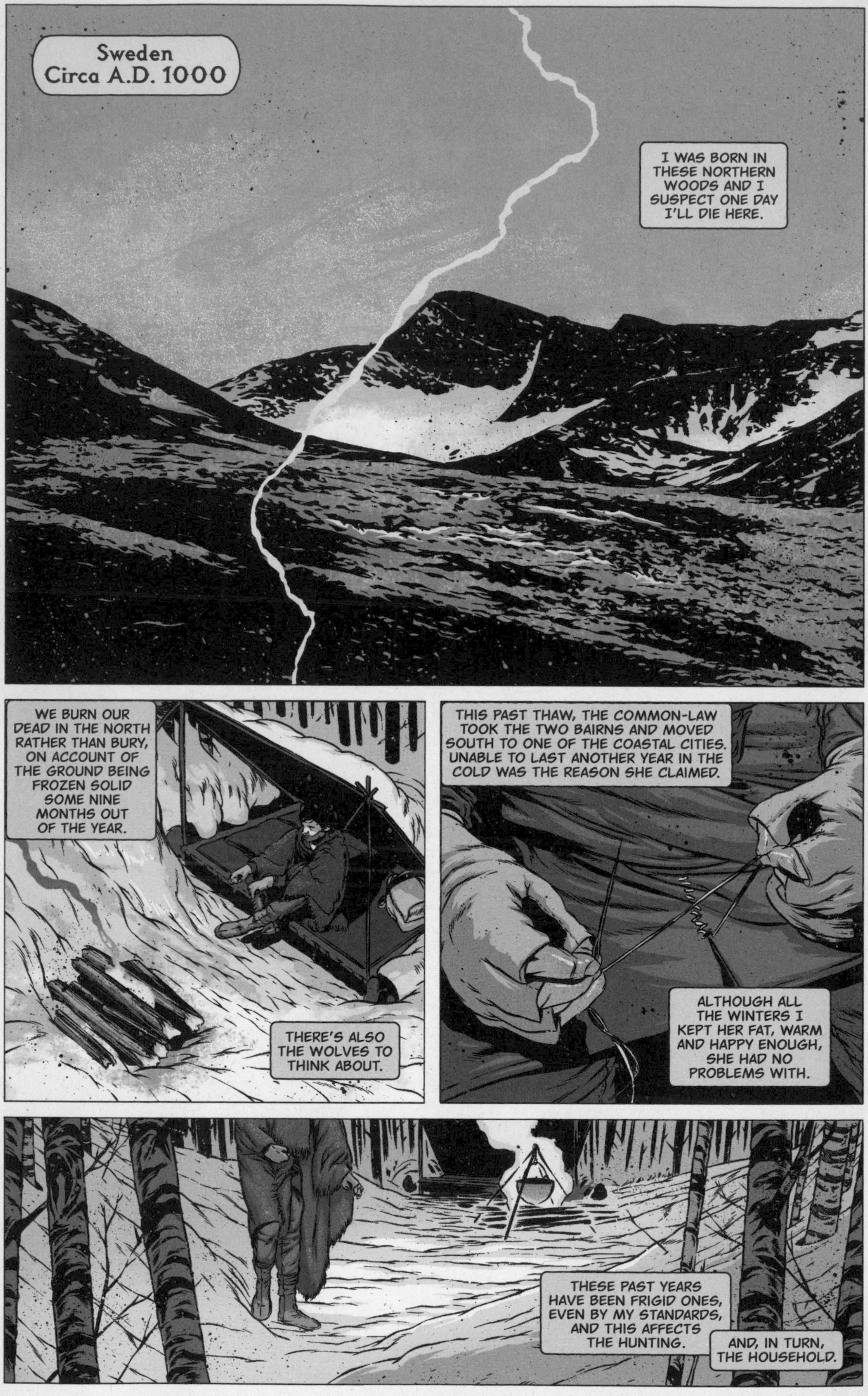
Sweden
Circa A.D. 1000
I WAS BORN IN THESE NORTHERN WOODS AND I SUSPECT ONE DAY I'LL DIE HERE.
WE BURN OUR DEAD IN THE NORTH RATHER THAN BURY, ON ACCOUNT OF THE GROUND BEING FROZEN SOLID SOME NINE MONTHS OUT OF THE YEAR.
THERE'S ALSO THE WOLVES TO THINK ABOUT.
THIS PAST THAW, THE COMMON-LAW TOOK THE TWO BAIRNS AND MOVED SOUTH TO ONE OF THE COASTAL CITIES. UNABLE TO LAST ANOTHER YEAR IN THE COLD WAS THE REASON SHE CLAIMED.
ALTHOUGH ALL THE WINTERS I KEPT HER FAT, WARM AND HAPPY ENOUGH, SHE HAD NO PROBLEMS WITH.
THESE PAST YEARS HAVE BEEN FRIGID ONES, EVEN BY MY STANDARDS, AND THIS AFFECTS THE HUNTING.
AND, IN TURN, THE HOUSEHOLD.

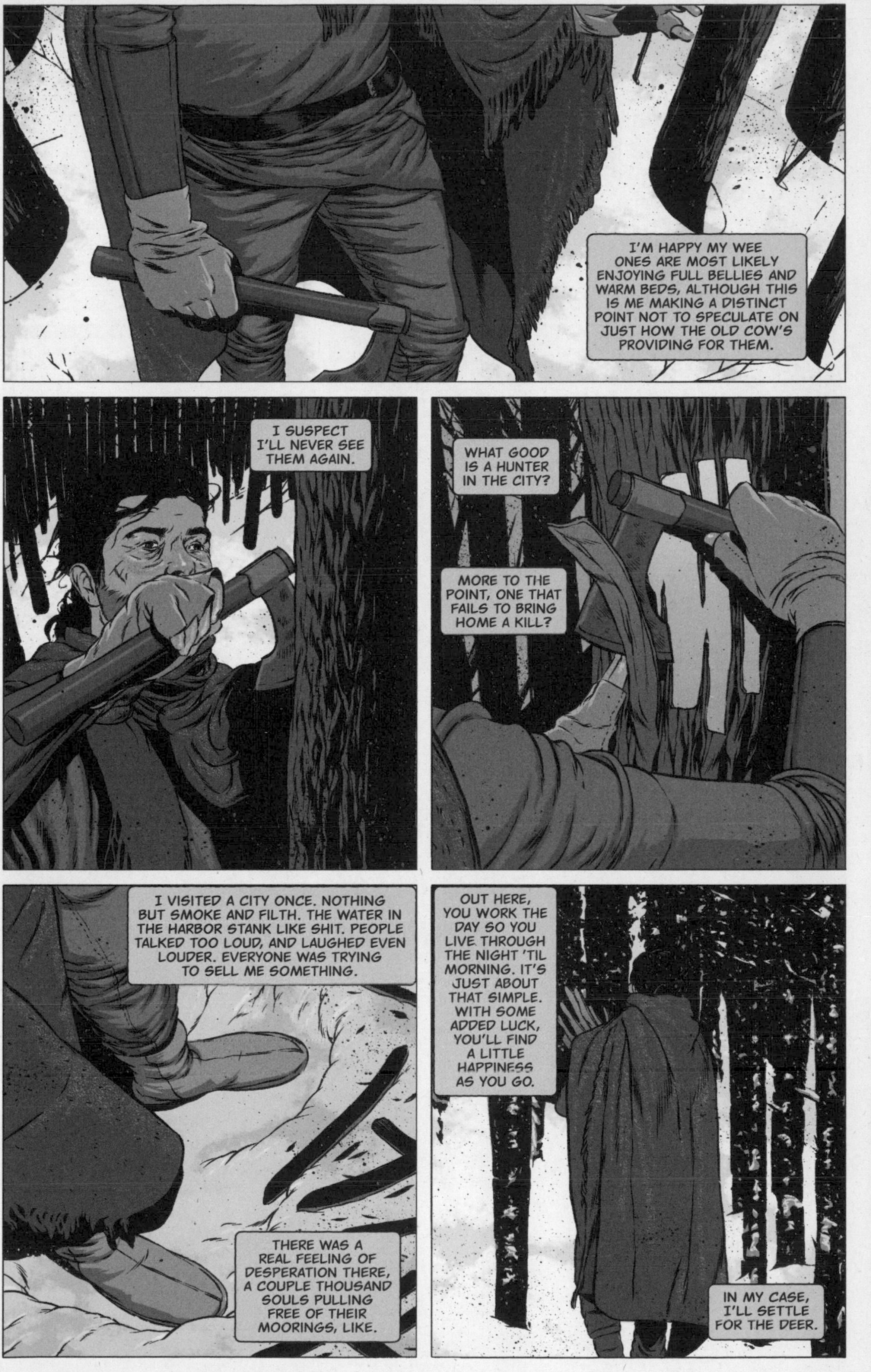
I'M HAPPY MY WEE ONES ARE MOST LIKELY ENJOYING FULL BELLIES AND WARM BEDS, ALTHOUGH THIS IS ME MAKING A DISTINCT POINT NOT TO SPECULATE ON JUST HOW THE OLD COW'S PROVIDING FOR THEM.
I SUSPECT I'LL NEVER SEE THEM AGAIN.
WHAT GOOD IS A HUNTER IN THE CITY?
MORE TO THE POINT, ONE THAT FAILS TO BRING HOME A KILL?
I VISITED A CITY ONCE. NOTHING BUT SMOKE AND FILTH. THE WATER IN THE HARBOR STANK LIKE SHIT. PEOPLE TALKED TOO LOUD, AND LAUGHED EVEN LOUDER. EVERYONE WAS TRYING TO SELL ME SOMETHING.
THERE WAS A REAL FEELING OF DESPERATION THERE, A COUPLE THOUSAND SOULS PULLING FREE OF THEIR MOORINGS, LIKE.
OUT HERE, YOU WORK THE DAY SO YOU LIVE THROUGH THE NIGHT 'TIL MORNING. IT'S JUST ABOUT THAT SIMPLE. WITH SOME ADDED LUCK, YOU'LL FIND A LITTLE HAPPINESS AS YOU GO.
IN MY CASE, I'LL SETTLE FOR THE DEER.

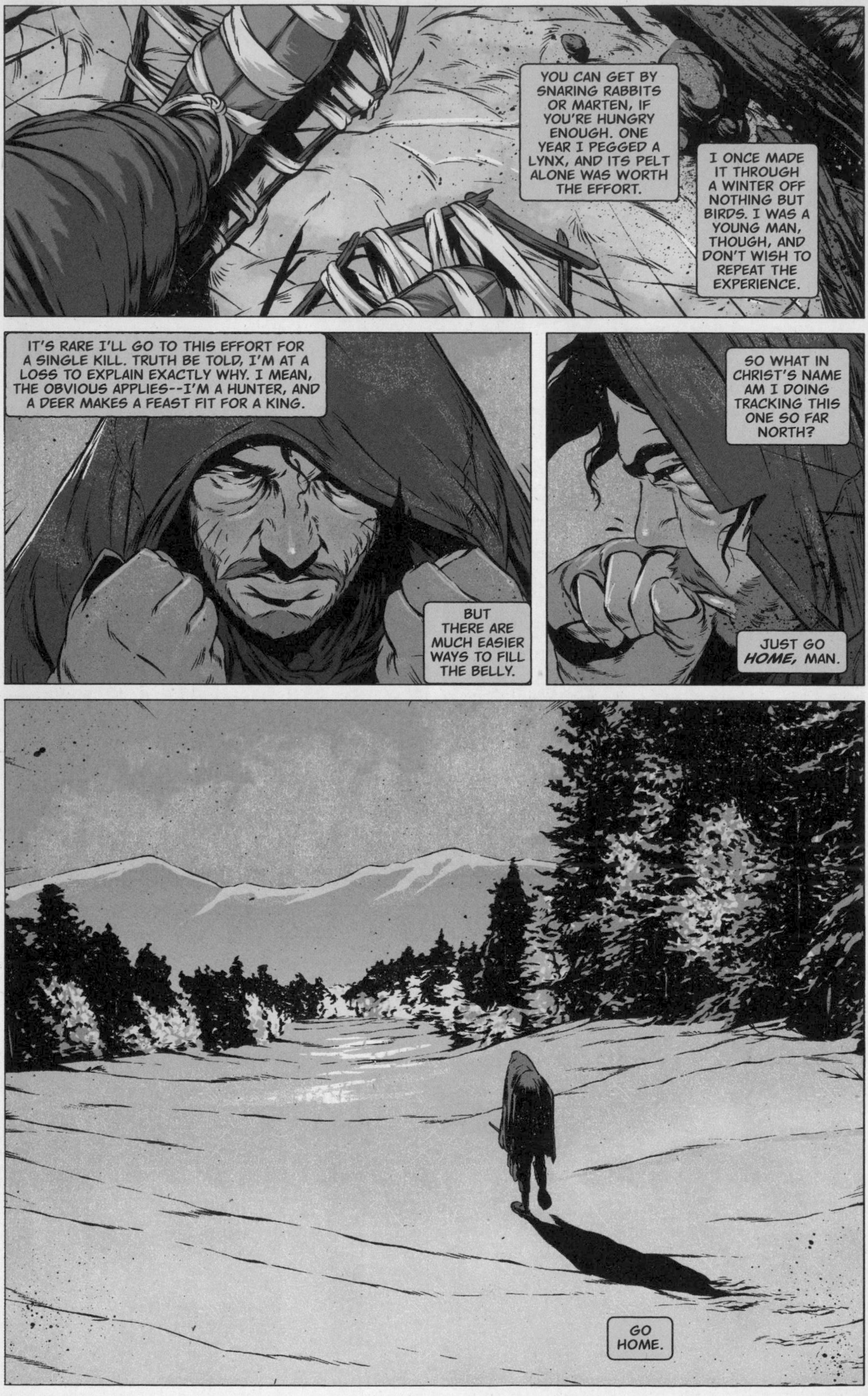
YOU CAN GET BY SNARING RABBITS OR MARTEN, IF YOU'RE HUNGRY ENOUGH. ONE YEAR I PEGGED A LYNX, AND ITS PELT ALONE WAS WORTH THE EFFORT.
I ONCE MADE IT THROUGH A WINTER OFF NOTHING BUT BIRDS. I WAS A YOUNG MAN, THOUGH, AND DON'T WISH TO REPEAT THE EXPERIENCE.
IT'S RARE I'LL GO TO THIS EFFORT FOR A SINGLE KILL. TRUTH BE TOLD, I'M AT A LOSS TO EXPLAIN EXACTLY WHY. I MEAN, THE OBVIOUS APPLIES--I'M A HUNTER, AND A DEER MAKES A FEAST FIT FOR A KING.
BUT THERE ARE MUCH EASIER WAYS TO FILL THE BELLY.
SO WHAT IN CHRIST'S NAME AM I DOING TRACKING THIS ONE SO FAR NORTH?
JUST GO *HOME,* MAN.
GO HOME.

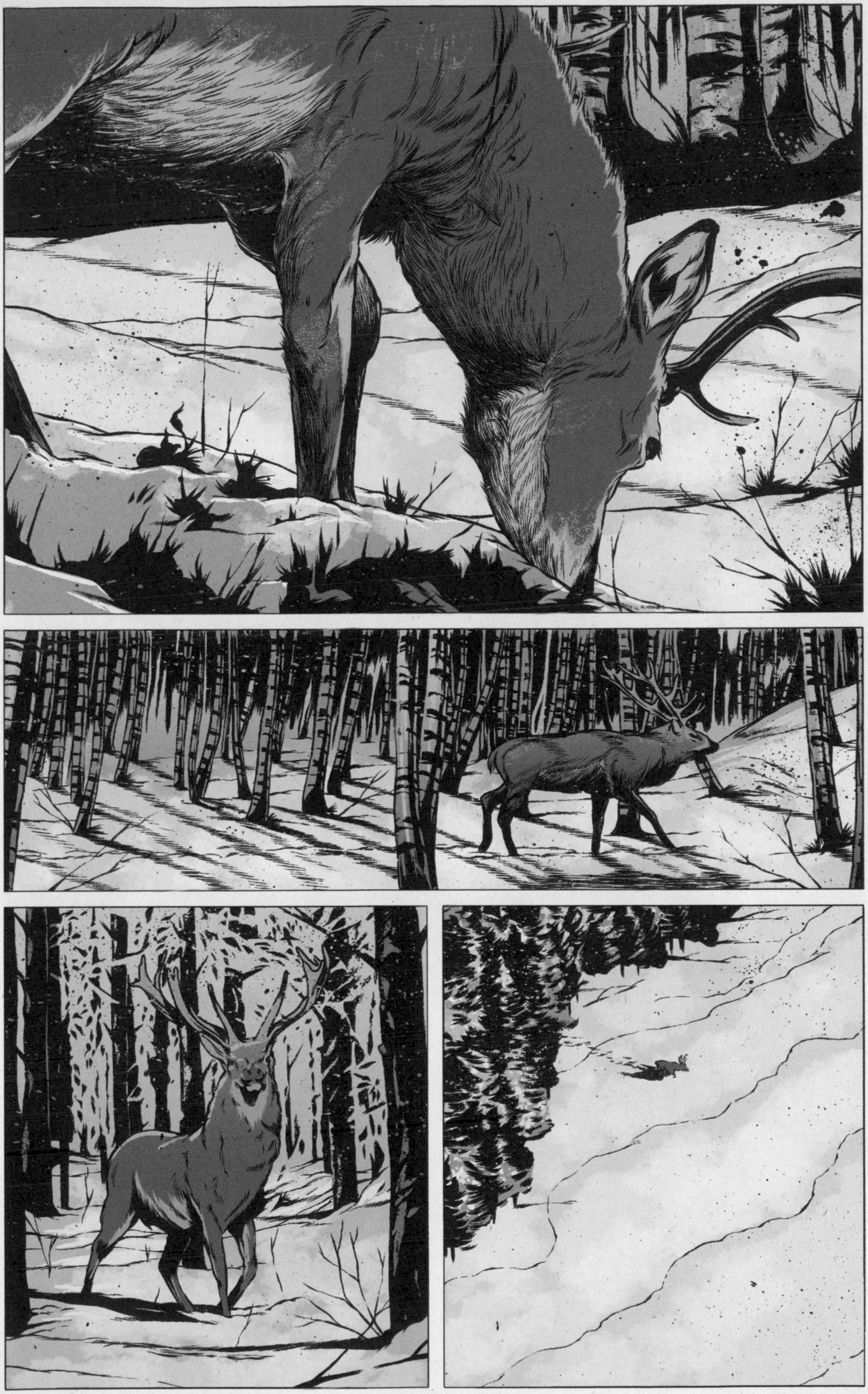

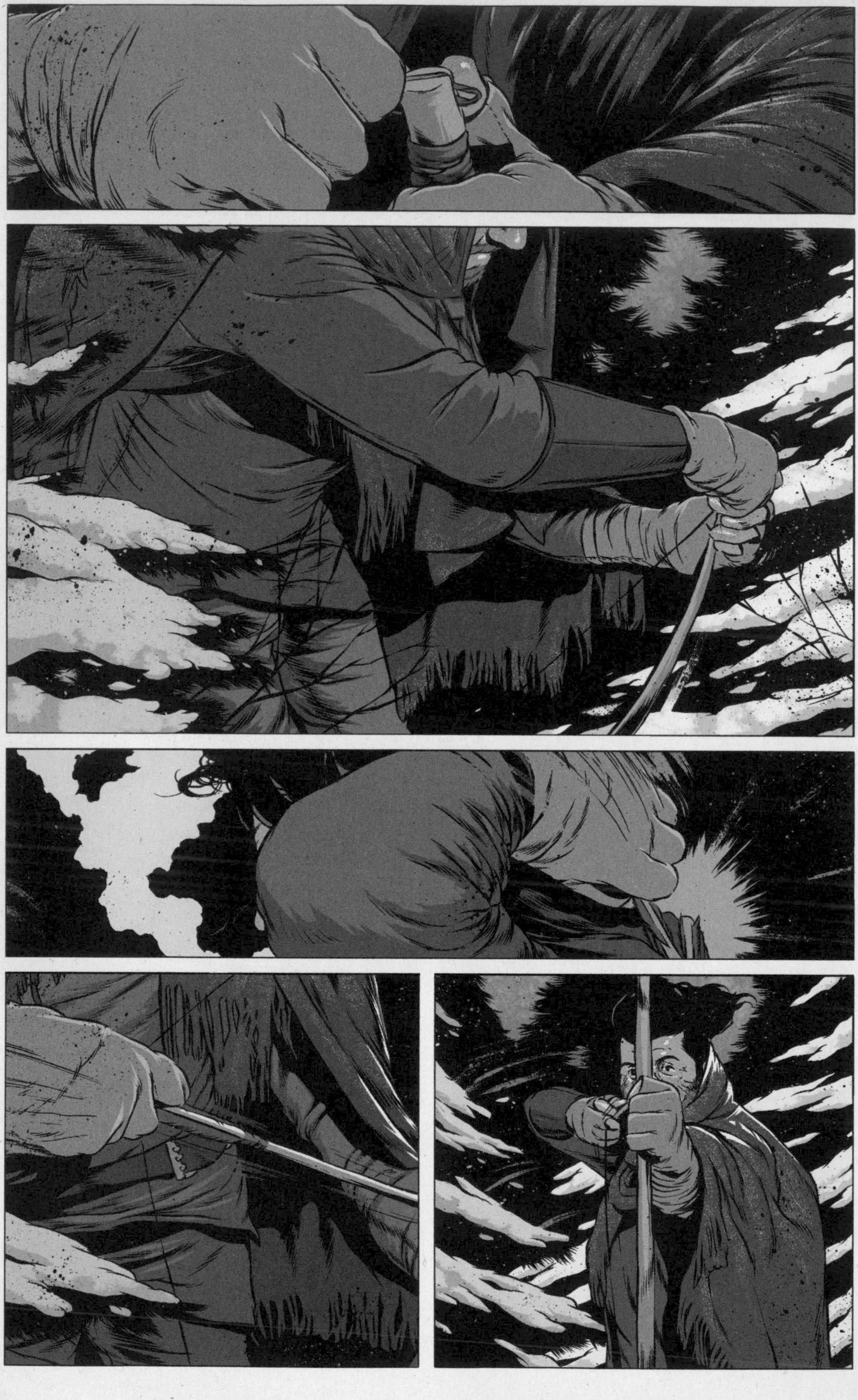

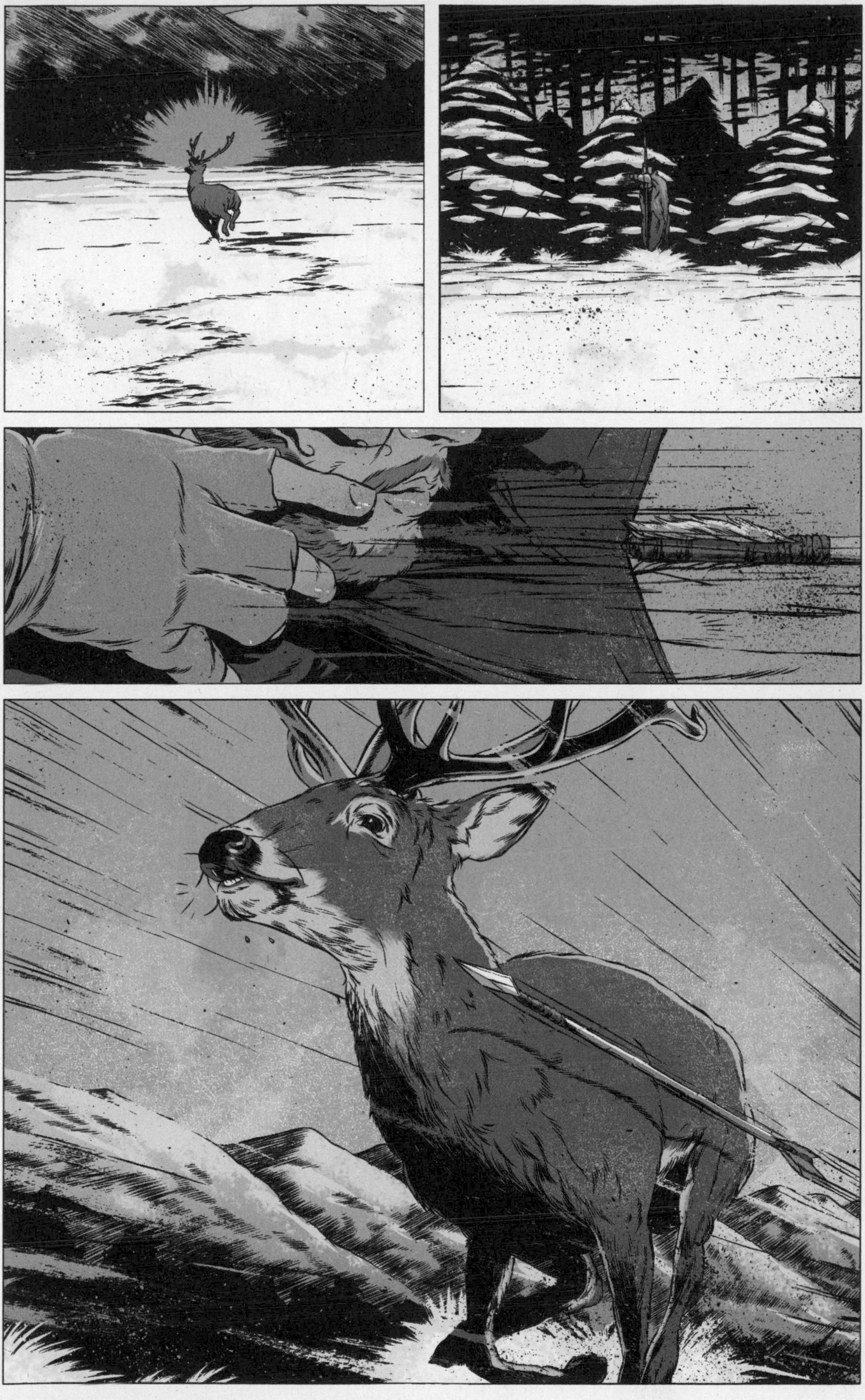

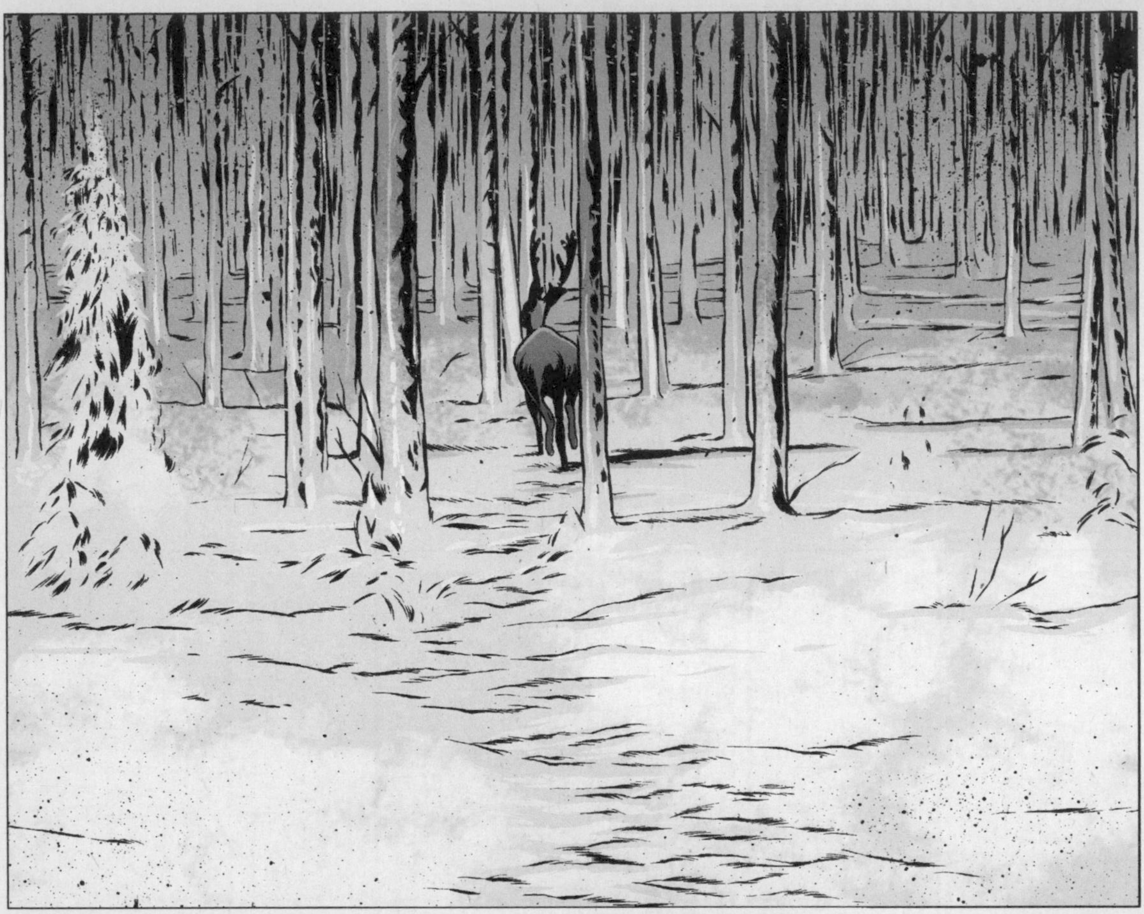

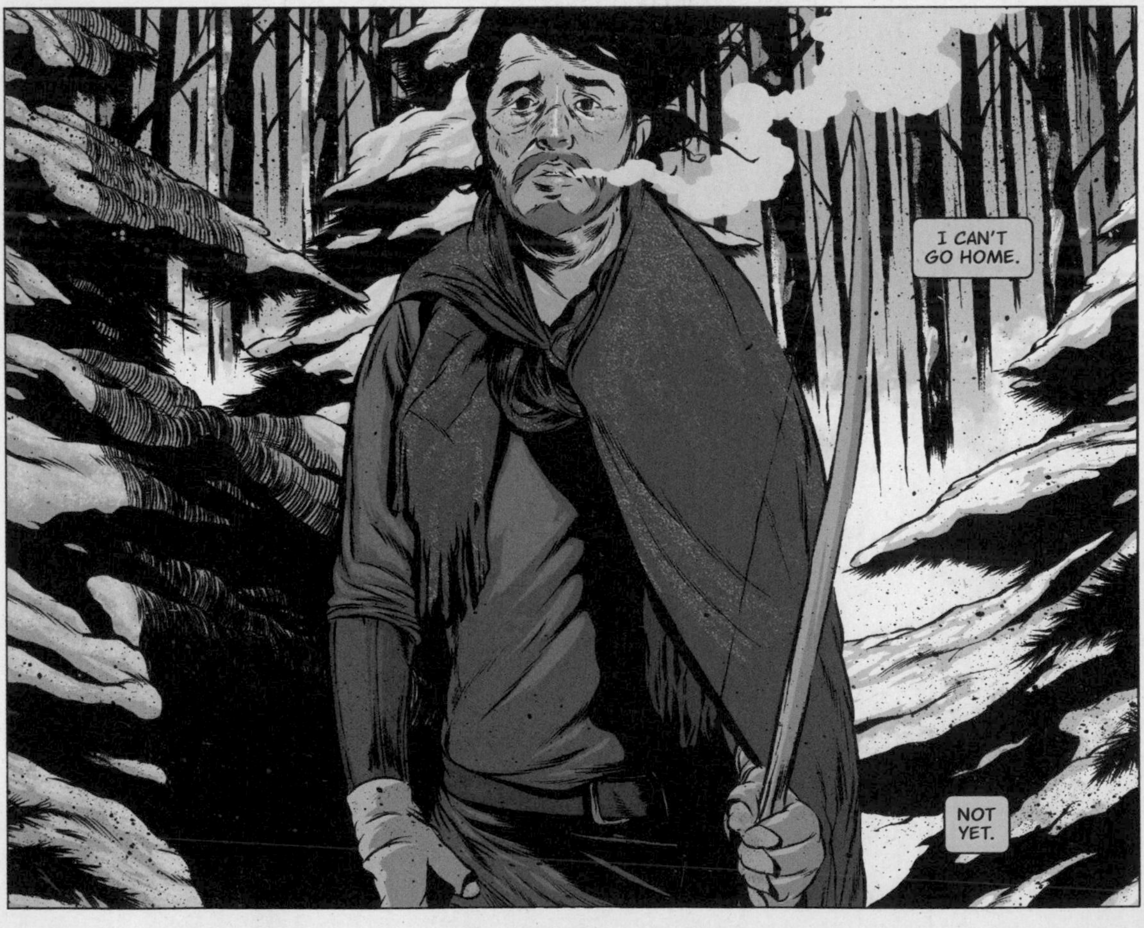
I CAN'T GO HOME.
NOT YET.

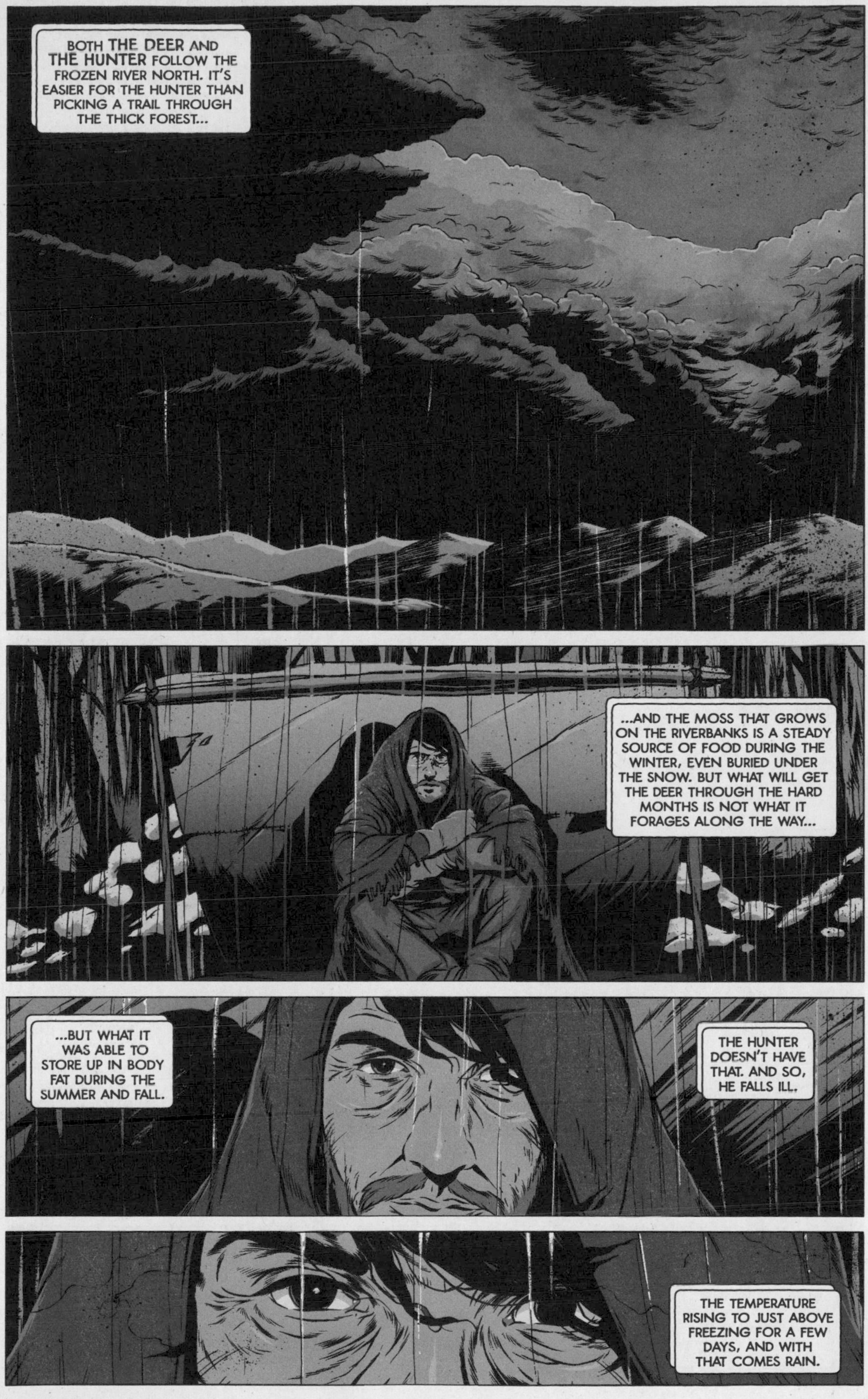
BOTH THE DEER AND THE HUNTER FOLLOW THE FROZEN RIVER NORTH. IT'S EASIER FOR THE HUNTER THAN PICKING A TRAIL THROUGH THE THICK FOREST...
...AND THE MOSS THAT GROWS ON THE RIVERBANKS IS A STEADY SOURCE OF FOOD DURING THE WINTER, EVEN BURIED UNDER THE SNOW. BUT WHAT WILL GET THE DEER THROUGH THE HARD MONTHS IS NOT WHAT IT FORAGES ALONG THE WAY...
...BUT WHAT IT WAS ABLE TO STORE UP IN BODY FAT DURING THE SUMMER AND FALL.
THE HUNTER DOESN'T HAVE THAT. AND SO, HE FALLS ILL.
THE TEMPERATURE RISING TO JUST ABOVE FREEZING FOR A FEW DAYS, AND WITH THAT COMES RAIN.

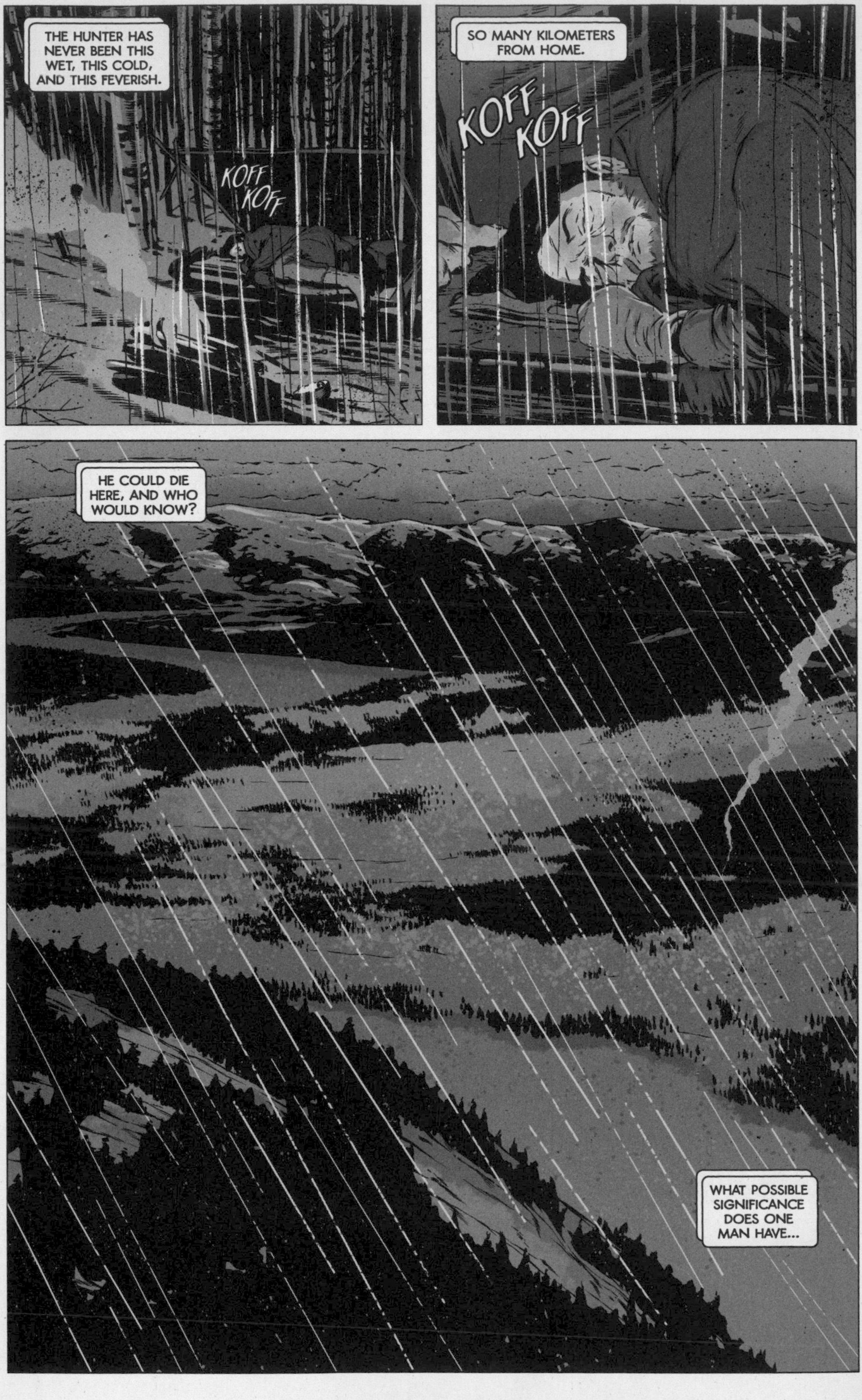
THE HUNTER HAS NEVER BEEN THIS WET, THIS COLD, AND THIS FEVERISH.
KOFF KOFF
SO MANY KILOMETERS FROM HOME.
KOFF KOFF
HE COULD DIE HERE, AND WHO WOULD KNOW?
WHAT POSSIBLE SIGNIFICANCE DOES ONE MAN HAVE...

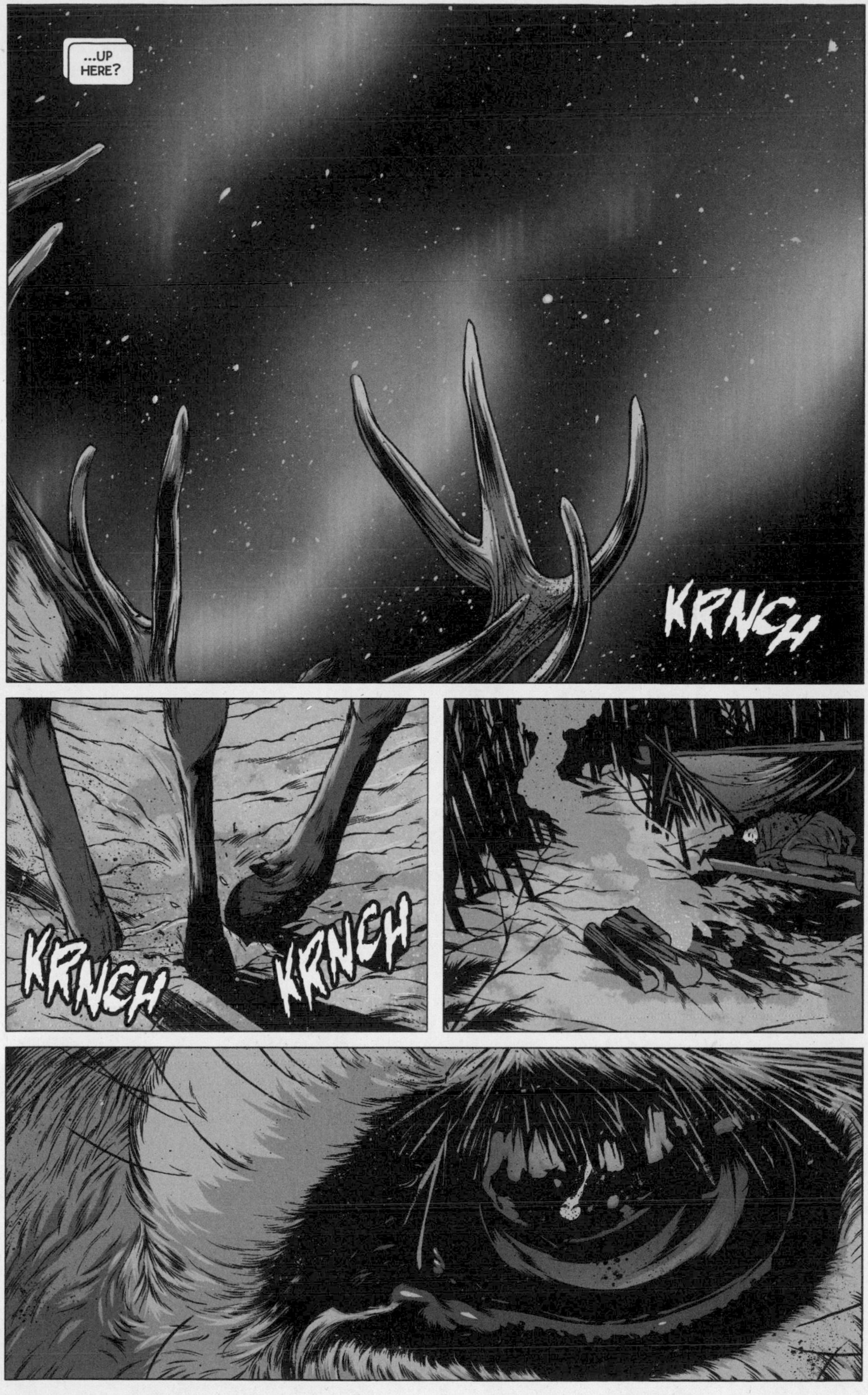
...UP HERE?
KRNCH
KRNCH
KRNCH

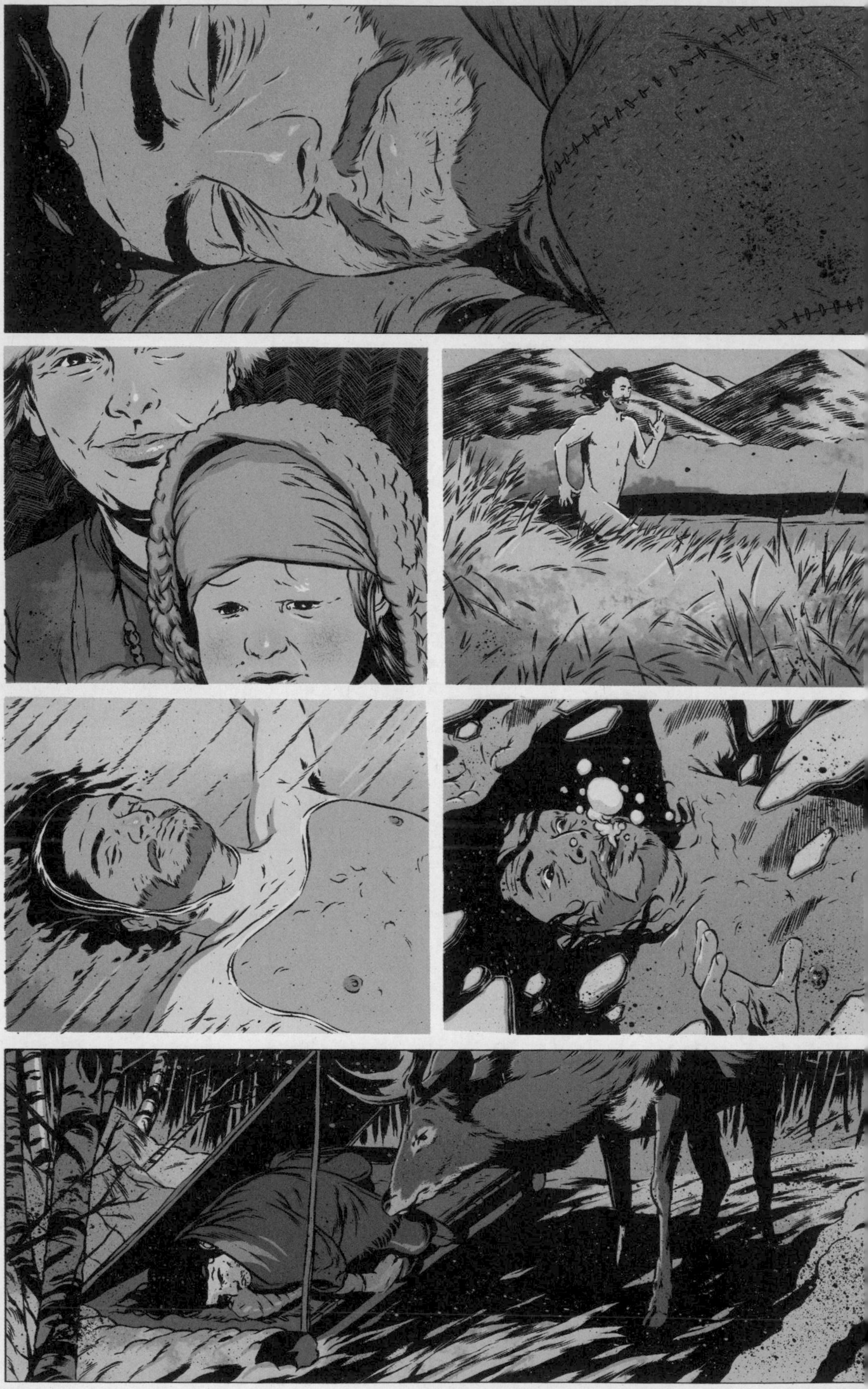

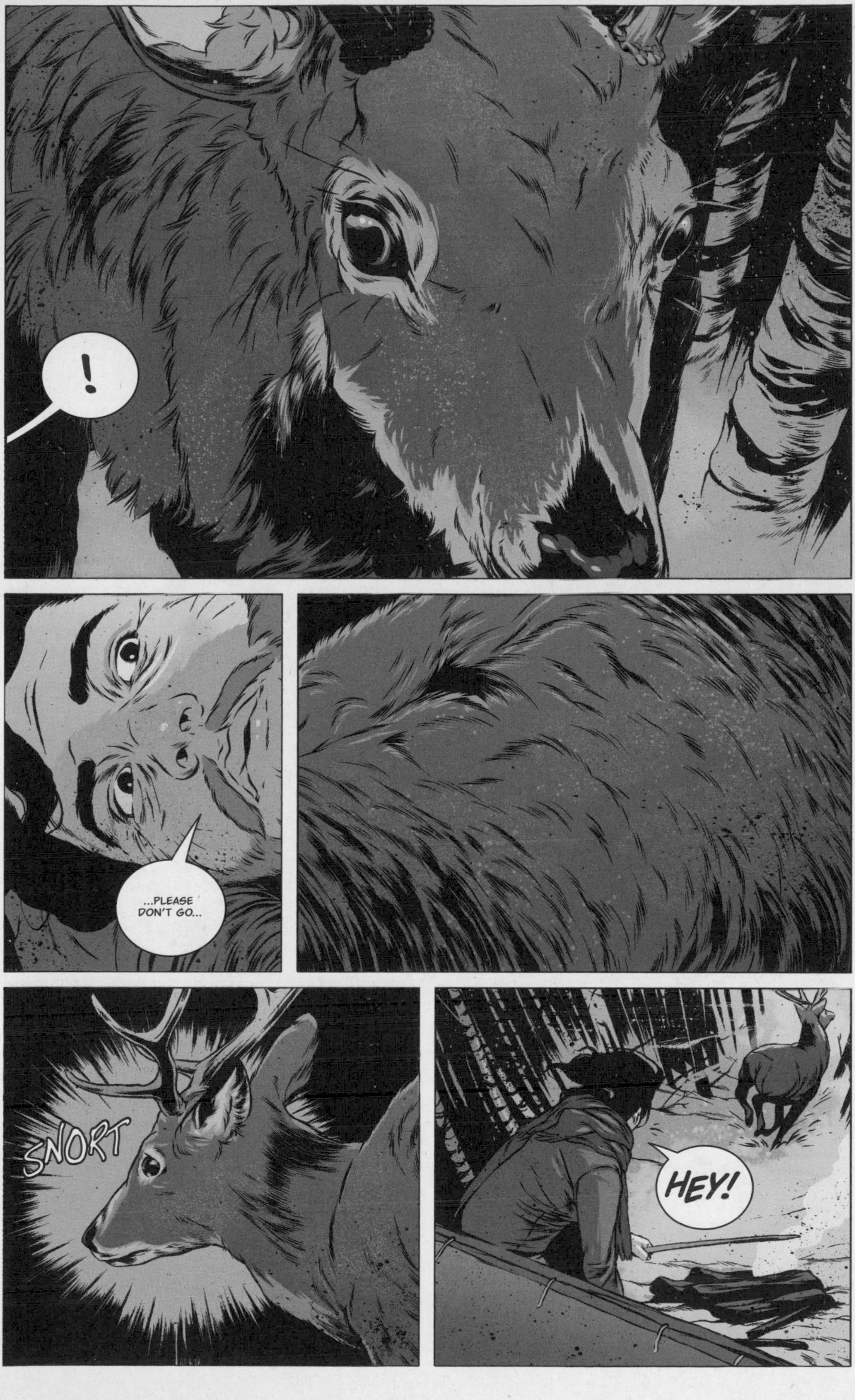
!
...PLEASE DON'T GO...
SNORT
HEY!

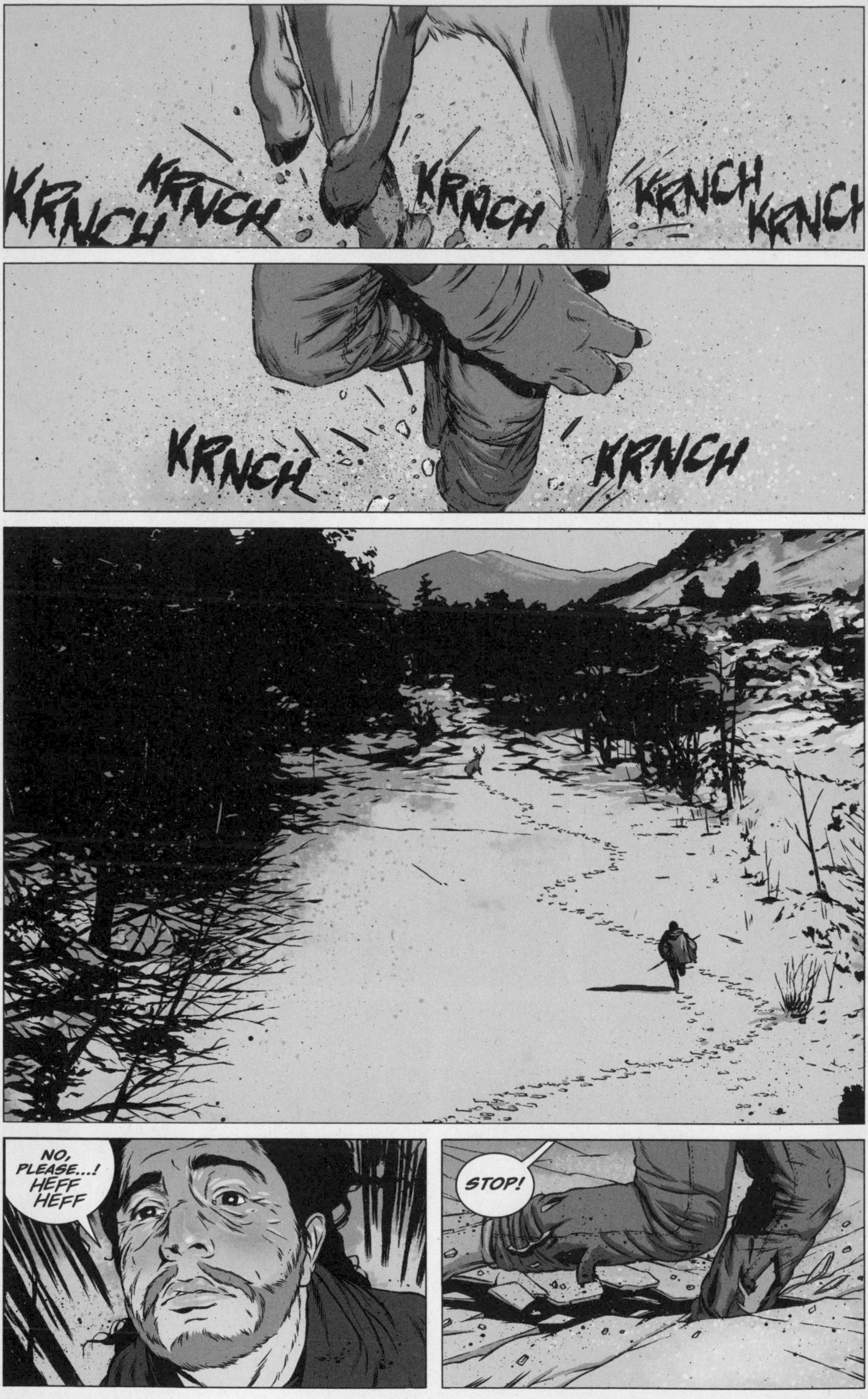
KRNCH
KRNCH
KRNCH
KRNCH
KRNCH
KRNCH
KRNCH
NO, PLEASE...! HEFF HEFF
STOP!

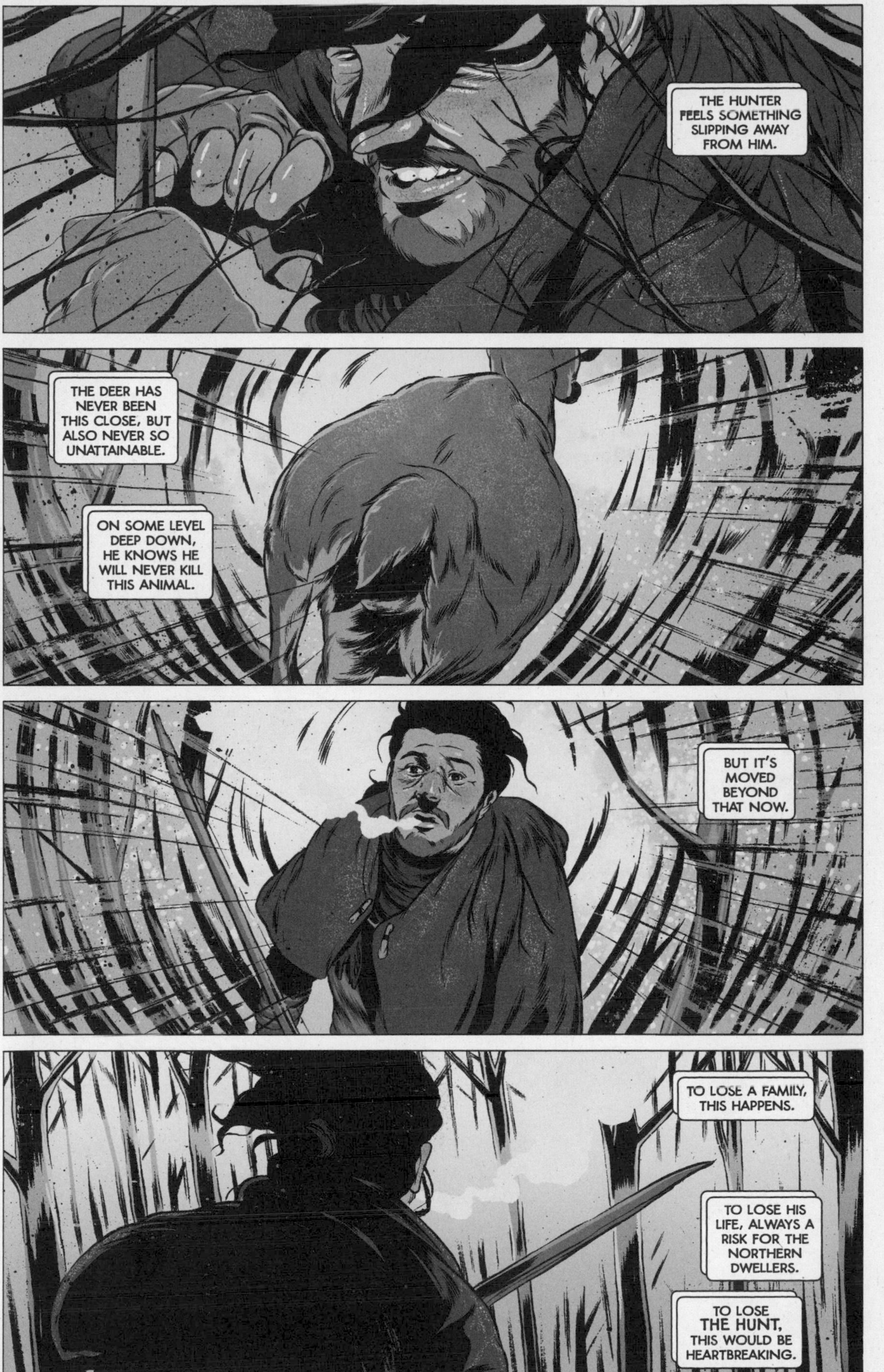
THE HUNTER FEELS SOMETHING SLIPPING AWAY FROM HIM.
THE DEER HAS NEVER BEEN THIS CLOSE, BUT ALSO NEVER SO UNATTAINABLE.
ON SOME LEVEL DEEP DOWN, HE KNOWS HE WILL NEVER KILL THIS ANIMAL.
BUT IT'S MOVED BEYOND THAT NOW.
TO LOSE A FAMILY, THIS HAPPENS.
TO LOSE HIS LIFE, ALWAYS A RISK FOR THE NORTHERN DWELLERS.
TO LOSE THE HUNT, THIS WOULD BE HEARTBREAKING.

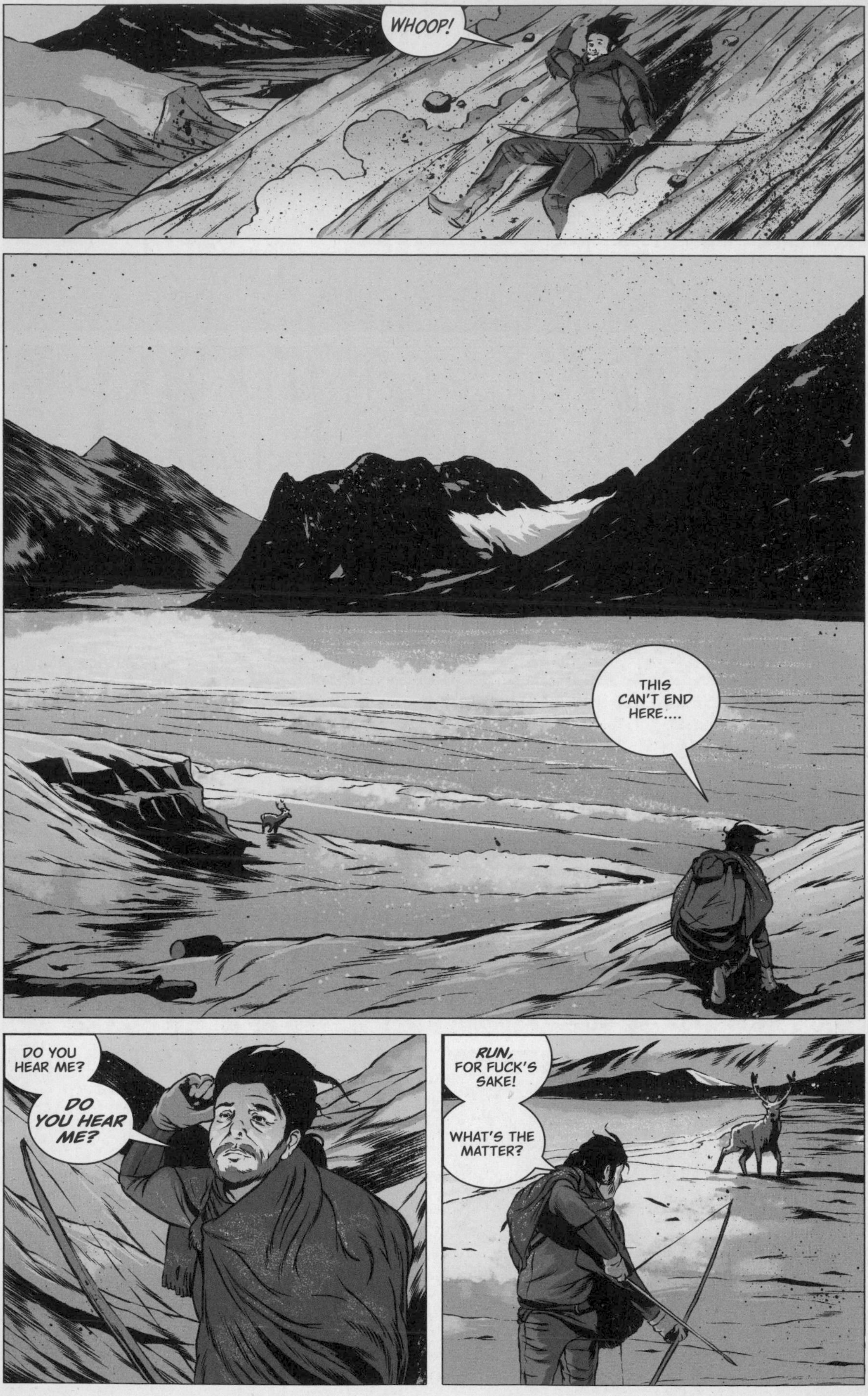
WHOOP!
THIS CAN'T END HERE....
DO YOU HEAR ME?
DO YOU HEAR ME?
RUN, FOR FUCK'S SAKE!
WHAT'S THE MATTER?

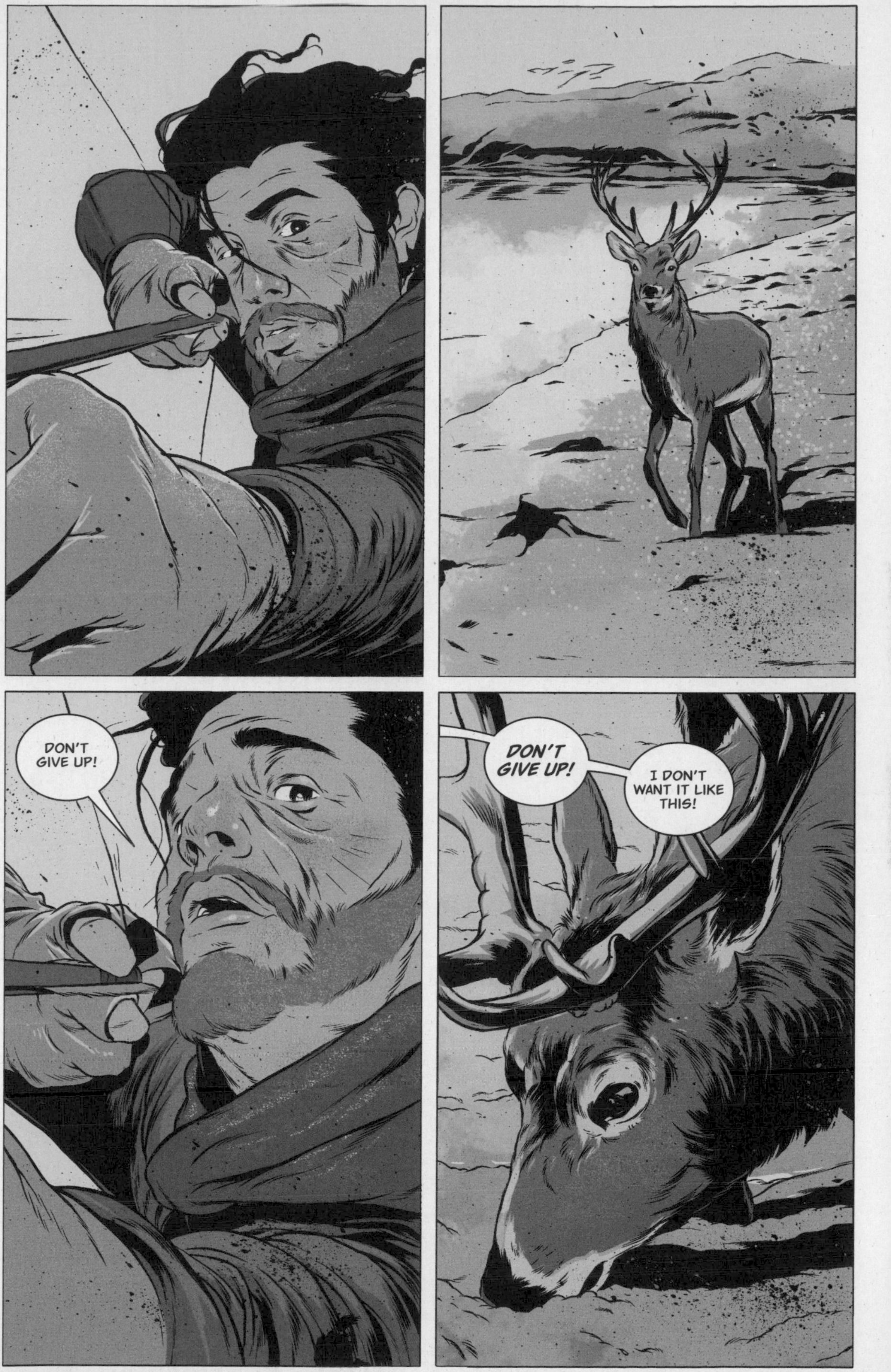
DON'T GIVE UP!
DON'T GIVE UP!
I DON'T WANT IT LIKE THIS!

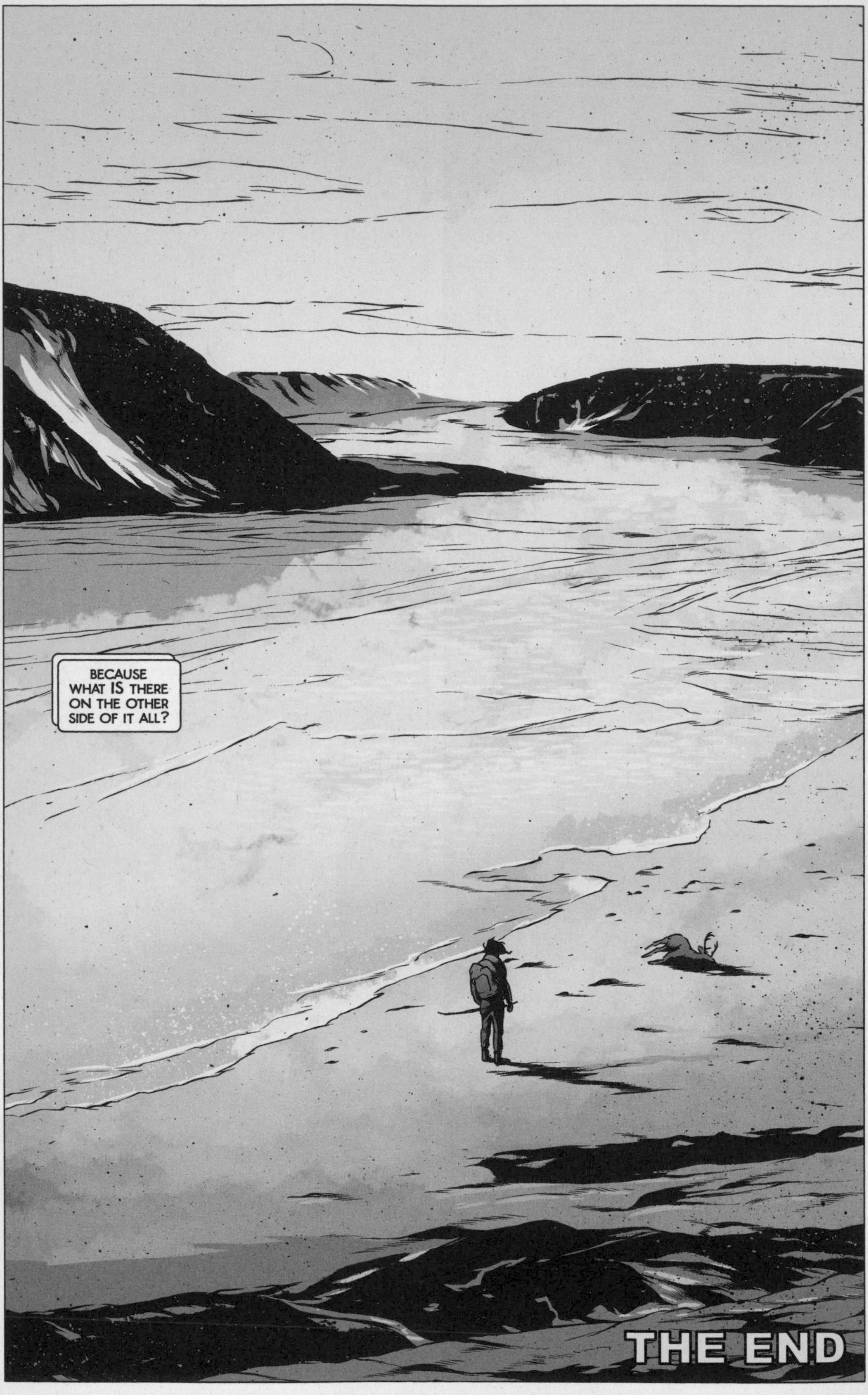
BECAUSE WHAT IS THERE ON THE OTHER SIDE OF IT ALL?
THE END

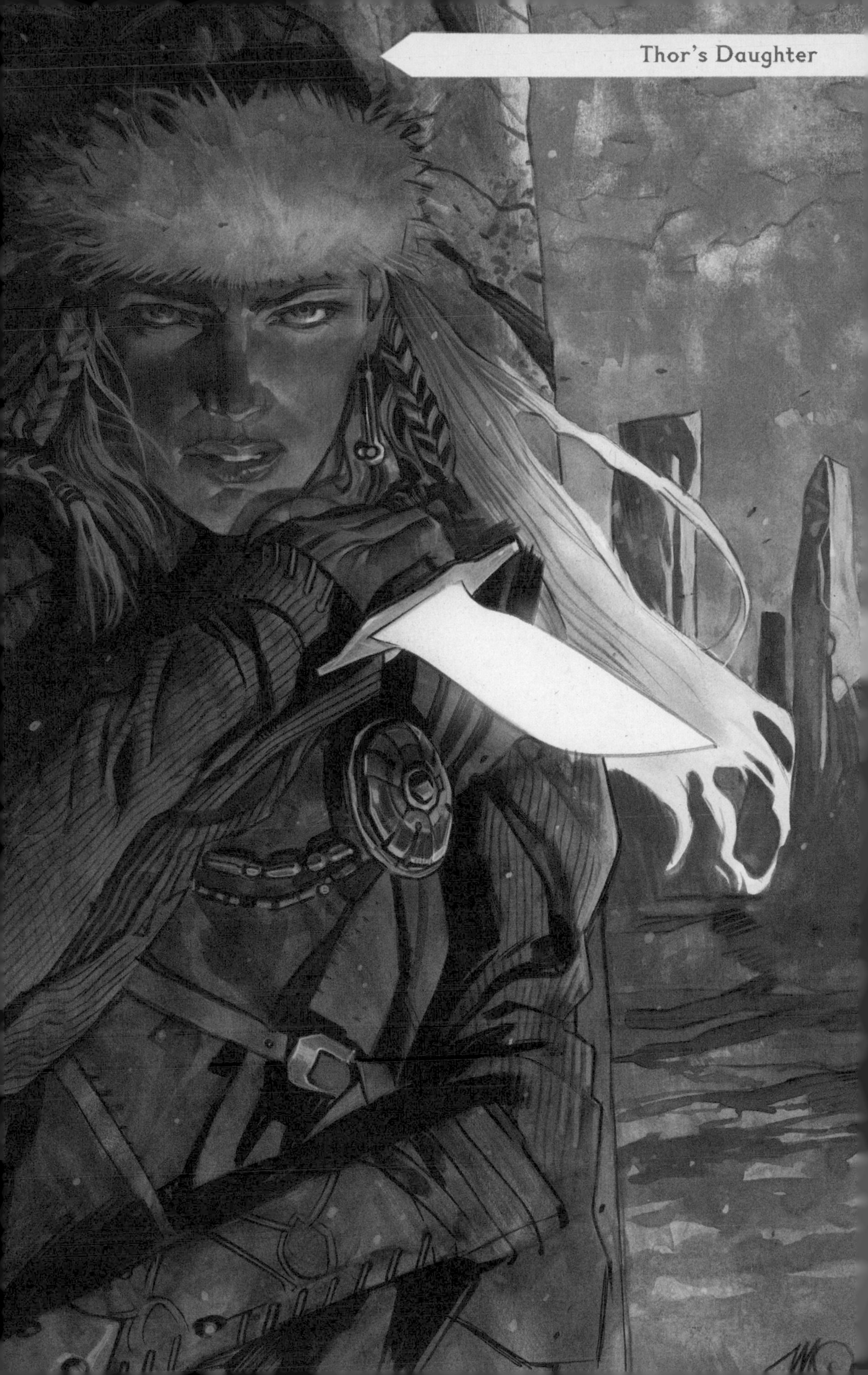

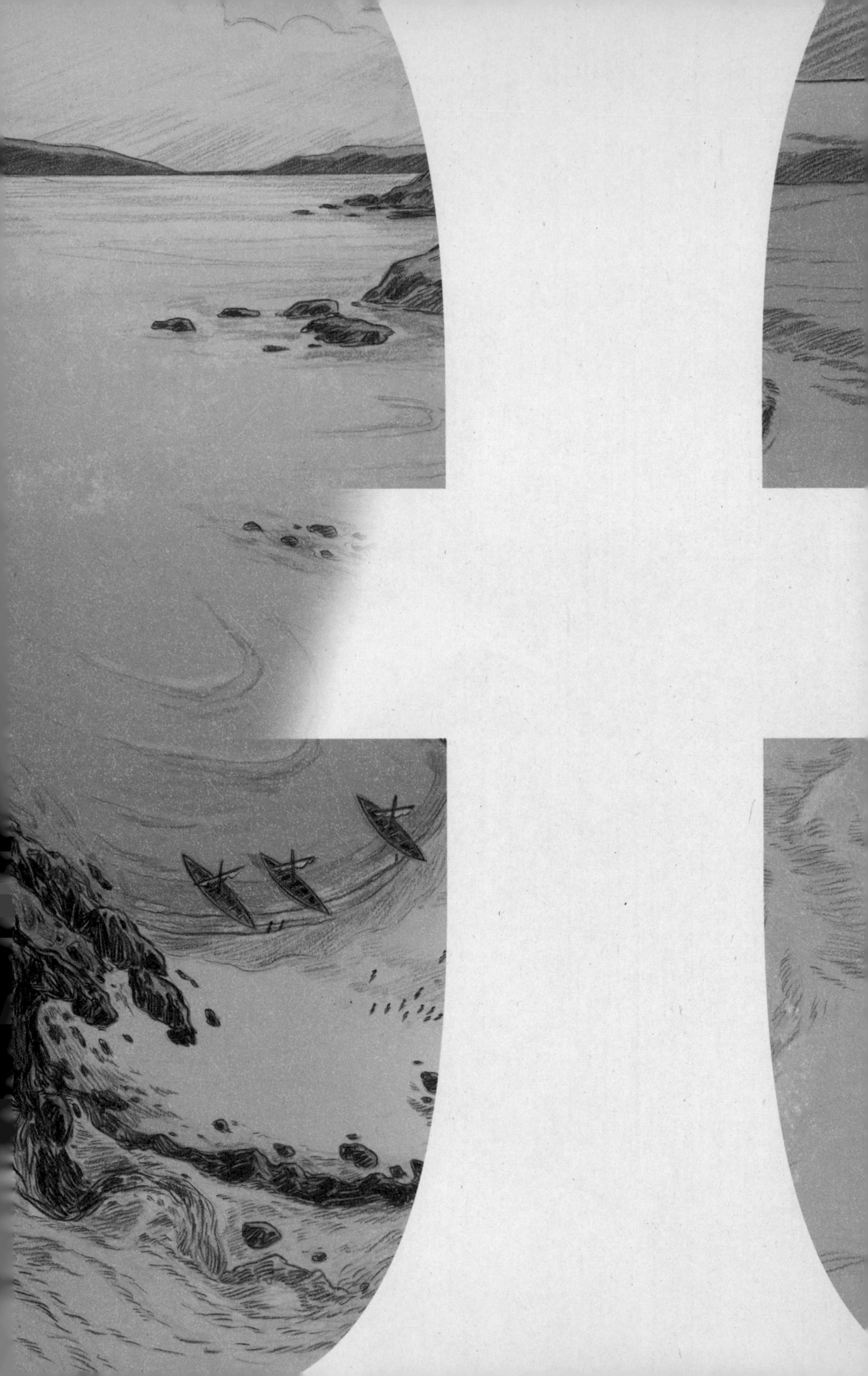

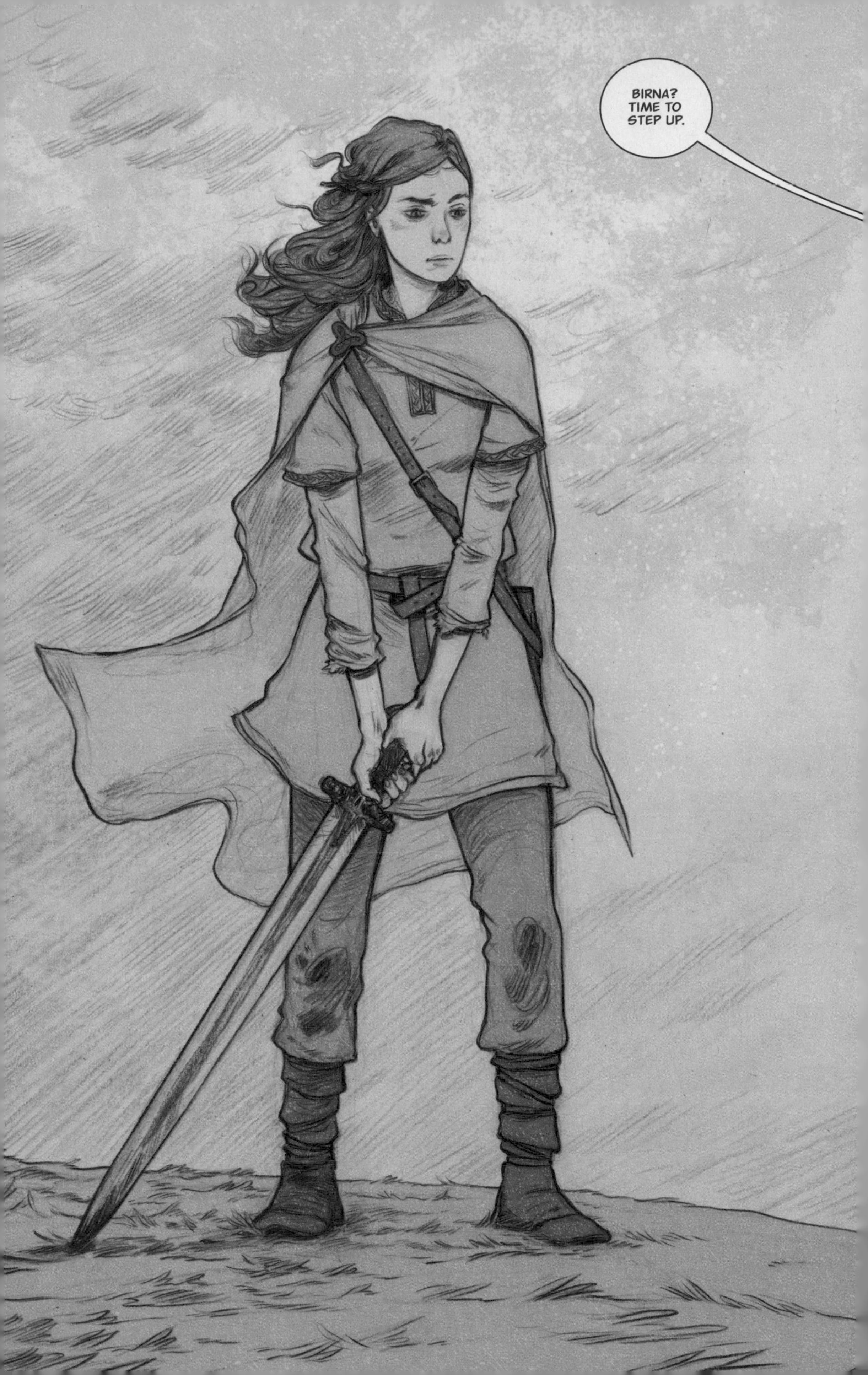
BIRNA? TIME TO STEP UP.

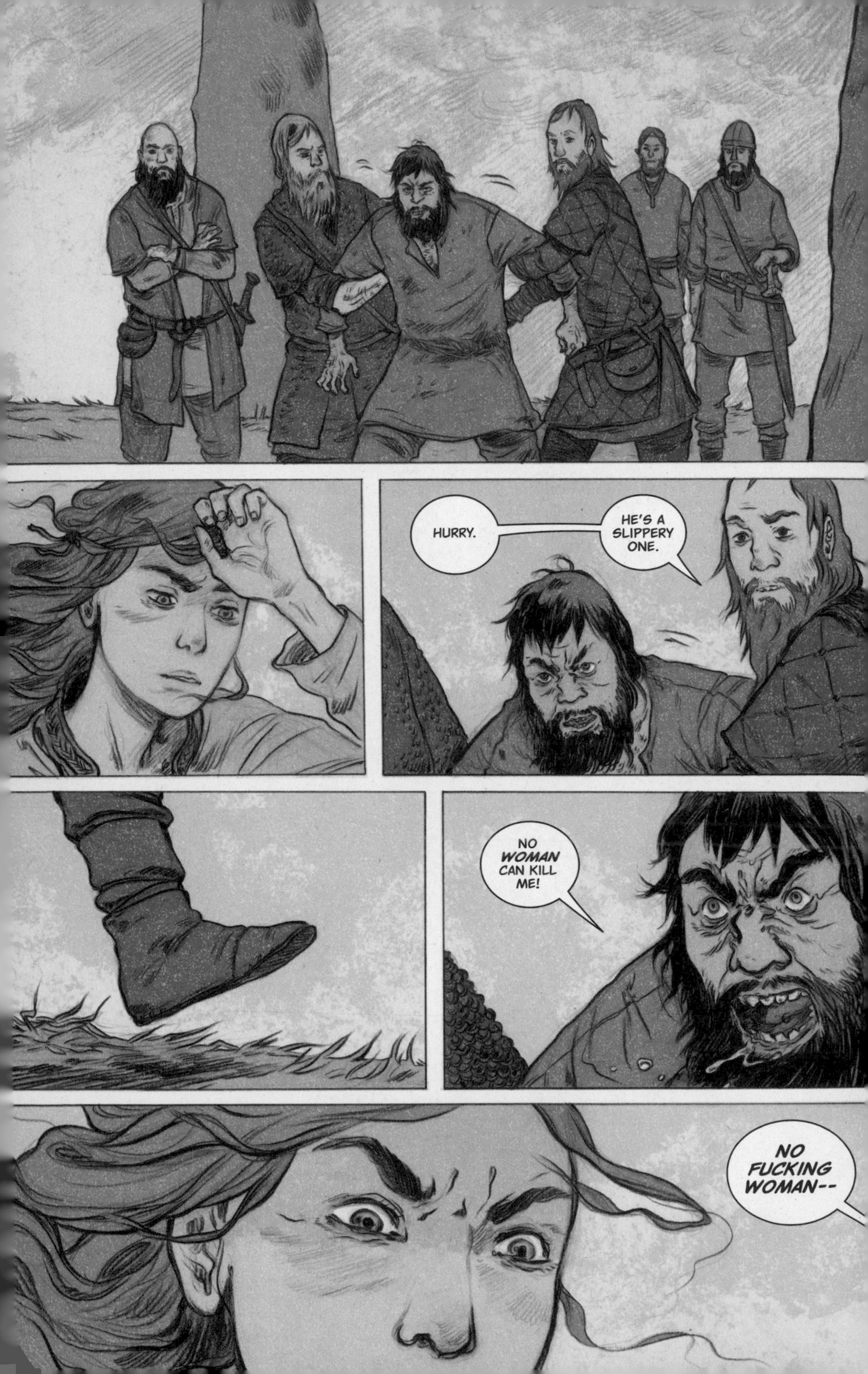
HURRY.
HE'S A SLIPPERY ONE.
NO *WOMAN* CAN KILL ME!
NO FUCKING WOMAN--

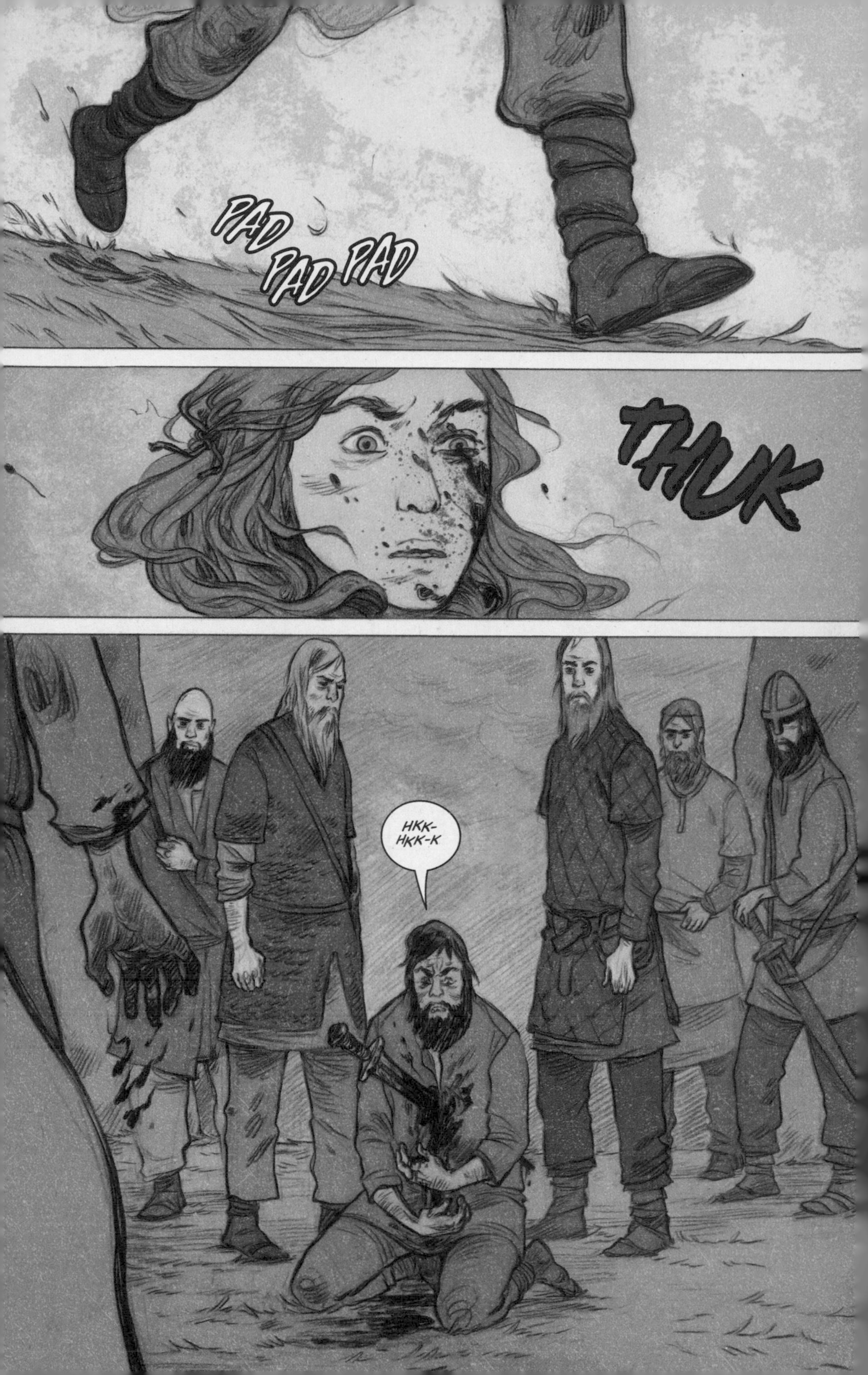
PAD PAD PAD
THUK
HKK-
HKK-K

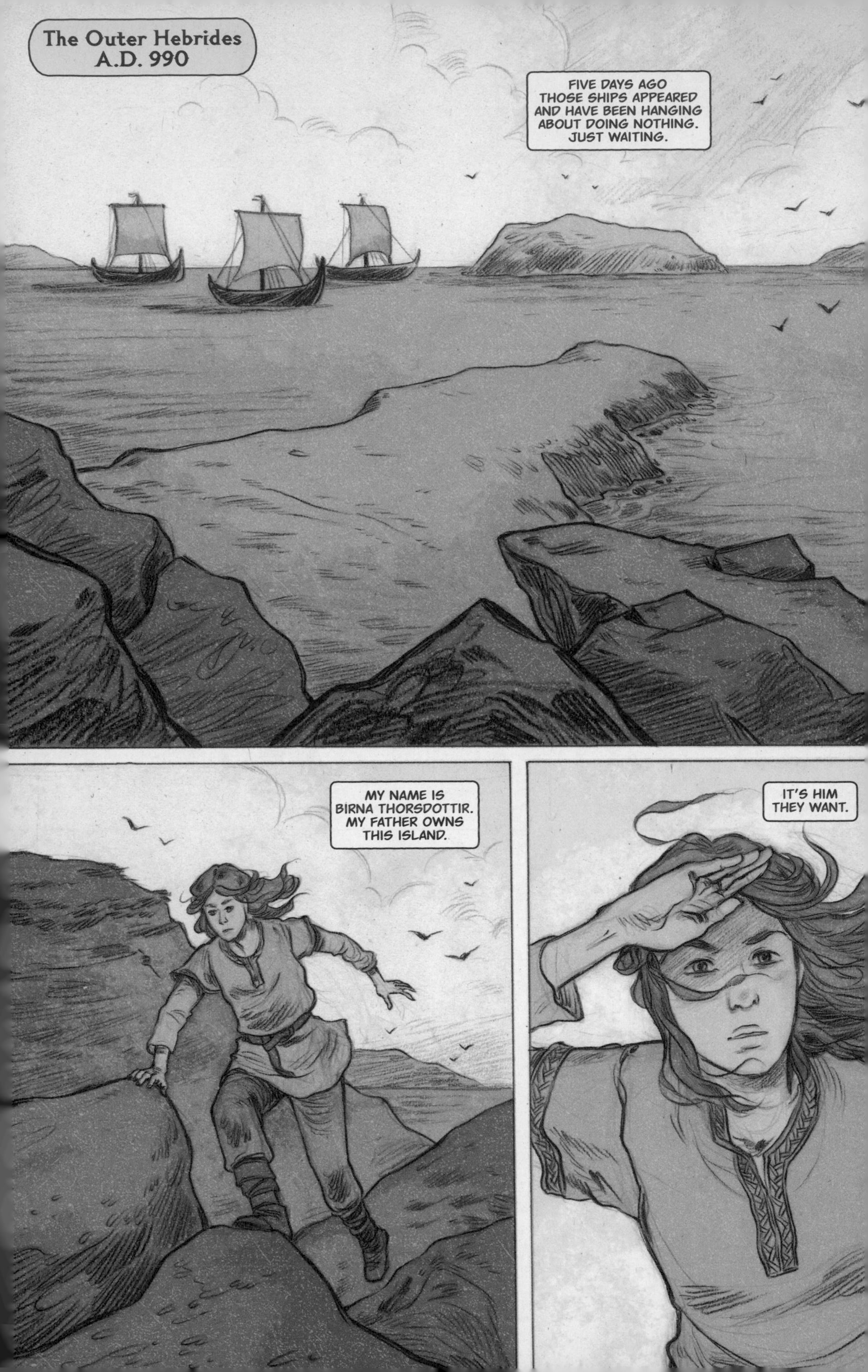
The Outer Hebrides
A.D. 990
FIVE DAYS AGO THOSE SHIPS APPEARED AND HAVE BEEN HANGING ABOUT DOING NOTHING. JUST WAITING.
MY NAME IS BIRNA THORSDOTTIR. MY FATHER OWNS THIS ISLAND.
IT'S HIM THEY WANT.

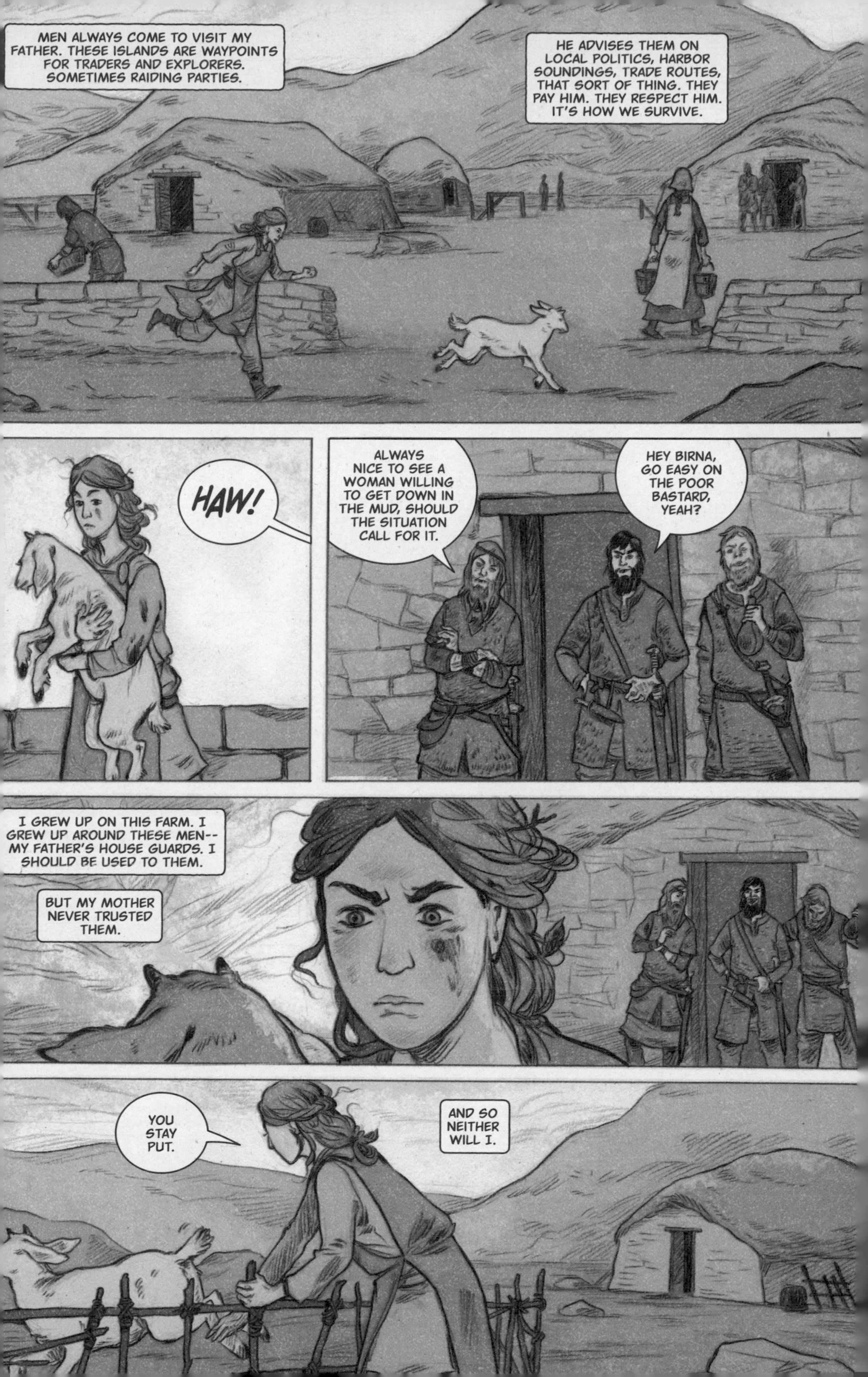
MEN ALWAYS COME TO VISIT MY FATHER. THESE ISLANDS ARE WAYPOINTS FOR TRADERS AND EXPLORERS. SOMETIMES RAIDING PARTIES.
HE ADVISES THEM ON LOCAL POLITICS, HARBOR SOUNDINGS, TRADE ROUTES, THAT SORT OF THING. THEY PAY HIM. THEY RESPECT HIM. IT'S HOW WE SURVIVE.
HAW!
ALWAYS NICE TO SEE A WOMAN WILLING TO GET DOWN IN THE MUD, SHOULD THE SITUATION CALL FOR IT.
HEY BIRNA, GO EASY ON THE POOR BASTARD, YEAH?
I GREW UP ON THIS FARM. I GREW UP AROUND THESE MEN-- MY FATHER'S HOUSE GUARDS. I SHOULD BE USED TO THEM.
BUT MY MOTHER NEVER TRUSTED THEM.
YOU STAY PUT.
AND SO NEITHER WILL I.

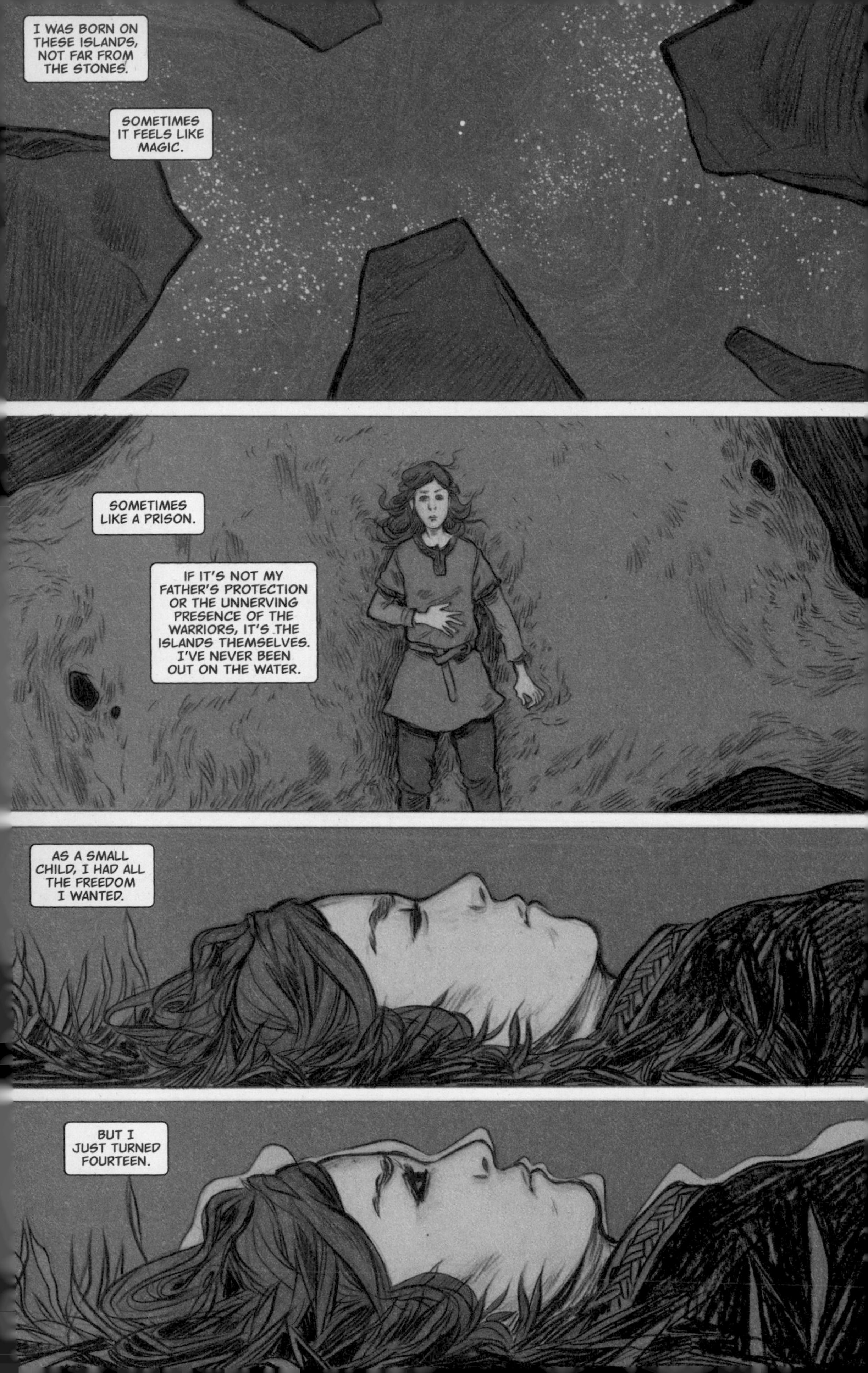
I WAS BORN ON THESE ISLANDS, NOT FAR FROM THE STONES.
SOMETIMES IT FEELS LIKE MAGIC.
SOMETIMES LIKE A PRISON.
IF IT'S NOT MY FATHER'S PROTECTION OR THE UNNERVING PRESENCE OF THE WARRIORS, IT'S THE ISLANDS THEMSELVES. I'VE NEVER BEEN OUT ON THE WATER.
AS A SMALL CHILD, I HAD ALL THE FREEDOM I WANTED.
BUT I JUST TURNED FOURTEEN.

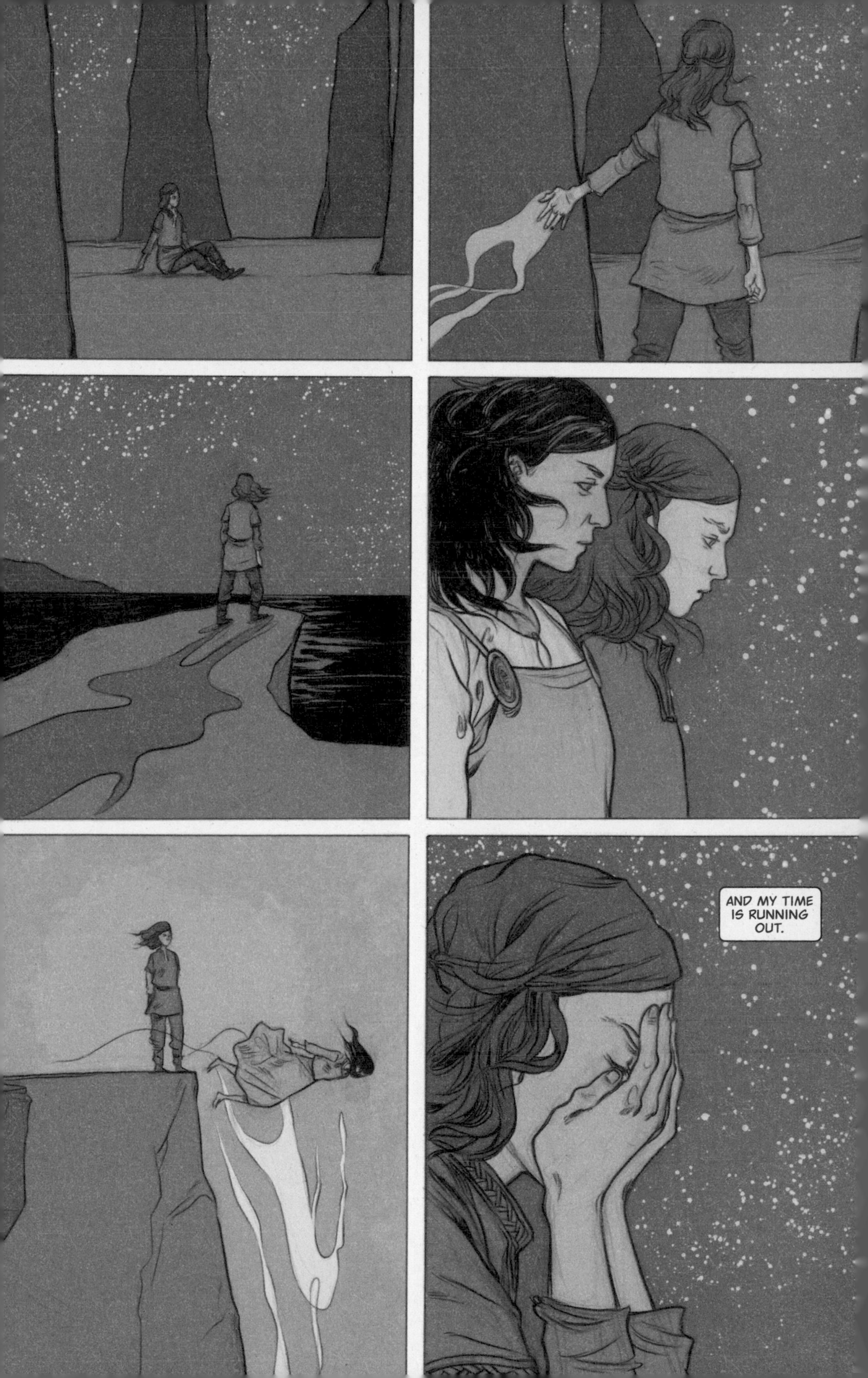
AND MY TIME IS RUNNING OUT.

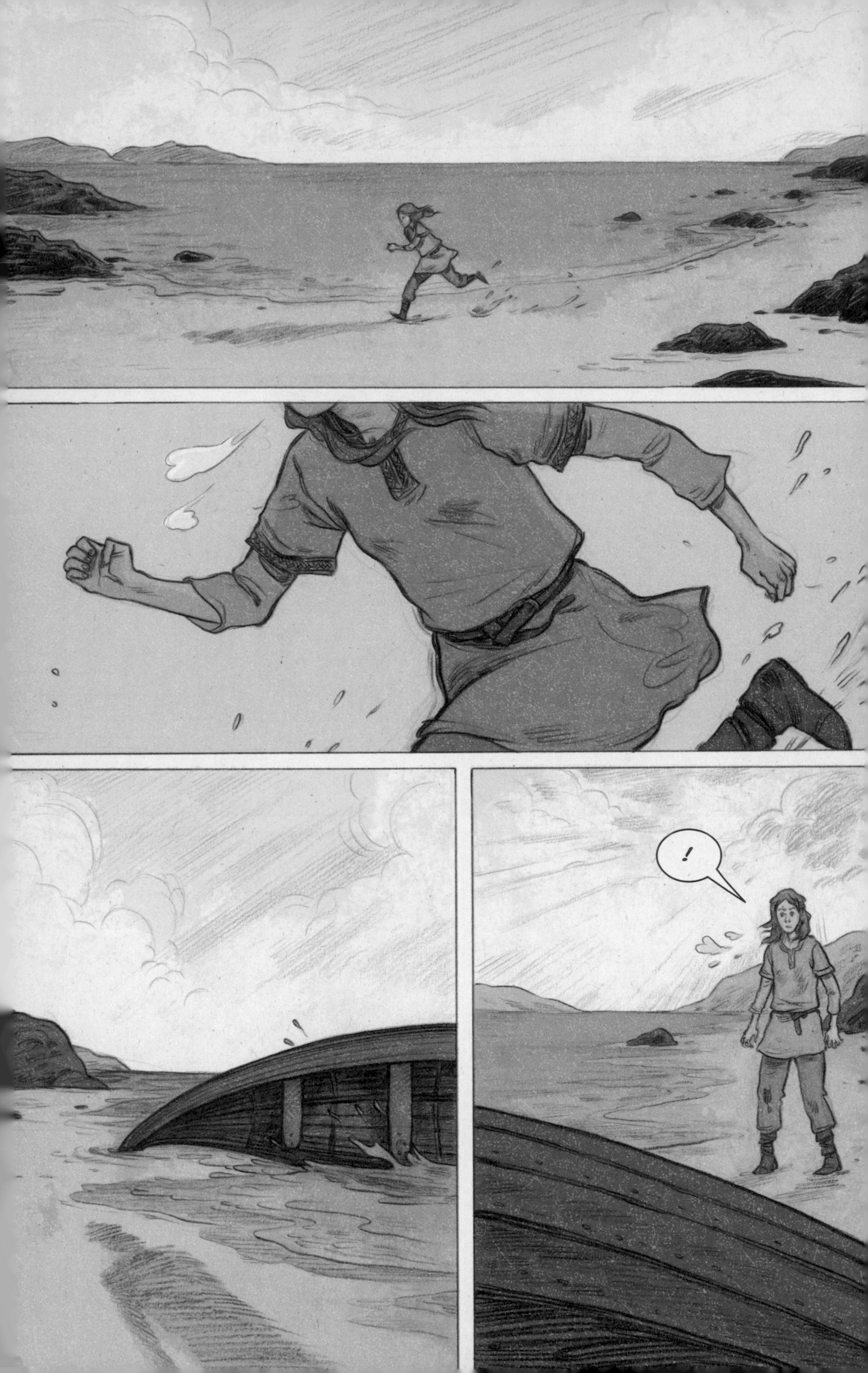
!

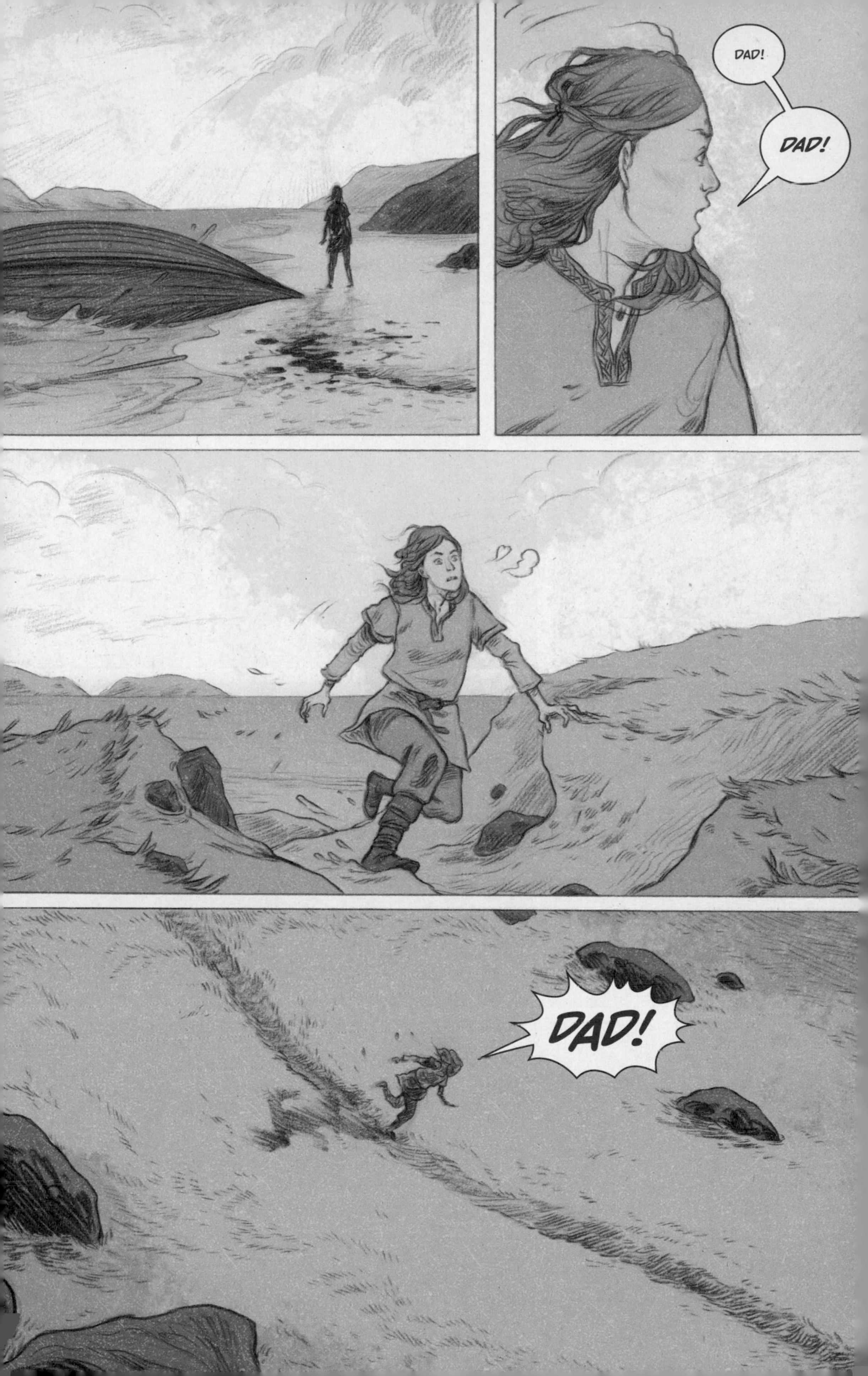
DAD!
DAD!
DAD!

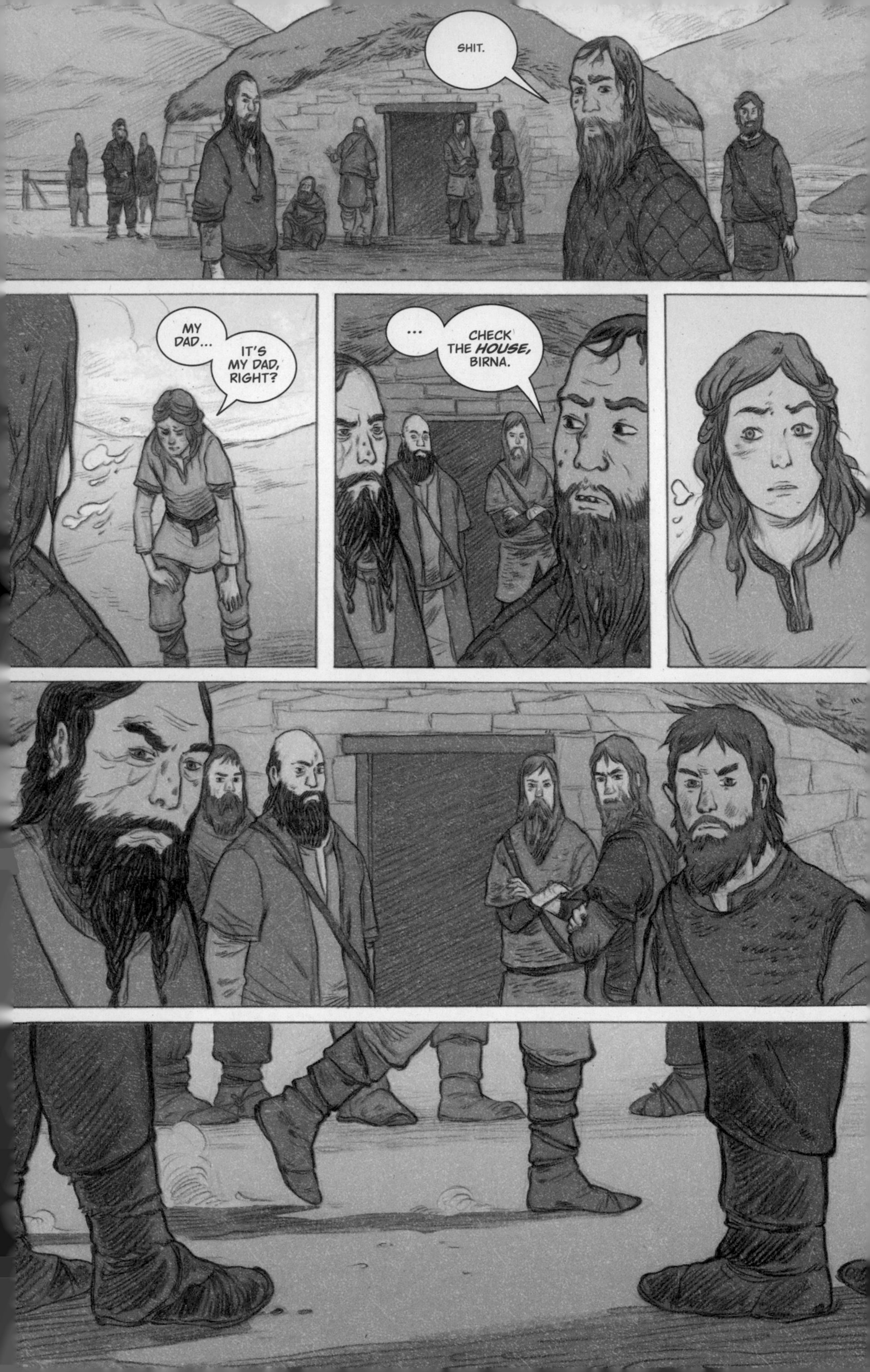
SHIT.
MY DAD...
IT'S MY DAD, RIGHT?
...
CHECK THE *HOUSE,* BIRNA.

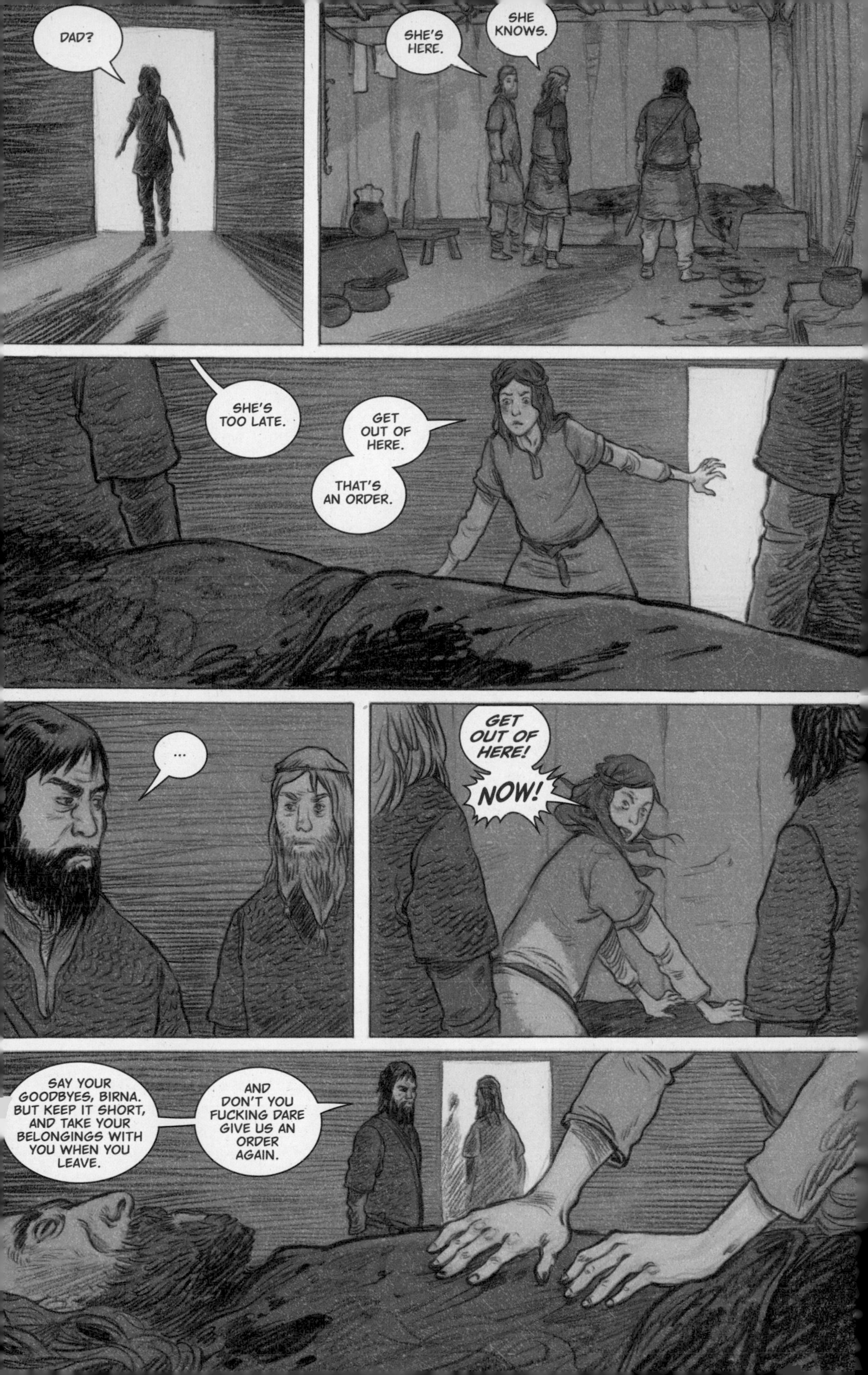
DAD?
SHE'S HERE.
SHE KNOWS.
SHE'S TOO LATE.
GET OUT OF HERE.
THAT'S AN ORDER.
...
GET OUT OF HERE!
NOW!
SAY YOUR GOODBYES, BIRNA. BUT KEEP IT SHORT, AND TAKE YOUR BELONGINGS WITH YOU WHEN YOU LEAVE.
AND DON'T YOU FUCKING DARE GIVE US AN ORDER AGAIN.

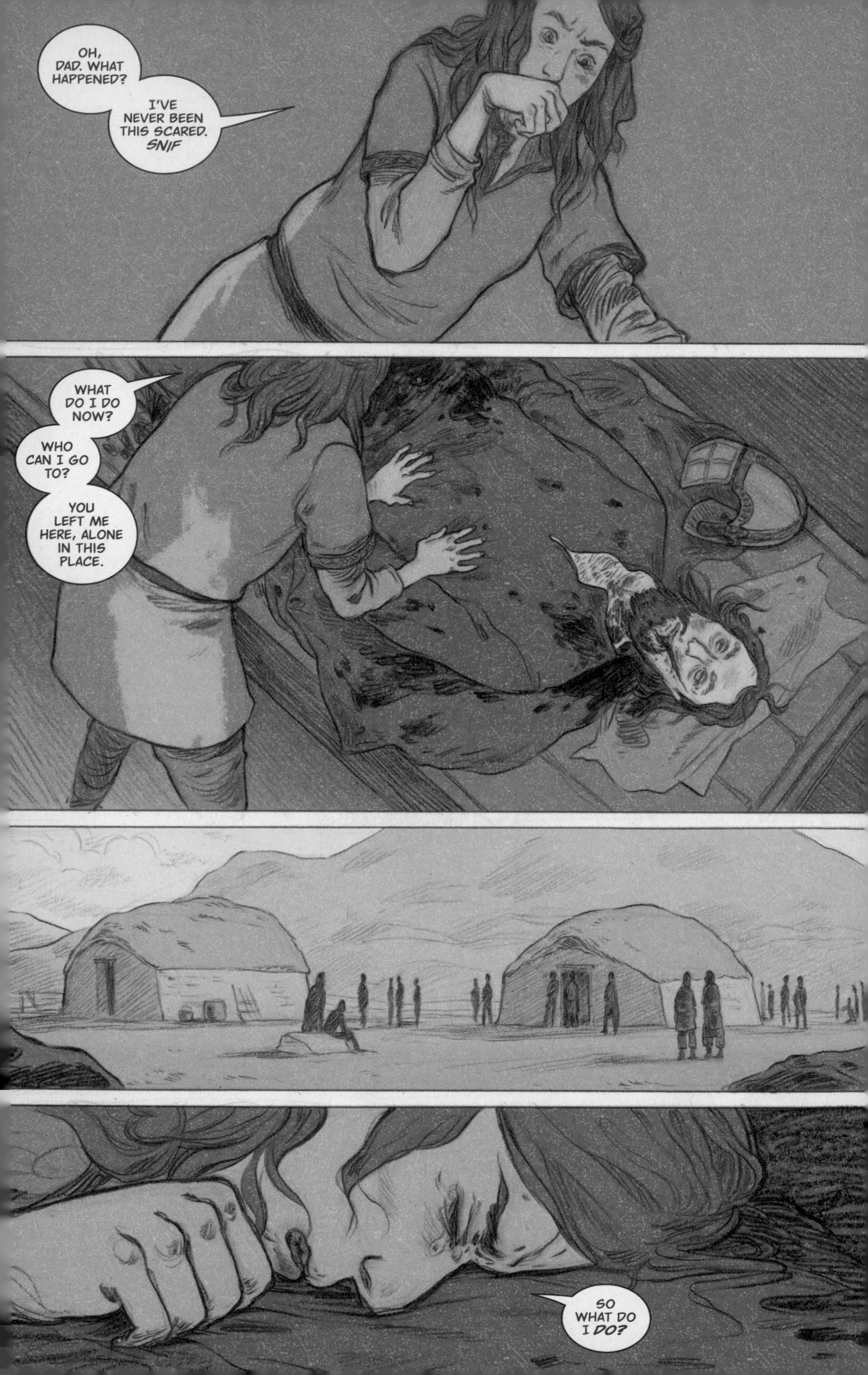
OH, DAD. WHAT HAPPENED?
I'VE NEVER BEEN THIS SCARED. *SNIF*
WHAT DO I DO NOW?
WHO CAN I GO TO?
YOU LEFT ME HERE, ALONE IN THIS PLACE.
SO WHAT DO I *DO?*

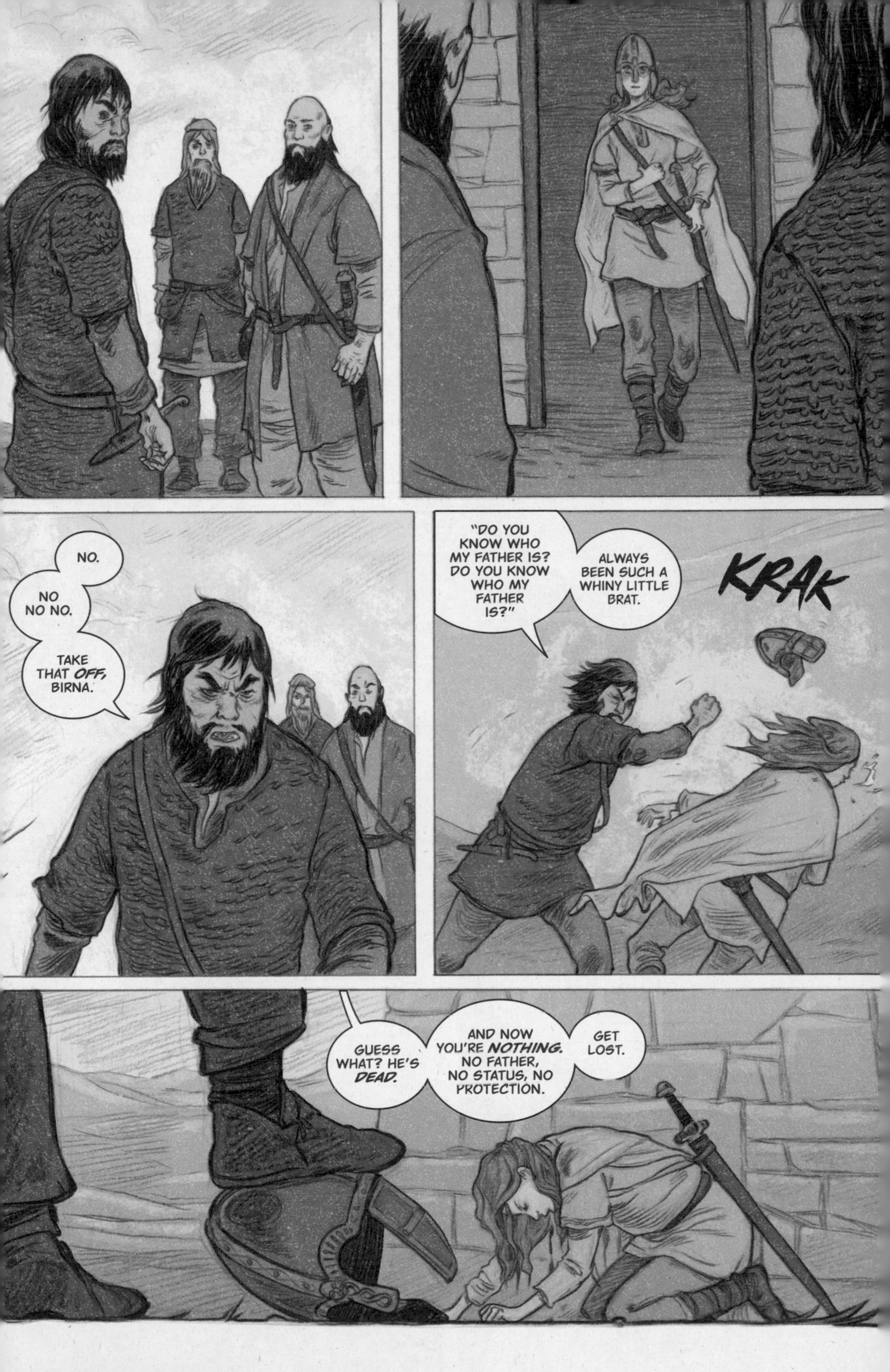
NO.
NO NO NO.
TAKE THAT OFF, BIRNA.
"DO YOU KNOW WHO MY FATHER IS? DO YOU KNOW WHO MY FATHER IS?"
ALWAYS BEEN SUCH A WHINY LITTLE BRAT.
KRAK
GUESS WHAT? HE'S DEAD.
AND NOW YOU'RE NOTHING. NO FATHER, NO STATUS, NO PROTECTION.
GET LOST.

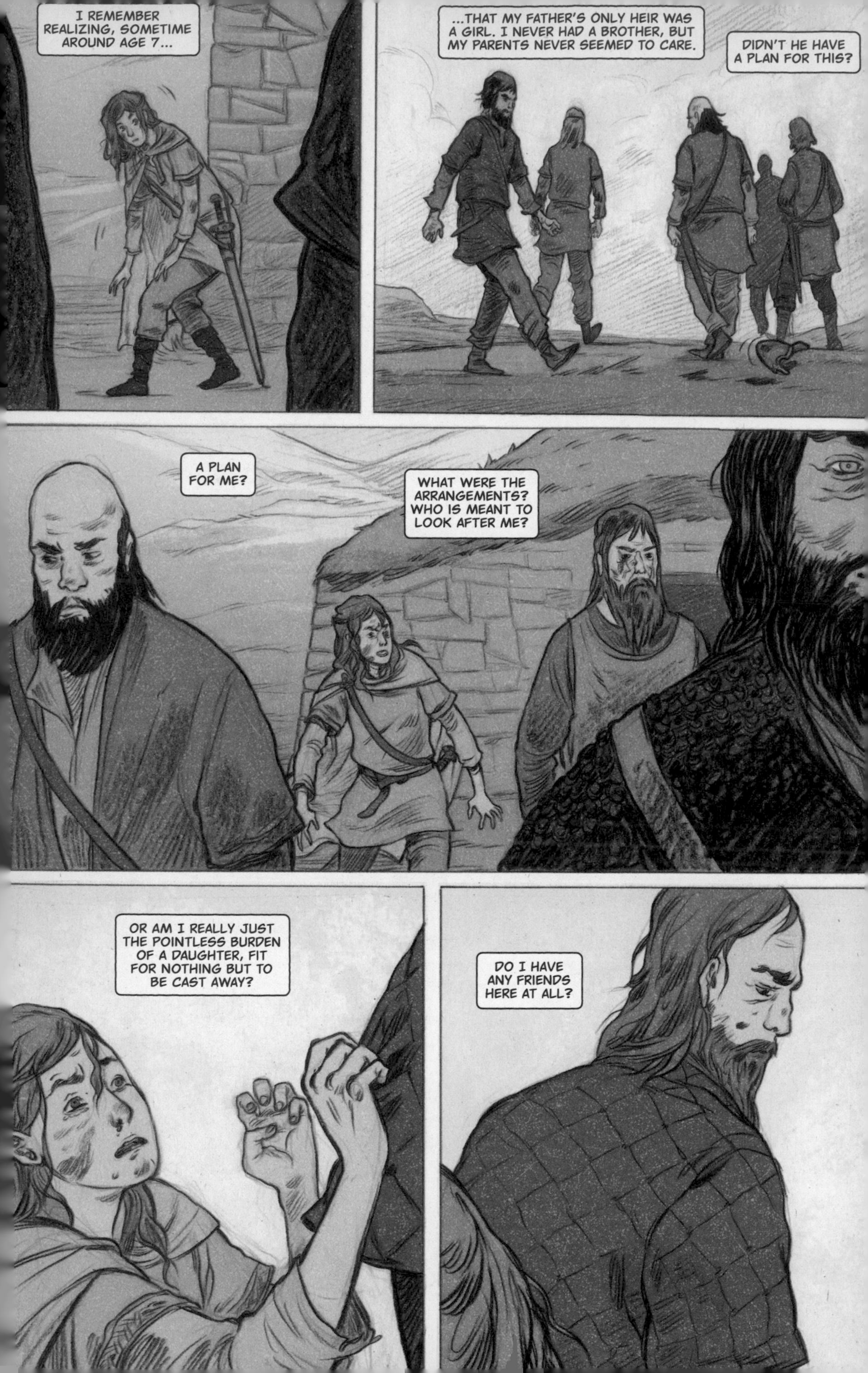
I REMEMBER REALIZING, SOMETIME AROUND AGE 7...
...THAT MY FATHER'S ONLY HEIR WAS A GIRL. I NEVER HAD A BROTHER, BUT MY PARENTS NEVER SEEMED TO CARE.
DIDN'T HE HAVE A PLAN FOR THIS?
A PLAN FOR ME?
WHAT WERE THE ARRANGEMENTS? WHO IS MEANT TO LOOK AFTER ME?
OR AM I REALLY JUST THE POINTLESS BURDEN OF A DAUGHTER, FIT FOR NOTHING BUT TO BE CAST AWAY?
DO I HAVE ANY FRIENDS HERE AT ALL?

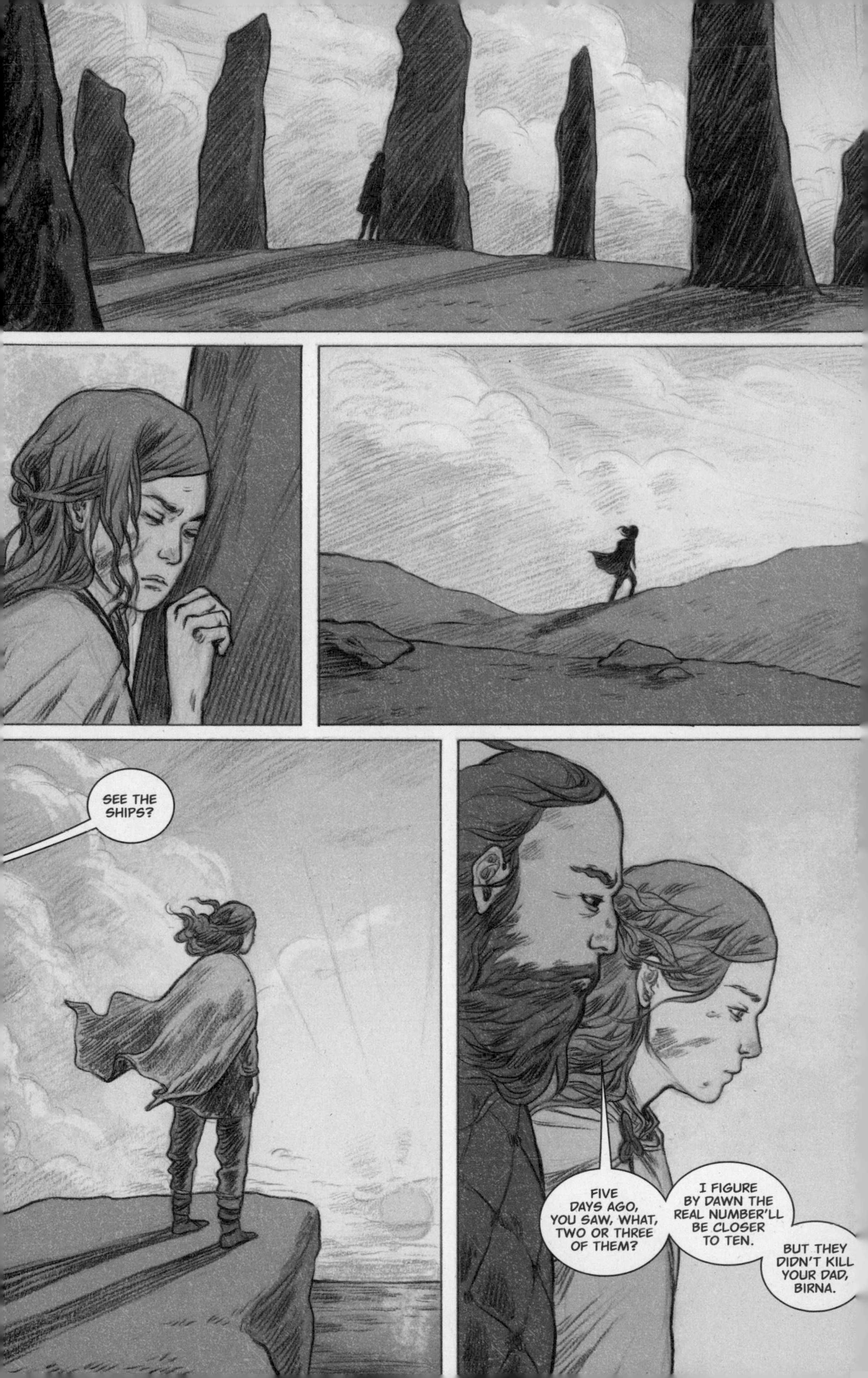
SEE THE SHIPS?
FIVE DAYS AGO, YOU SAW, WHAT, TWO OR THREE OF THEM?
I FIGURE BY DAWN THE REAL NUMBER'LL BE CLOSER TO TEN.
BUT THEY DIDN'T KILL YOUR DAD, BIRNA.

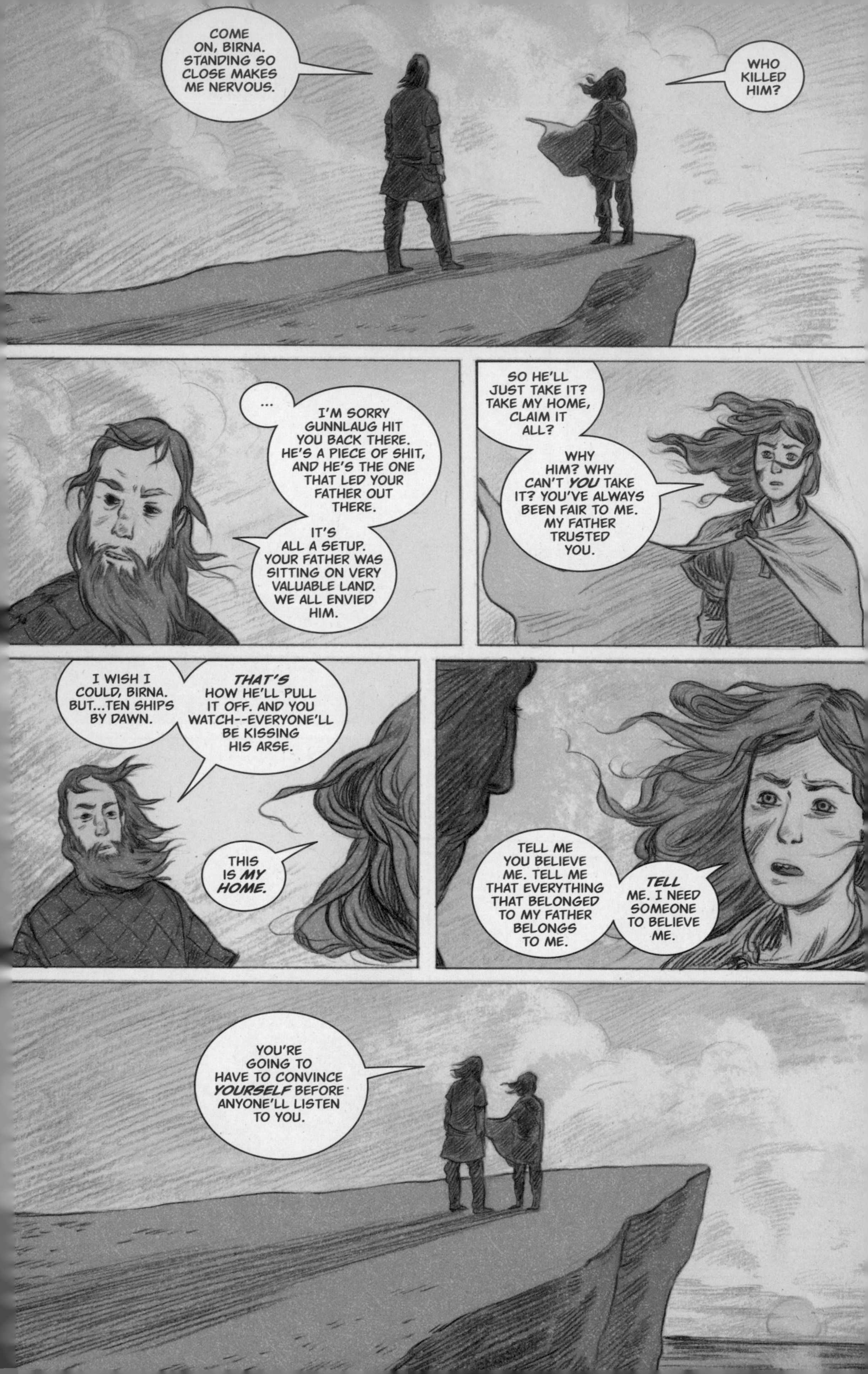
COME ON, BIRNA. STANDING SO CLOSE MAKES ME NERVOUS.
WHO KILLED HIM?
...
I'M SORRY GUNNLAUG HIT YOU BACK THERE. HE'S A PIECE OF SHIT, AND HE'S THE ONE THAT LED YOUR FATHER OUT THERE.
IT'S ALL A SETUP. YOUR FATHER WAS SITTING ON VERY VALUABLE LAND. WE ALL ENVIED HIM.
SO HE'LL JUST TAKE IT? TAKE MY HOME, CLAIM IT ALL?
WHY HIM? WHY CAN'T *YOU* TAKE IT? YOU'VE ALWAYS BEEN FAIR TO ME. MY FATHER TRUSTED YOU.
I WISH I COULD, BIRNA. BUT...TEN SHIPS BY DAWN.
THAT'S HOW HE'LL PULL IT OFF. AND YOU WATCH--EVERYONE'LL BE KISSING HIS ARSE.
THIS IS *MY HOME.*
TELL ME YOU BELIEVE ME. TELL ME THAT EVERYTHING THAT BELONGED TO MY FATHER BELONGS TO ME.
TELL ME. I NEED SOMEONE TO BELIEVE ME.
YOU'RE GOING TO HAVE TO CONVINCE *YOURSELF* BEFORE ANYONE'LL LISTEN TO YOU.

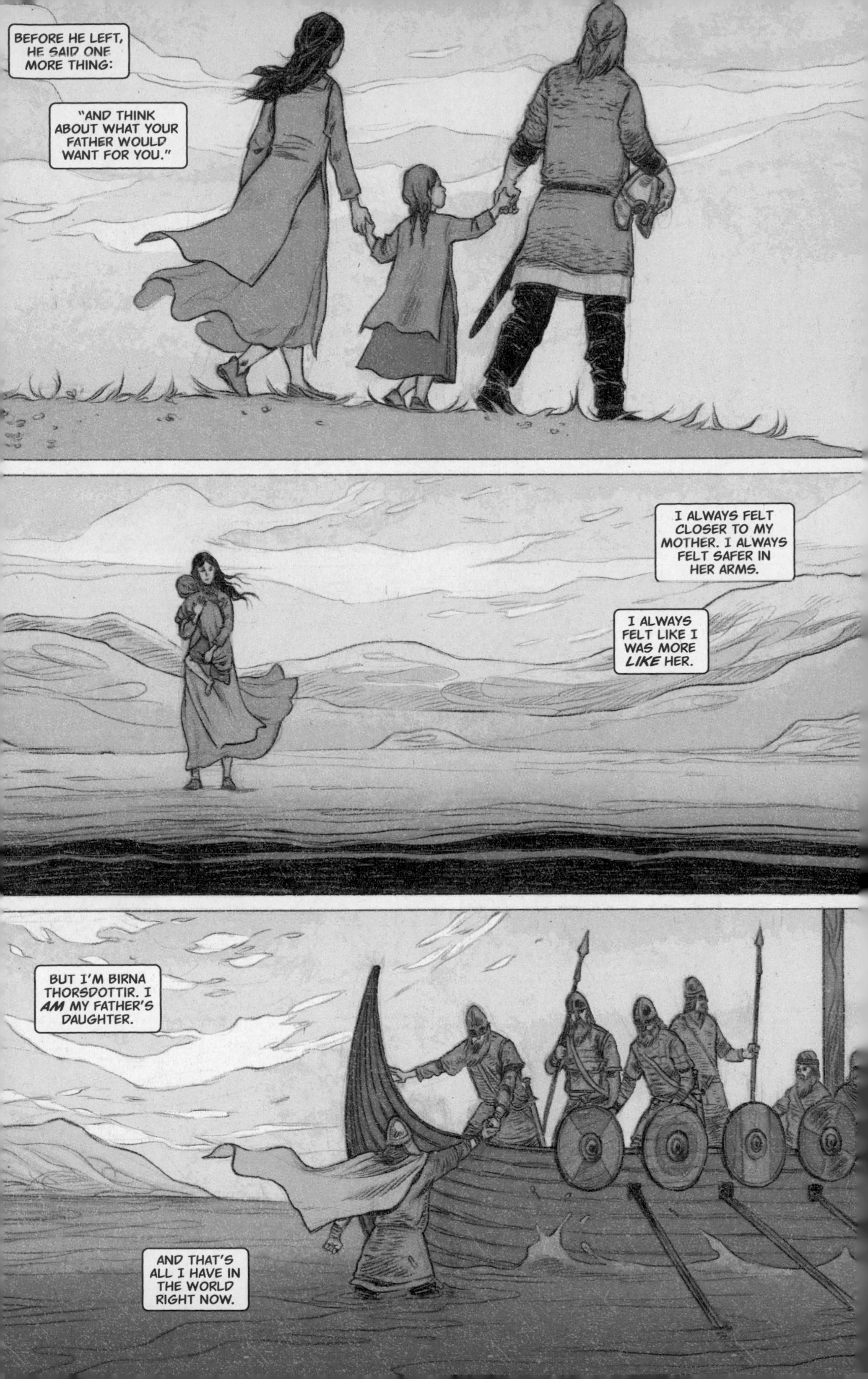
BEFORE HE LEFT, HE SAID ONE MORE THING:
"AND THINK ABOUT WHAT YOUR FATHER WOULD WANT FOR YOU."
I ALWAYS FELT CLOSER TO MY MOTHER. I ALWAYS FELT SAFER IN HER ARMS.
I ALWAYS FELT LIKE I WAS MORE *LIKE* HER.
BUT I'M BIRNA THORSDOTTIR. I *AM* MY FATHER'S DAUGHTER.
AND THAT'S ALL I HAVE IN THE WORLD RIGHT NOW.

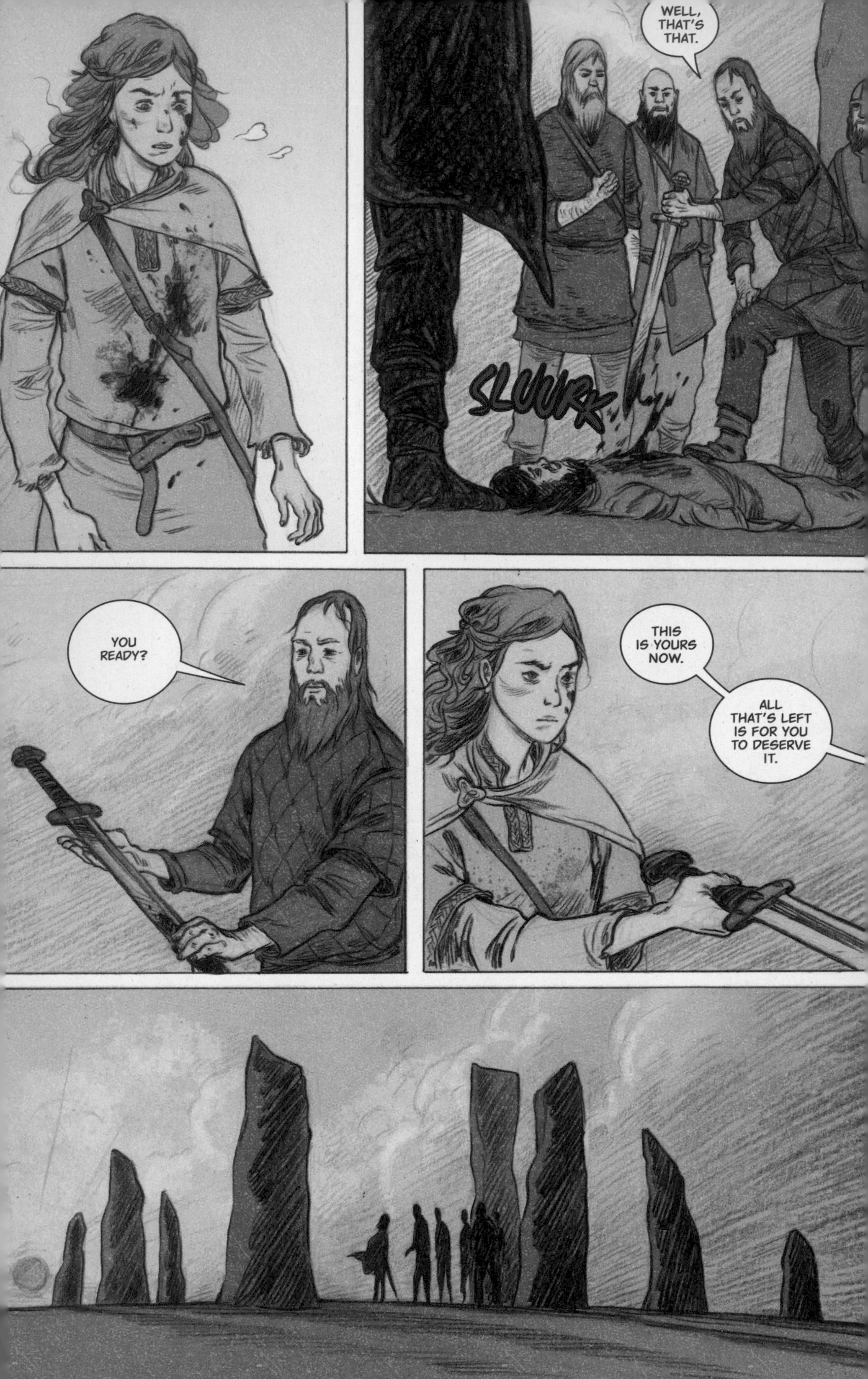
WELL, THAT'S THAT.
SLUURK
YOU READY?
THIS IS YOURS NOW.
ALL THAT'S LEFT IS FOR YOU TO DESERVE IT.

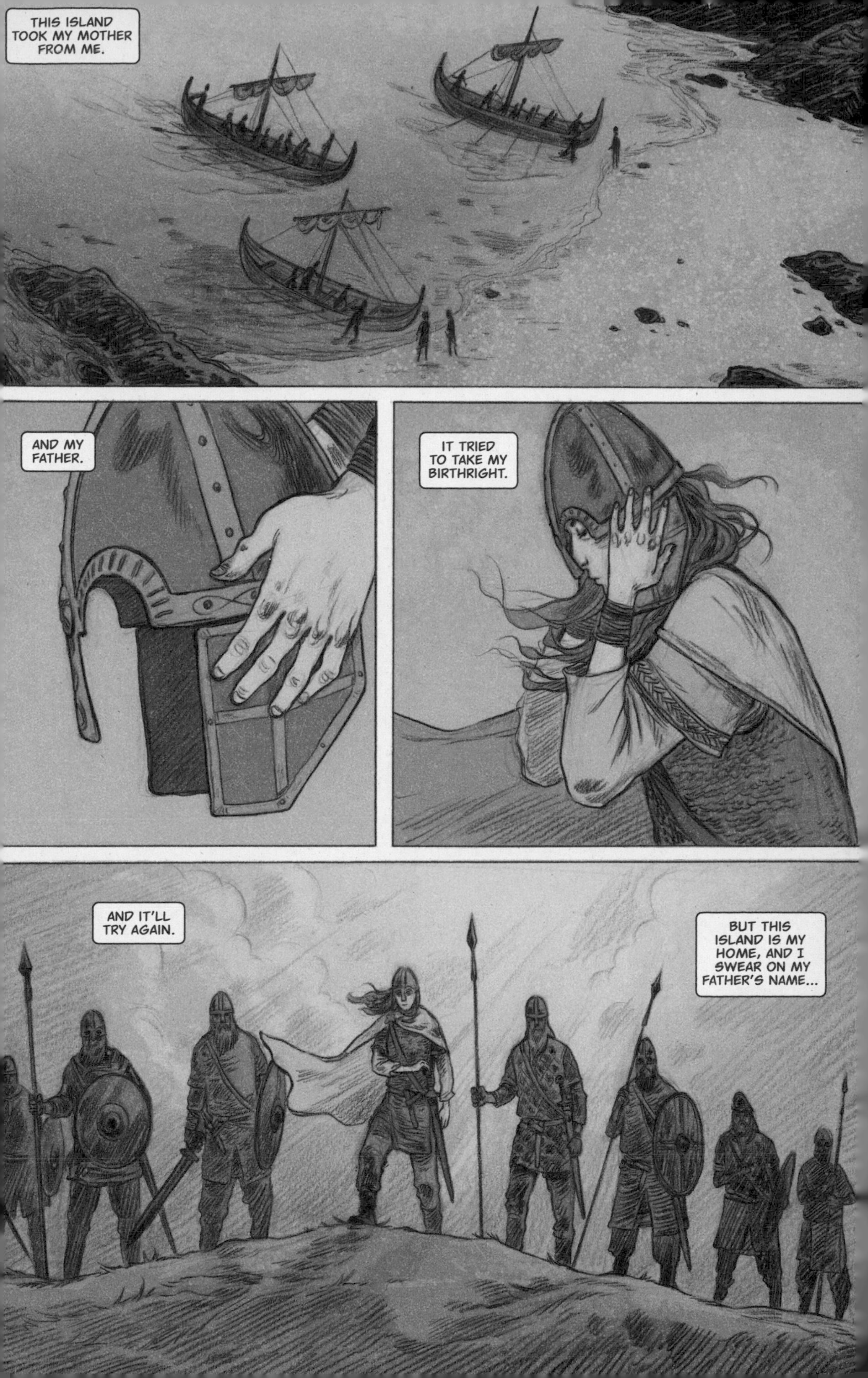
THIS ISLAND TOOK MY MOTHER FROM ME.
AND MY FATHER.
IT TRIED TO TAKE MY BIRTHRIGHT.
AND IT'LL TRY AGAIN.
BUT THIS ISLAND IS MY HOME, AND I SWEAR ON MY FATHER'S NAME...

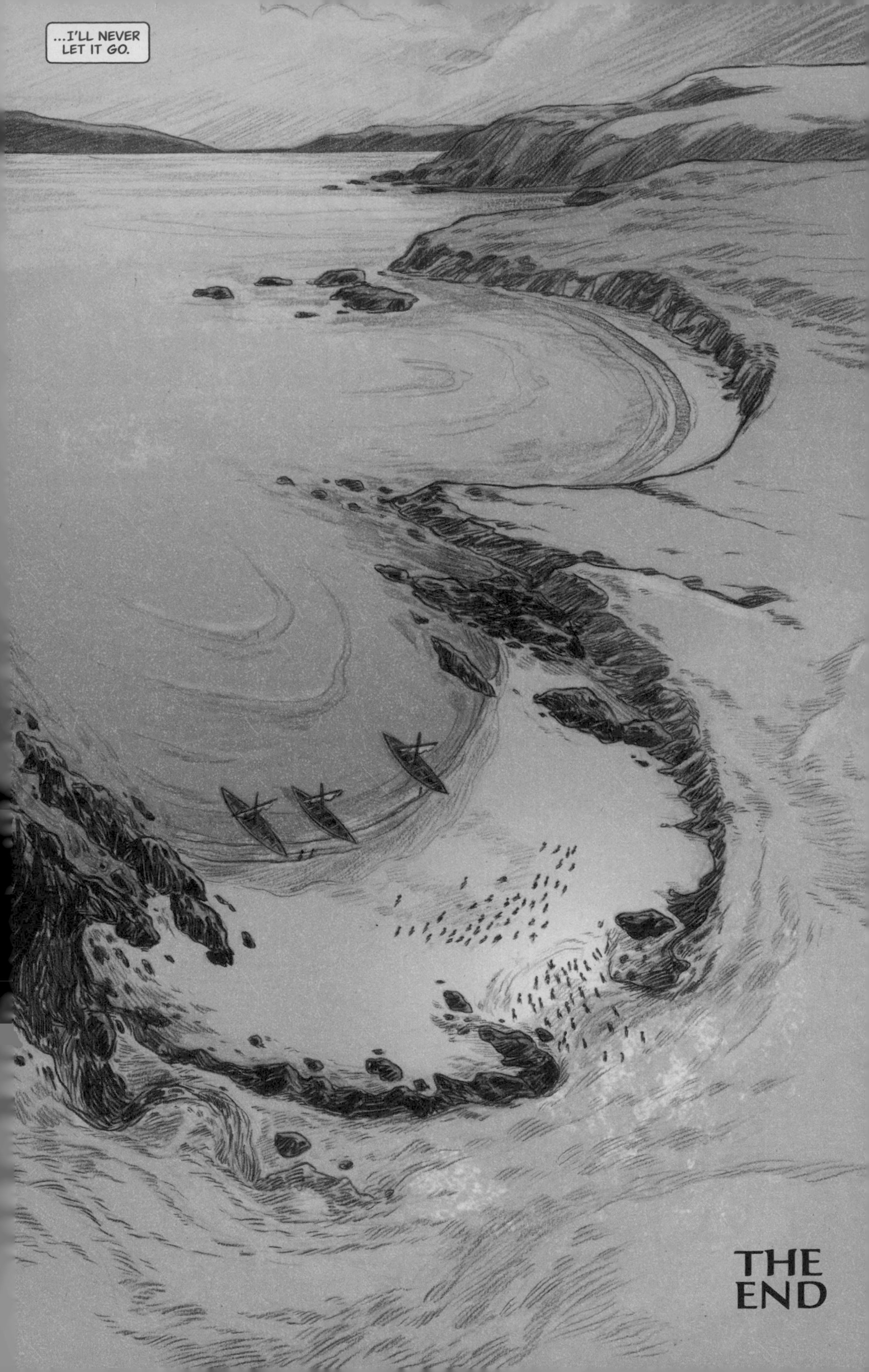
...I'LL NEVER LET IT GO.
THE END

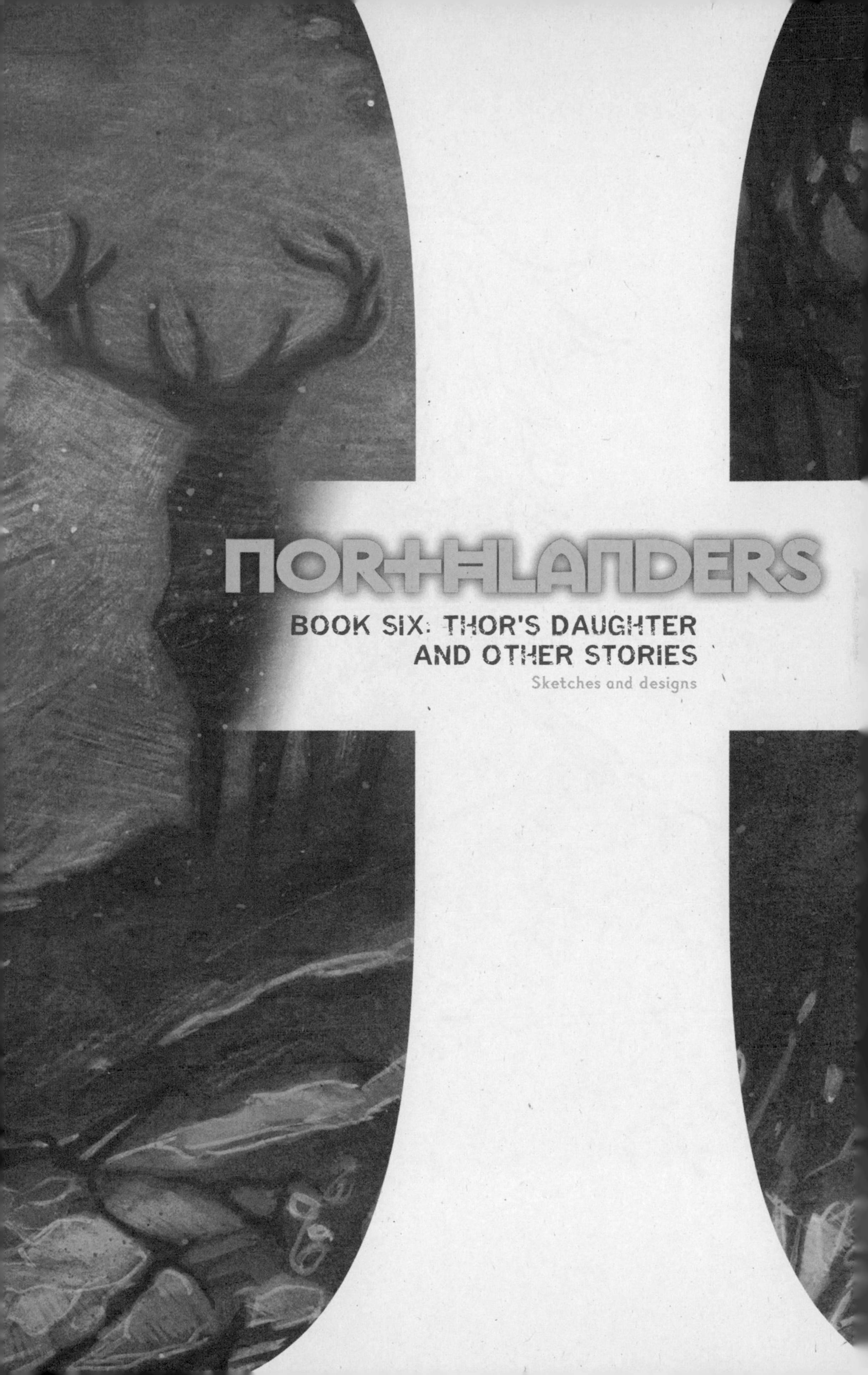

NORTHLANDERS

BOOK SIX: THOR'S DAUGHTER AND OTHER STORIES

Sketches and designs

The Siege of Paris
character sketches by
SIMON GANE

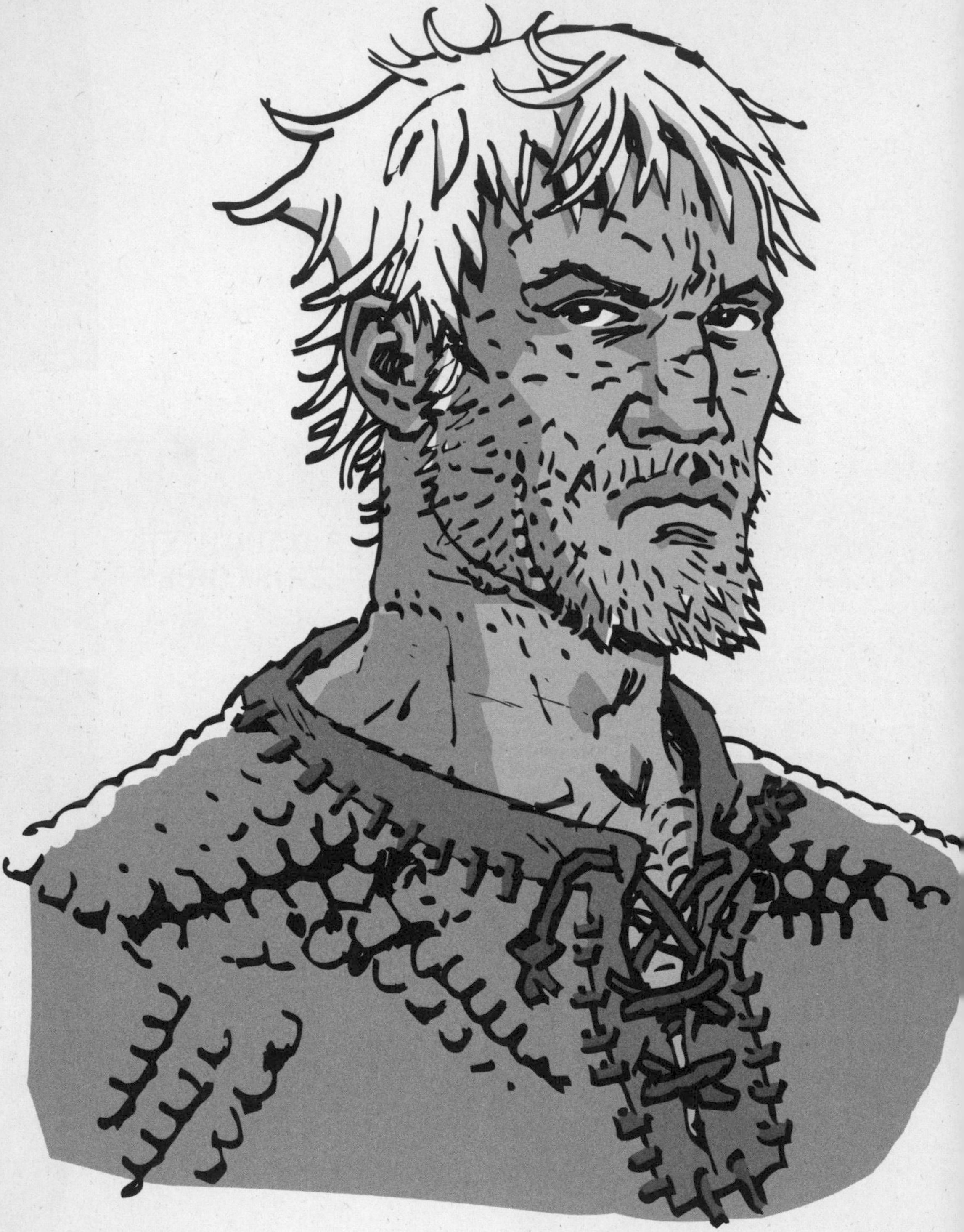

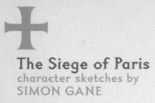

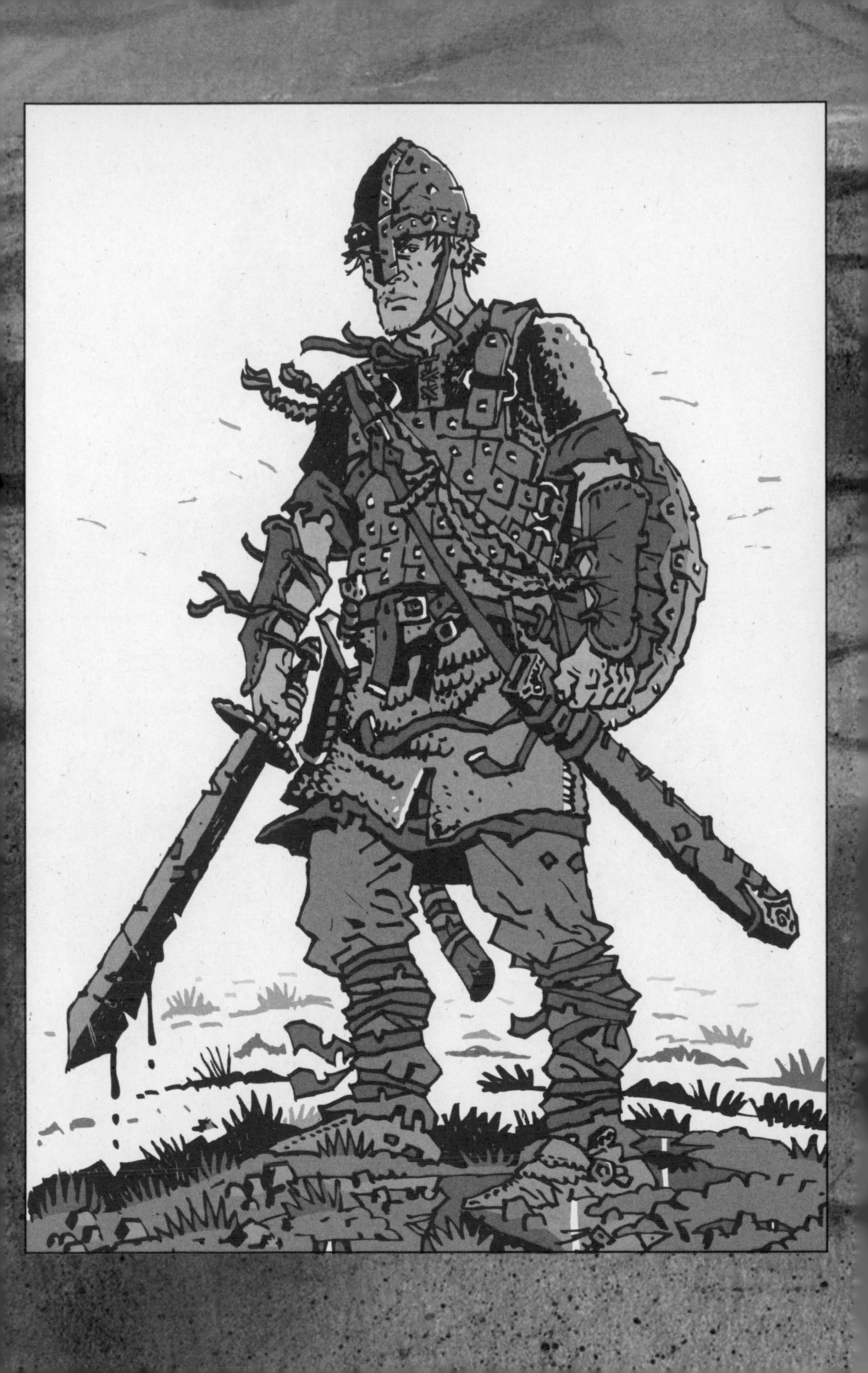

The Siege of Paris
character sketches by
SIMON GANE

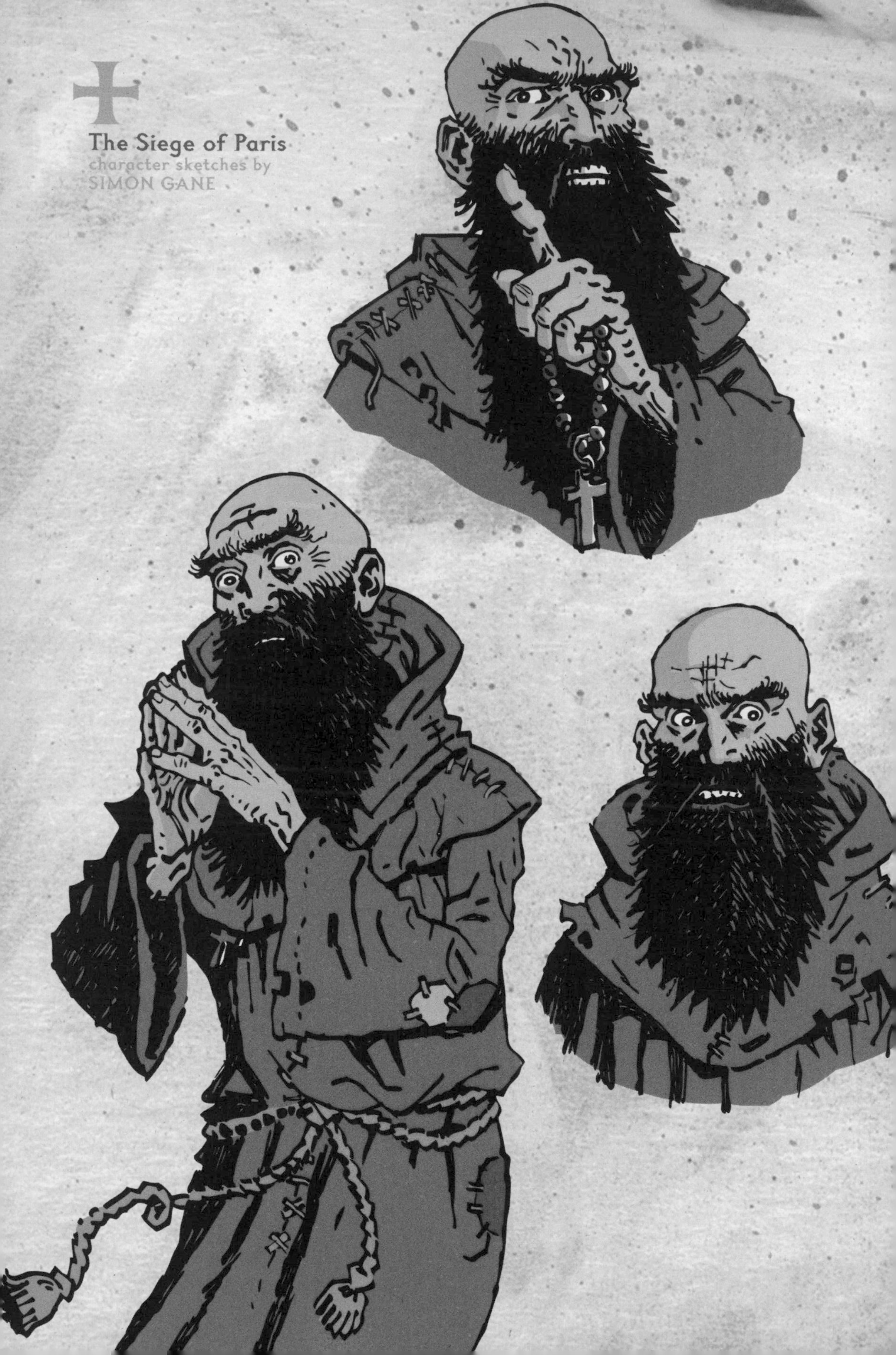

THOR'S DAUGHTER

character sketches by
MARIAN CHURCHLAND

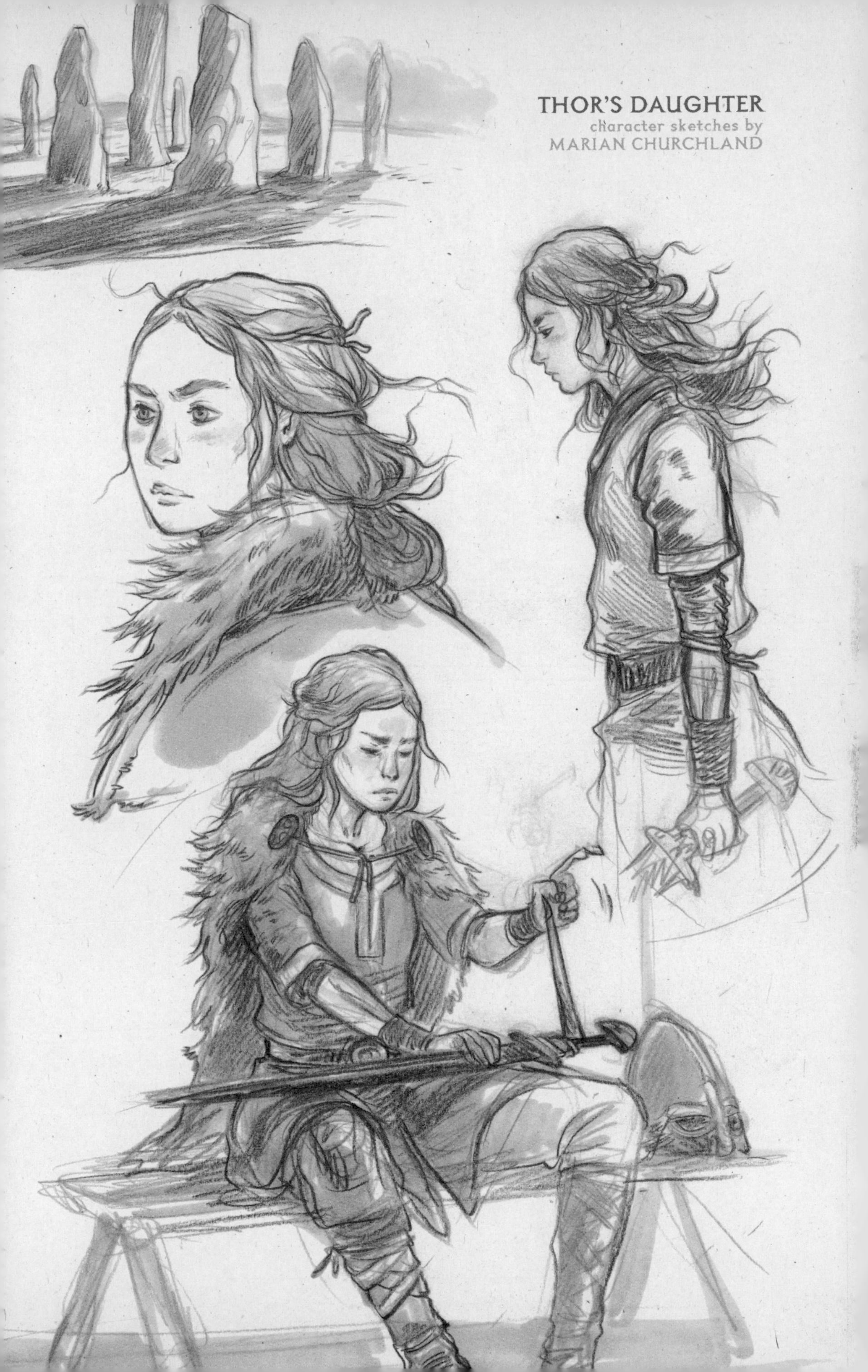

Cover sketches by MASSIMO CARNEVALE

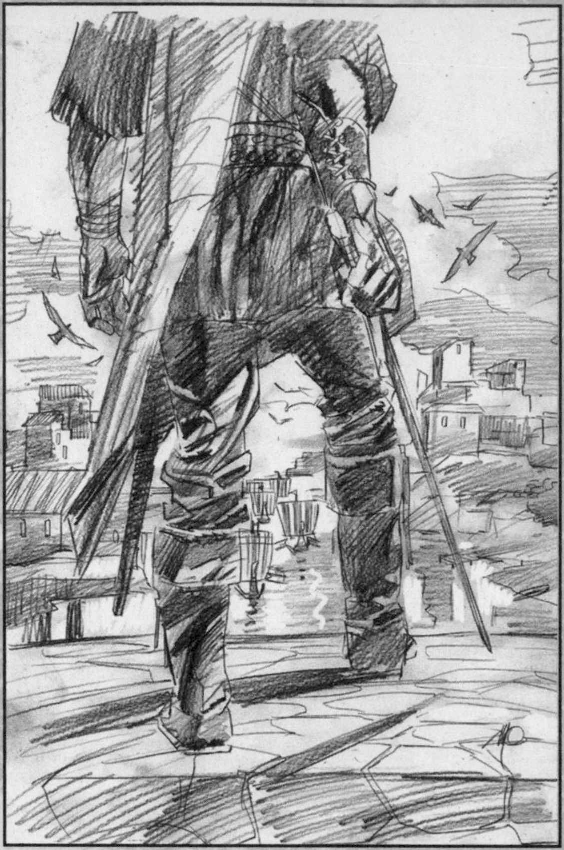
Cover 37 sketch

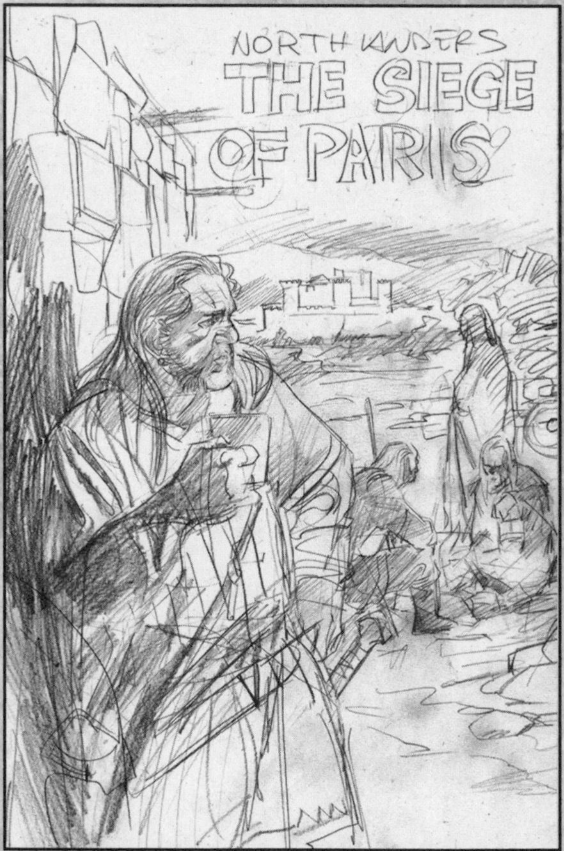
NORTHLANDERS
THE SIEGE OF PARIS
Cover 38 sketch

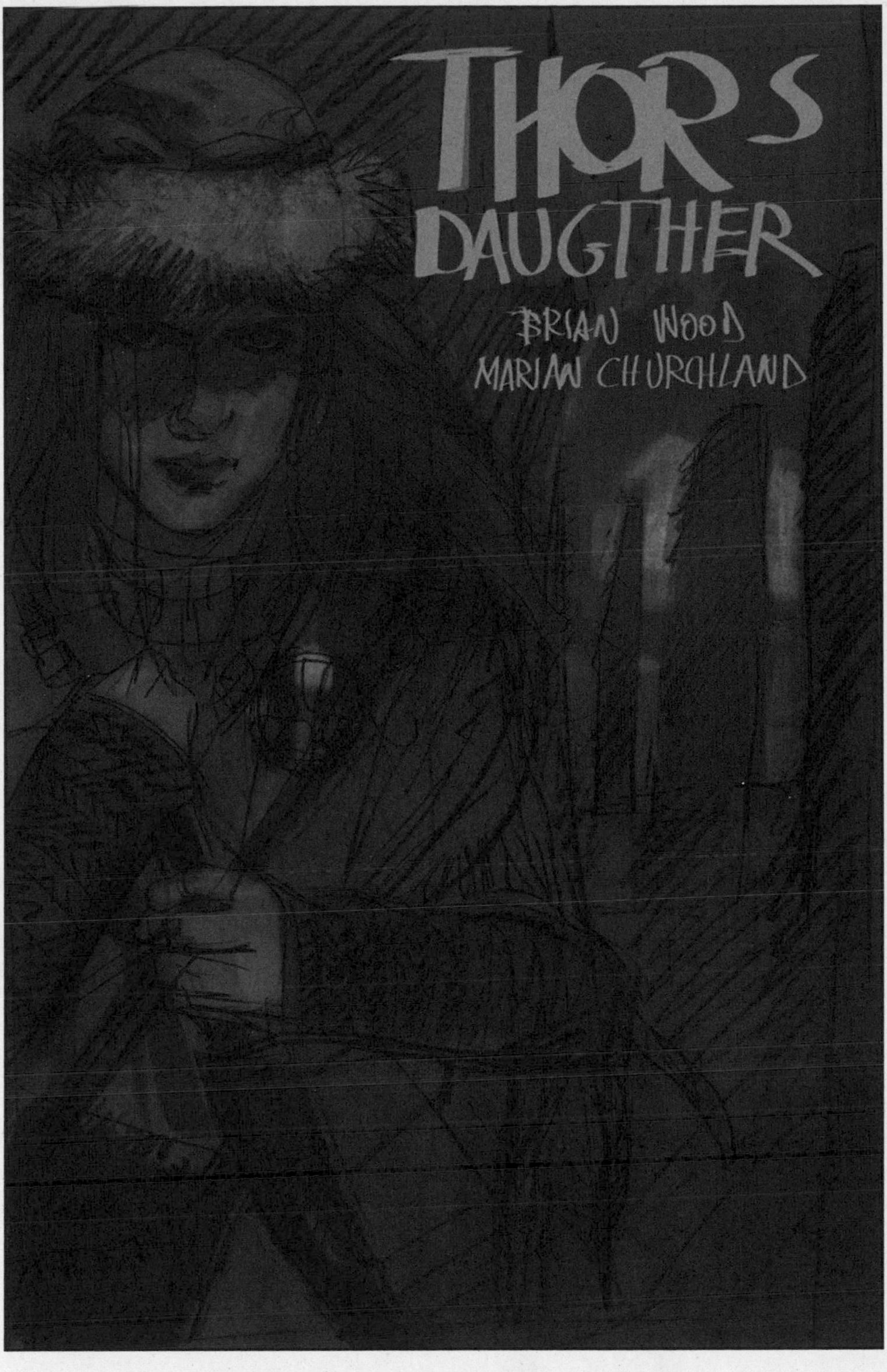
THORS
DAUGTHER
BRIAN WOOD
MARIAN CHURCHLAND

Cover 41 sketch

Cover sketches by
MASSIMO CARNEVALE

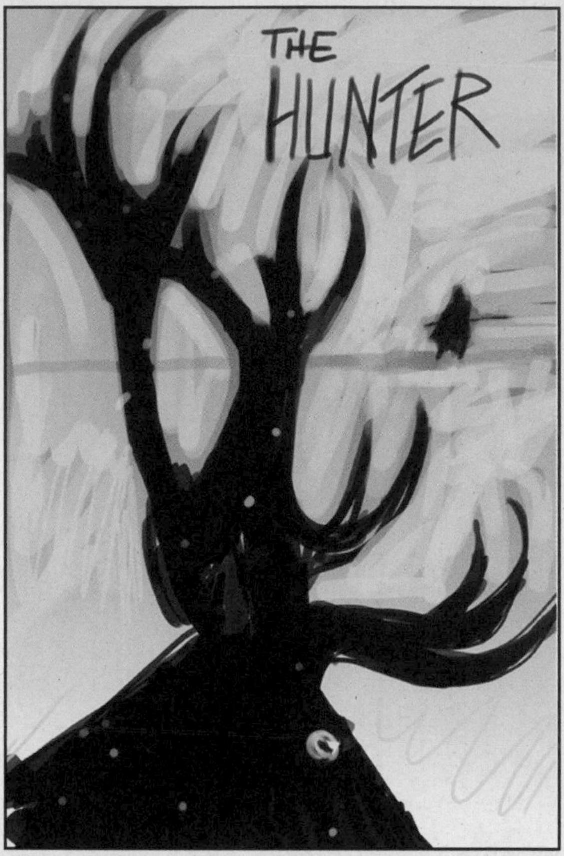
THE
HUNTER

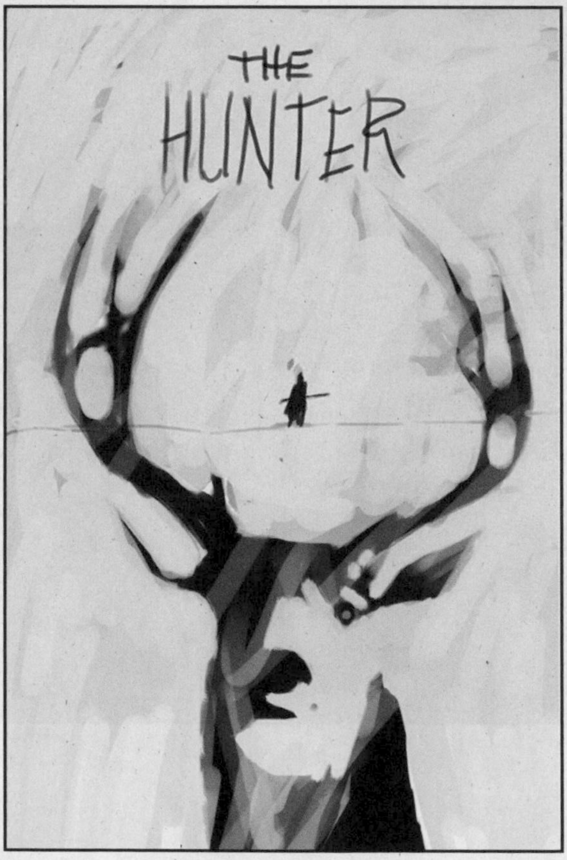
THE
HUNTER

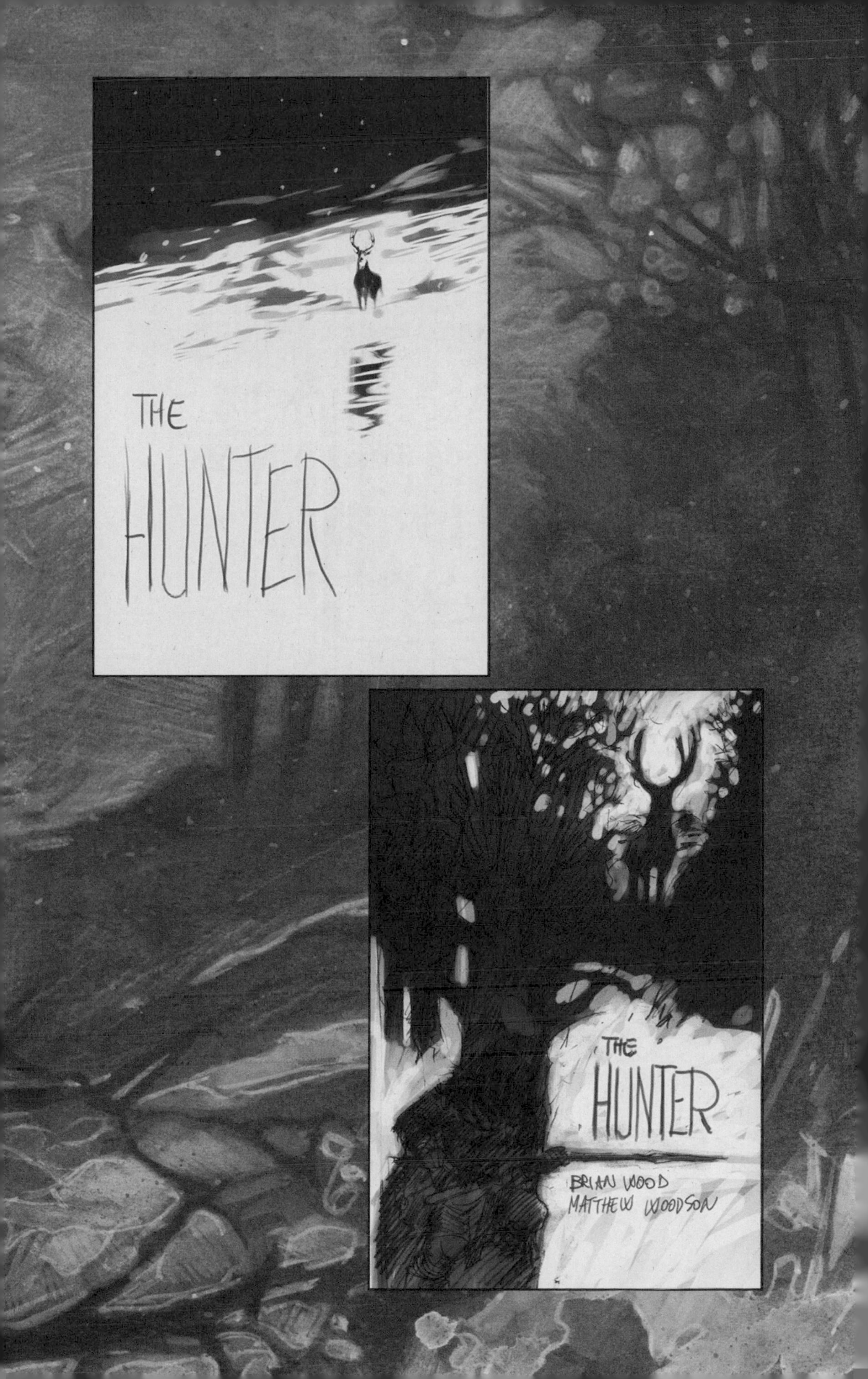
THE HUNTER
THE HUNTER
BRIAN WOOD
MATTHEW WOODSON

THE HUNT
page layouts by
MATTHEW WOODSON

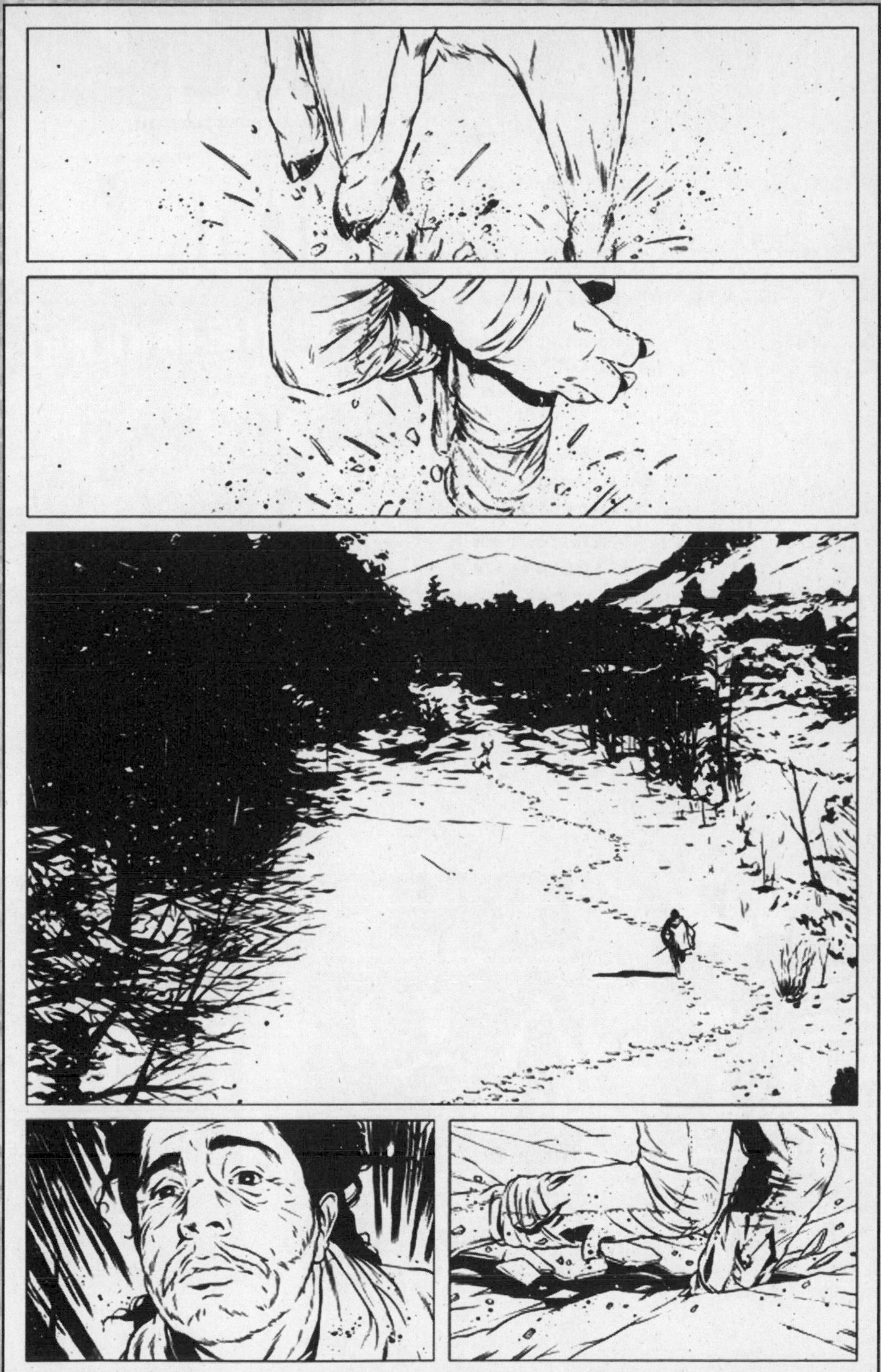

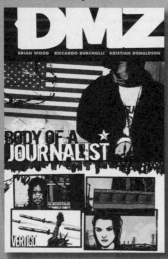

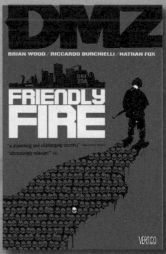